# once a·day

# men&women of the Bible

## DEVOTIONAL

The Livingstone Corporation

ZONDERVAN®

We want to hear from you. Please send your comments about this book to us in care of zreview@zondervan.com. Thank you.

ZONDERVAN

*Once-A-Day Men and Women of the Bible Devotional*
Copyright © 2003, 2012 by the Livingstone Corporation

Requests for information should be addressed to:
Zondervan, *Grand Rapids, Michigan* 49530

Library of Congress Cataloging-in-Publication Data

Once-a-day men and women of the Bible devotional.
        p.  cm.
    Includes bibliographical references and index.
    ISBN  978-0-310-44078-9 (softcover : alk. paper)
    1. Bible — Biography — Meditations.  2. Men in the Bible — Meditations.  3. Women in the Bible — Meditations.  4. Devotional calendars.
    BS571.O68    2012
    220.9'2 — dc23                                                                          2012018162

*Cover design: Faceout Studio and Jamie DeBruyn*
*Interior design: Sherri Hoffman and Jamie DeBruyn*
*Livingstone Editors: Michael Kendrick; Daryl Lucas*
*Livingstone Project Manager: Dave Veerman*
*Livingstone Project Staff: Joel Bartlett, Bruce Barton, Mary Horner Collins, Jack Crabtree, Mark Fackler, Peter Gregory, Rosalie Krusemark, Mary Ann Lackland, Daryl Lucas, Kirk Luttrell, Michael Kendrick, Kathleen Ristow, Thomas Ristow, Betsy Todt Schmitt, Ashley Taylor, Linda Taylor, David R. Veerman, Linda Washington, Neil Wilson, Len Woods*

*Printed in the United States of America*

12 13 14 15 16 17 18 /DCI/ 20 19 18 17 16 15 14 13 12 11 10 9 8 7 6 5 4 3 2 1

# ABOUT THE LIVINGSTONE CORPORATION

Since our inception in September 1988, Livingstone has helped Christian publishers produce 169 specialty Bibles and more than 500 trade books, devotionals, gift and specialty books, studies and curriculum products. Each year we produce about 70 new titles, including Bibles, reference products, trade books, children's books, studies, and curriculum. Our products have won 11 Gold Medallion awards and have been Gold Medallion finalists more than 30 times.

## OUR VISION

Our vision is to glorify and enjoy God in and through our lives, relationships and services and support the advancement of the Good News of Jesus Christ.

## OUR MISSION

Livingstone's mission is to provide superior ideation, content, design and composition services for religious publishers worldwide.

## OUR MOTTO

Ideas to Marketplace. This saying expresses our core brand promise to clients and reflects both the breadth and depth of our capabilities to deliver convenient and effective solutions for marketplace success.

## LEARN FROM GOD'S PEOPLE

*You learned it from Epaphras, our dear fellow servant, who is a faithful minister of Christ on our behalf.*                    COLOSSIANS 1:7

Biographies fascinate us. Take a look at a nonfiction best-seller list, and there will be a few life stories of celebrities or historical greats. We are curious to learn how these people think and behave. We want to know about their personal habits. In short, we want to understand what lifts them beyond the ordinary.

*Once-a-Day Men and Women of the Bible Devotional* is a collection of short episodes from the lives of men and women who played a role in the unfolding of God's plan. More than a retelling of facts, each reading is designed to illustrate a principle that can be applied to one's own spiritual life. *Once-a-Day Men and Women of the Bible Devotional* covers a wide range of personalities—from humble people who obeyed God wholeheartedly to kings and rebels whose evil was their undoing. Each story concludes with a prayer prompt for your own personal application and Scripture references for further study.

*Once-a-Day Men and Women of the Bible Devotional* can be used individually, with other Scripture reading plans or for family devotions. Teachers and small group leaders as well can use the book as a resource for developing more extensive studies of prominent Bible people. However you choose to use *Once-a-Day Men and Women of the Bible Devotional*, we hope that it will help you develop the character God wants to create in you.

# day1

## AARON
### A CROWD-PLEASER

*"They gave me the gold."* EXODUS 32:24

Aaron was senior pastor in a congregation of approximately half a million people, but he still made mistakes, and one of them was colossal. One day the people wanted an idol—something physical and visible—around which to rally, and Aaron gave in. He supervised construction of the golden calf. He did not even raise a protest or urge an alternative.

Had Aaron lost his marbles? Confronted by Moses, he certainly tried to play the part of innocent bystander caught in the middle of a movement bigger than he could stop. It was as if the people had thrown him their gold, and *presto!*—here's this calf thing.

"Due to circumstances beyond my control" may be a reasonable excuse for losing an umbrella in a hurricane, but there's no good reason to entertain pagan worship. Aaron, spiritual leader of Israel, should have stood stronger for God's truth. The lesson he learned carried a high price.

Aaron is an example of what can happen when we let the popular wind blow us away—far away—from God's ideal for us. Aaron should have and could have held on. God would have seen to the rabble rebels. In this new year, when "isms" or ideologies can sometimes appear appealing, keep your loyalty rooted in the one true God. ✤

### PRAYER

*Heavenly Father, keep me loyal to you ...*

### READ

Aaron's story is told in Exodus 1:1—Deuteronomy 10:6 (the story of the Golden Calf is located in Exodus 32). Aaron is also mentioned in Hebrews 5.

## AARON
### *A TEAM PLAYER*

*"You are to say everything I command you, and your brother Aaron is to tell Pharaoh to let the Israelites go."*                                                    Exodus 7:2

Older than Moses by three years, Aaron was chosen by God to be Moses' spokesman to Pharaoh; he later was given the job of high priest for the Israelites. Together Moses and Aaron would lead the people to a land of promise, far away from Egyptian whips and chain gangs. Aaron did not have Moses' strength of will or visionary leadership, but he could speak with clarity and (usually) followed loyally. He stood at Moses' side through many confrontations with Pharaoh and his magicians.

Capable lieutenants turn good leaders into great ones. Few worthy projects are accomplished by individuals acting alone. Teamwork is the key, and a staff of trusted helpers can be a leader's greatest resource. A choirmaster is useless without a choir. God increased the strength of each one, Moses and Aaron, by their joint appointment to lead the exodus.

We play at the top of our game when, as part of a motivated team of people, our personalities and talents are stretched to reach important goals for God's kingdom. Your role may be spokesperson, "go-fer" or crew chief. Whatever the assignment, God deserves your best.                                                    ♣

**PRAYER**

*Lord, grant me the wisdom to know whom to follow ...*

**READ**

Aaron's story is told in Exodus 1:1 — Deuteronomy 10:6. Aaron also is mentioned in Hebrews 5.

## ABEL
### *GIVE YOUR BEST*

*Abel also brought an offering—fat portions from some of the firstborn of his flock.*

GENESIS 4:4

Every child who knows the Bible and every adult who has committed to coming under a church's roof likely knows the name of this second son—Abel. He is the youth whose life was snuffed out by his own brother's jealous blow.

Exactly why God favored Abel's offering is unknown to us, but not to them. They knew. The pristine world was not so cluttered with noise and distraction that God's will could be anything less than crystal clear. Cain was not sure he liked God's ways; Abel, on the other hand, brought his offering with a smile on his lips and a song in his heart.

Likewise, God's will for us today is clear enough. We know that loving service is the centerpiece, while greed and pride are spoilers. We know that "our way or no way" is offensive to God. We know that God wants our devotion no matter the cost.

Today give your best to God. Check to make sure your heart is trusting in God's care, your mind is devoted to knowing the Lord deeply, and your will is eager to please the sovereign Creator.    ❖

**PRAYER**

*Lord, I offer you . . .*

**READ**

Abel's story is told in Genesis 4. He also is mentioned in Matthew 23:35; Luke 11:51 and Hebrews 11:4; 12:24.

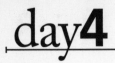 **day4**

## ABEL
### *SPEAKING WITHOUT WORDS*

*By faith Abel still speaks, even though he is dead.*  HEBREWS 11:4

It's odd that a person can "speak" so effectively through centuries and millennia, even though the Bible does not record a single word from his mouth. Cain, the perpetrator, gets to talk at some length in Abel's story (see Genesis 4:1–14). In her recorded story, Eve speaks. Adam also had his say. But what do we hear from Abel? Nothing. He did, however, demonstrate several recognizable qualities: obedience (he brings the offering God desired) and eagerness (one cannot read of Abel without sensing that he enjoyed pleasing God).

Abel was also the victim of extreme violence. Abel follows his brother Cain to the field and dies with a look of shock and vulnerability in his eyes, as millions have since. Abel's story reminds us of the evil that darkens our world, of lives lost to treachery and hatred. His death begs for moral judgment, for God to make things right again.

And that is exactly what God promises to do, through the victory of Jesus Christ, our Savior. On Easter morning, Abel's life—and yours—was bought back eternally, forever, by God's mighty power. Jesus said, "I am the way and the truth and the life," (John 14:6). Today and each day of your life, trust Jesus Christ, God's Son, our Savior, for life eternal.  ❖

**PRAYER**

*Jesus, I acknowledge that you are the way ...*

**READ**

Abel's story is told in Genesis 4. He also is mentioned in Matthew 23:35; Luke 11:51 and Hebrews 11:4; 12:24.

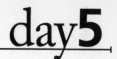

## ABIATHAR
### *THE GIFT OF MERCY*

*To Abiathar the priest the king said, "Go back to your fields in Anathoth. You deserve to die, but I will not put you to death now."*  1 KINGS 2:26

God mercifully allowed Abiathar to avoid certain death twice during his lifetime. The first time, he escaped with nothing but the ephod—a special robe identifying him as a priest—on his back. A vengeful King Saul had all the priests and their families in the city of Nob killed for helping David, but David welcomed Abiathar into his protection.

David trusted Abiathar for many years. But instead of a lifetime of gratefulness to God and loyalty to David, Abiathar eventually conspired against David and Solomon, God's choice for the next king. This time Solomon showed Abiathar tremendous mercy, and he lost only his priestly position as punishment for his disloyalty.

Many times throughout our lives we are given second chances and experience great mercy. Perhaps you have been given another chance in a damaged relationship or an important opportunity you thought you'd wasted. While some people would call it good luck, we know it to be a gift from the merciful hand of God. Like Abiathar, we may neglect to express our gratefulness to God and to others for their graciousness. Make it a point this week to reflect on the "second chances" you have received recently and express your thanks for them.  ❖

**PRAYER**

*Father God, thank you for . . .*

**READ**

Abiathar's story is found in 1 Samuel 22:6 — 23:13 and 1 Kings 1:1 — 2:27.

# day6

## ABIGAIL
### *STEPPING INTO THE LINE OF FIRE*

*[Abigail] fell at his feet and said: "Pardon your servant, my lord."*   1 SAMUEL 25:24

The beautiful wife of pugnacious Nabal had nothing to apologize for. She was putting out her husband's fire. Nabal had refused to supply provisions for David's troops, though they had protected his property. Stunned at Nabal's discourtesy, David was en route to avenge the insult. Abigail stood between them, sensibly handling the tension, negotiating a settlement.

Her speech to David is a brilliant example of strength, cleverness and dignity. First and foremost, Abigail deflected blame from Nabal to herself, which put David in an awkward position; he could hardly take revenge on a beautiful and defenseless woman. Then she reminded David of God's sure justice—David didn't need to take revenge because God would do it for him. Finally, she advised David in light of his coming greatness. After all, why clutter his good conscience with a hasty act of violence against a fool?

Abigail did not have to answer for her husband's actions. Yet she did because she recognized that a greater evil would result if David followed through on his emotional venting: inappropriate vengeance and the death of innocent people.

It takes practice to learn the difference between meddling in business that's not your own (bad—see Proverbs 26:17) and wounding a friend (good—see Proverbs 27:6). When someone smart is about to do something dumb, don't be afraid to consider stepping in the line of fire. Even better, when you see a fight coming, ask God to show you a smart way to end it.                                    ✤

### PRAYER

*Show me, Lord, when to confront . . .*

### READ

Abigail's story is told in 1 Samuel 25:1 — 2 Samuel 2:7.

## ABIGAIL
### *EXPECTING A RESCUE*

*David and his men wept aloud until they had no strength left to weep.*    1 SAMUEL 30:4

What turmoil racked David's life! He had abandoned his homeland, become a warrior for the countrymen of Goliath, intended to march against Saul and battle fellow Israelites, was rejected by Philistine generals and now the Amalekites had ravaged Ziklag. It was so bad that David's own men were close to mutiny.

To make matters worse, Abigail was a hostage. The beautiful voice of reason and faith who had at once cooled David's bloodlust (see 1 Samuel 25 and the devotion at January 6) and warmed his heart—this winsome woman whose looks could tame a lion, whose grace under fire had stopped David in his tracks—was a captive of the Amalekites.

David prayed and sought the counsel of godly advisers. Then he led his men to the recovery of all the captives and stolen property.

At some point in the melee that wrecked the Amalekites' party, David approached his precious bride, grateful beyond words to see her alive and well, eager to celebrate God's deliverance with her.     ❖

**PRAYER**

*Lord, I am in need of your deliverance ...*

**READ**

Abigail's story is told in 1 Samuel 25:1—2 Samuel 2:7.

## ABIJAH
### *HALFHEARTED DEVOTION*

*His heart was not fully devoted to the LORD his God, as the heart of David his forefather had been.*                                                                    1 KINGS 15:3

An armed confrontation with King Jeroboam (of Israel) brought a crisis into Abijah's life. His army of Judah was half the size of Israel's forces. To make matters worse, Jeroboam demonstrated his tactical superiority by surrounding Abijah's army. Faced with such overwhelming odds, Abijah acted on what he knew about his heavenly Father, rather than on what he had learned from his earthly father, Rehoboam. He stated that God's reputation was at stake in the conflict between Israel and Judah. Army sizes didn't matter; what mattered was who was on God's side. Abijah's fiery speech hit the bull's-eye, and his army gained a crushing victory.

That victory on the battlefield, unfortunately, did not represent Abijah's true self at all. His speech, true as it was, constitutes the sum total of his good deeds recorded in Scripture. Sadly, King Abijah fits this description better: "His heart was not fully devoted to the LORD his God."

A moment in the spotlight does not a star make. God is looking for people who will cling to him day in and day out, not just in an emergency. Does that describe you?                                                                                  ❖

**PRAYER**

*Take my heart, O God . . .*

**READ**

For more on Abijah, see 1 Kings 15:1–8 and 2 Chronicles 13:1–22.

## ABIMELEK
### *PRAY FOR THE DAY*

*On one stone murdered his seventy brothers.*      JUDGES 9:5

Abimelek was a cold-blooded man. To secure his own future, he ended the lives of 69 half-brothers, Gideon's children. (Abimelek was Gideon's son by a concubine in Shechem.) Killing so many is not easy. It takes planning, teamwork and a certain heartless poise. One must be deaf to cries for mercy, one victim after another. One must regard the murders as a job, a task, a career step. The messiness of the killing field must not deter one from his purpose: to secure political control.

Abimelek could handle mass murder, but apparently he couldn't count. By God's mercy, one half-brother, Jotham, escaped. Didn't Abimelek count the corpses? Didn't he know one was still alive? Only three years after the massacre at Ophrah, a speech by Jotham and a rebellious spirit among the people of Shechem toppled Abimelek, who died dishonorably, the victim of a dropped millstone. In more ways than one, Abimelek had never learned to look up.

Viciousness still claims its victims. Peace is still a fragile truce with evil. The day is coming, however, when a just God will judge brutality and vindicate the suffering of the innocent. Until that time, injustice, evil and bloodshed can and should compel us to pray for the day of the Lord.      ❖

### PRAYER

*Lord, bring about your justice ...*

### READ

Abimelek's story is told in Judges 8:31 — 9:57. He is also mentioned in 2 Samuel 11:21.

# day 10

## ABISHAG
### *WE MATTER TO GOD*

*She took care of the king and waited on him.*                    1 KINGS 1:4

Chosen for her youth and beauty, Abishag found herself one day the live-in nurse of the great but old King David. Her job was to keep the king warm. Within months her patient had died. We know little about their relationship except that they never had sex.

Soon after David's death, Abishag became a bargaining chip in the power struggle between his sons, Solomon and Adonijah, and his widow, Bathsheba. For Adonijah, Abishag was probably little more than a possible angle to renew his claim on the throne of David. Bathsheba, herself acquainted with being treated as an object, may have been trying to do Abishag a favor as well as to pacify Adonijah. Solomon gave his half-brother no room for doubt. He assumed Adonijah was planning to use Abishag to fight for the throne. The behavior of all three family members makes one fact clear: no one cared what Abishag thought. She might as well have been listed with the furniture.

There are many situations in life in which people are sometimes treated as objects—both on purpose and in ignorance. In fact, you may occasionally be hurt by such treatment. Family members may withhold appreciation. Co-workers may treat you like just another office machine. Resist these invitations to hopelessness or resentment by remembering that God knows your true worth. He knows you intimately and will always treat you as the specially created person you are.     ♣

### PRAYER

*Father, thank you for your love . . .*

### READ

Abishag's story is told in 1 Kings 1:1–4; 2:13–24.

# day11

## ABISHAI
### LOYAL TO A FAULT

*Abishai son of Zeruiah came to David's rescue.*  2 SAMUEL 21:17

Fearless Abishai saved the king's life by jumping in front of a screaming Philistine who was ready to kill and able to do it. We have no details except that David was exhausted and Abishai jumped in to stop the Philistine's sword.

Fearless Abishai was both a general's ideal soldier and worst nightmare. He was loyal to his king to a fault. Anything David wanted, Abishai would do—and more. Abishai was reckless with regard to his own safety, the Israelite equivalent of a modern-day Special Forces officer who stops at no obstacle and calculates no risk. Those qualities were also his weakness, for Abishai would act without thinking. His loyalty to David would have driven him to kill even more, in the name of serving the king, had David not stopped him on three separate occasions.

Great leaders need Abishai's courage, but they also need something more: moral judgment. Abishai's extreme loyalty to David was too much. God urges that we learn restraint, wisdom, insight and discretion (see Proverbs 2:1–22; 3:13–35). Responsible leaders need to discern when to back off and when to pursue, to press toward a goal and yet show mercy along the way. Serve your king, your spouse or your friend, but do not worship them.  ❖

### PRAYER

*Lord, I worship you alone ...*

### READ

Abishai's story is told in 2 Samuel 18:1—23:19. He is also mentioned in 1 Samuel 26:1–13 and 1 Chronicles 2:16; 11:20; 18:12; 19:11,15.

# day12

## ABNER
### *LEARNING FROM PAST MISTAKES*

*Abner replied, "Who are you who calls to the king?"*     1 SAMUEL 26:14

Abner was the man who made Saul's kingship a political reality. He organized and commanded a large army, and did so with a general's instincts. Against the Philistine Goliath, Abner played a strategic waiting game that paid off when David stepped forward. Years later, outwitted by the renegade David (see 1 Samuel 26), Abner conceded his mistake, but not before crushing David's ego with a stunning verbal comeback. Here's the setting:

Under cover of night, David stole past Abner's sentries, taking Saul's own spear and canteen, glorious souvenirs that would surely embarrass the entire Israelite high command. At dawn David climbed upon a rock on a hill opposite Saul and began to taunt, in effect saying, "Look what I've got!" Abner, who knew very well who was boasting, answered David with aplomb, covering his own astonishment and at the same time minimizing David's feat.

Abner survived the episode, while lesser leaders would have found themselves demoted or jailed. He could take a hit without falling apart. He could muster an army to fight another day. He was a cat who always landed on his feet.

The next time you're caught in an embarrassing bind, own up to the situation—face the music head on, without falling apart, and God will see you through.     ✤

### PRAYER

*Lord God, I admit that I...*

### READ

Abner's story is told in 1 Samuel 14:50—2 Samuel 4:12. Abner is also mentioned in 1 Kings 2:5,32 and 1 Chronicles 26:28; 27:16–22.

## ABNER
### *THE NEED FOR DECISIVENESS*

*Abner said to him, "Go back home!" So he went back.*   2 SAMUEL 3:16

Abner was a practical man. First and only commander of the army of his cousin Saul, Abner could make decisions, issue orders and force compliance. Abner was a "can-do" general.

Contrast Abner with poor Paltiel, who had become second husband to Michal, Saul's daughter (see 1 Samuel 25:43–44). When David finally had the power to demand that Michal be returned to him, Paltiel was brokenhearted. Abner, escorting Michal to David as part of a plea bargain, had to deal with this emotionally distraught man. His words carried no sympathy. He simply gave Paltiel an order. And that order probably saved Paltiel's life.

Making decisions that affect other people stresses us. We hem and haw over options; we calculate risks; we stew over how they'll take it. Some people just can't decide because they feel trapped by all the possible outcomes.

But there are times when have to be like Abner—decisive. We may wish his hard exterior was softer and gentler. But Abner could assess a situation and move clearly to a decision that achieved important goals. The next time you're faced with a decision that affects others, pray with intensity, then act in faith with bravery and resolve.                                                   ❖

**PRAYER**

*Grant me your wisdom, Lord, to act …*

**READ**

Abner's story is told in 1 Samuel 14:50—2 Samuel 4:12. Abner is also mentioned in 1 Kings 2:5,32 and 1 Chronicles 26:28; 27:16–22.

## ABRAHAM
### THE RISK OF FAITH

*By faith Abraham, when called to go to a place he would later receive as his inheritance, obeyed and went.*        HEBREWS 11:8

Travel packages are offered with numerous insurance policies. Our material possessions of value—jewelry, hobby collections, etc.—have legal papers to assure passage of title to proper heirs. We have built layers of security around every important move we make.

In the ancient world, Abraham moved about by his wits, his strength and—unusual for his time—radical faith in one God, Jehovah, the "I AM."

Faith gave Abraham his security. God would be Abraham's protector; God would prosper his life; God would take fear from Abraham's heart and give him courage. God, who sent this man into foreign territory, would show him truth that no one had uncovered. All of this for Abraham, and all of it by faith.

Abraham could have said, "No way!" when God told him to move. After all, such a move would involve too little assurance and too much risk. Abraham, however, heard the Lord speak—alone, in visions, with unprecedented clarity—and believed.

Life today gains richness and meaning as we put our faith in God, stretching resources, exhausting energies, pressing toward promises generously given to us throughout the Bible's amazing story. We need to experience Abraham's freedom, the liberty and joy of trusting in our shield and reward. We need to trust in God.

❖

**PRAYER**

*Lord, you are my hiding place ...*

**READ**

Abraham's story is told in Genesis 11–25. Abraham is also mentioned in Exodus 2:24; Acts 7:2–8; Romans 4; Galatians 3; Hebrews 2; 6–7; 11 and James 2:21–24.

## ABRAHAM
### *TAKING GOD AT HIS WORD*

*"We will worship and then we will come back to you."*  GENESIS 22:5

What a twist! God promised a child to aged Abraham and Sarah, for which they waited many years. Finally the miracle birth occurred, bringing Abraham and Sarah great joy. Now, the boy was to be given back to God in sacrifice by his father's own hand.

With stunning immediacy, Abraham set out on the journey. What feelings rumbled in his heart as he and the youngster hiked is left to our imagination. We know only that he obeyed, believing God would provide a way to fulfill his promise. Hebrews says Abraham believed that God could raise the dead (see Hebrews 11:19).

Just about everything that happens to us tests our faith. We seem not to have enough money to give, though God says he will always meet our needs. Will we believe? We want to take revenge, but God says he will avenge. Will we believe? Christ died for our sins and says he will take them away if we will but trust in him. Will we believe? Accept God's promise and discover God's blessing.  ✤

### PRAYER

*Lord, I believe in your promise to ...*

### READ

Abraham's story is told in Genesis 11–25. Abraham is also mentioned in Exodus 2:24; Acts 7:2–8; Romans 4; Galatians 3; Hebrews 2; 6–7; 11 and James 2:21–24.

# day16

## ABSALOM
### *FALLEN YOUTH*

*"If only I were appointed judge in the land!"*                    2 SAMUEL 15:4

Absalom was the consummate politician. His smile and appearance were charming, his ability to "work the crowd" was without equal, his speeches were simple self-advertisements, and he had the right family connections. Absalom promised the people all that King David (his father) was apparently not delivering.

In retrospect, we see Absalom as a failed leader whose shallow character and outright treacheries spoiled his grand campaign promises. After Absalom died, people throughout Israel were saying, "We knew all along..." But many people had been fooled.

Who will win your allegiance and respect today? We need people of integrity and vision to accept leadership roles, but too often we get people of selfish ambition, greed and empty promises. The blame is ours. If we want leaders who exhibit virtue and a strong sense of servanthood, we must nurture them. We must pray for them as youngsters and work with them as protégés.

Support youth ministries in your church. Befriend neighborhood kids. Give kids responsibilities, especially in church, wherever you can. Be honest with them and expect them to be honest with you.                    ❖

### PRAYER

*Lord, today I pray for ...*

### READ

Absalom's story is told in 2 Samuel 3:3; 13–19.

# day17

## ACHAN
### THE COST OF SELF-CENTEREDNESS

*"Why have you brought this trouble on us?"*                                       JOSHUA 7:25

Achan stood open-mouthed with the other Israelites and watched God crush the fortified city of Jericho. He heard God say, "Keep away from the devoted things, so that you will not bring about your own destruction by taking any of them. Otherwise you will make the camp of Israel liable to destruction and bring trouble on it" (Joshua 6:18). But Achan chose to act on his desires rather than God's directions. He thought the robe he took was too beautiful to burn. And the gold and silver he hid? Surely God wouldn't miss a few items, right? Wrong!

Achan missed the reason for God's command. Because his perspective was self-centered, he couldn't see what was at stake. God was building a nation of people who understood that private actions lead to public consequences. Achan believed in the rule many live by today: "As long as no one else gets hurt or sees what I'm doing, I can do it." But his actions led to suffering and humiliation for the nation, and death for himself *and* his family.

We don't always know how our actions will affect other people, but it is a terrible mistake to assume they won't affect others at all. How many of your plans and actions today would be changed if someone was right beside you, watching you every moment? Remember, others are *always* involved. God doesn't miss anything.     ✤

### PRAYER

*Direct my will today, Lord . . .*

### READ

Achan's story is told in Joshua 7:1 – 26; 22:20 and 1 Chronicles 2:7.

## ADAM
### FAILURE, FRUSTRATION AND HOPE

*"I was afraid because I was naked; so I hid."*                     GENESIS 3:10

It is almost impossible to imagine what Adam's life was like in Eden. He was first and one-of-a-kind: no childhood, no parents, no schooling, no guilt, close contact with God, perfect world, a beautiful garden, knowing animals by name, a spouse created to be an ideal partner, only one rule to follow. Life today is vastly different.

Yet we can identify with Adam's struggles: (1) He's embarrassed to admit mistakes and wants to avoid confronting his problems. (2) His kids get into big trouble, spoiling many of his dreams for their future. (3) He works harder and gets less done as life goes on. (4) As an older adult, he has little to show for all his labors except a small farm and scattered grandchildren.

Yet even Adam had hope. Genesis 3:15 is God's first piece of Good News: Satan will be defeated; a Savior will come. That promise gave Adam hope, and still lifts us from the pits to the heavens, from "What's the use?" to "Praise the Lord!" When life seems barren and pointless, remember that even Adam, who had fallen the furthest, had this hope.

Jesus has come, salvation is won and the Bible promises another (second) coming at the end of time when all of our tears will be wiped away. Whenever you're discouraged, remember the Good News.                                        ✤

### PRAYER

*Lord, I need encouragement today because ...*

### READ

Adam's story is told in Genesis 1:26 — 5:5. Adam also is mentioned in 1 Chronicles 1:1; Luke 3:38; Romans 5:14; 1 Corinthians 15:22,45 and 1 Timothy 2:13 – 15.

## ADONIJAH
### *AMBITION WITHOUT WISDOM*

*Adonijah ... put himself forward and said, "I will be king."*     1 KINGS 1:5

Adonijah really, really wanted to be king of Judah. After all, he was the oldest living son of David. He was handsome, perhaps regal in appearance—so much so that two of David's advisers (Joab and Abiathar) gave him their support. But David had already promised his throne to Solomon. Adonijah's dreams and plans were in vain.

That didn't stop Adonijah. Hopelessly caught up in his own world, he hired a band of royal footmen and chariots to "prove" he was the king. He even performed the official sacrifices expected of a newly crowned king and sent invitations for his own coronation. His charade almost worked, but his willfulness ultimately led to his own death.

Adonijah was overly willful. He could neither recognize nor work within limits. For whatever reason, he was unwilling to respect the wishes of others or to accept God's will when it contradicted his own. His self-absorption led him to defy his father, deny God's sovereignty and eventually die.

Pursue your own plans within the will of God, not instead of or in spite of it. The limits he has placed on you will only help you to flourish.     ✤

**PRAYER**

*Lord, here are my plans ...*

**READ**

Adonijah's story is told in 1 Kings 1:5–53; 2:13–25.

# day20

## AGABUS
### BAD NEWS AND MORE BAD NEWS

*A prophet named Agabus came down from Judea.*                    ACTS 21:10

Agabus holds the distinction of being one of the few named prophets of New Testament times. We have two of his prophecies on record: He predicted a severe famine that would affect Judea, and he foretold Paul's imprisonment in Jerusalem. "I have bad news, and I have bad news," we might have heard him say.

However, Agabus's prophecies were not intended as declarations of doom. Rather, they offered information that could be used to prepare the right response. In the first instance, his prophecy stirred the church into action and the disciples provided help for the believers in Judea. In response to the second prophecy, Paul's companions panicked while Paul rightly took the news as advance notice of God's plan for him; he declared his devotion to Christ and got ready to go. Everyone learned from that.

Should Agabus have held his tongue because of "what people might think"? Of course not! He delivered God's words because that was his God-given job. God gave him a prophecy; he *had* to share it.

Don't be timid about serving God with the gifts he's given you just because you see some natural barrier. Many people around you need your words of *encouragement*, acts of *hospitality*, or whatever gifts you have to share. They *need* it.    ❖

PRAYER

*Lord, please use me ...*

READ

The story of Agabus is found in Acts 11:25–30; 21:10–14.

## AHAB
### *THE BLAME GAME*

*When [Ahab] saw Elijah, he said to him, "Is that you, you troubler of Israel?"*

1 KINGS 18:17

The labels we affix to people become a lens through which we view everything. The names we use can distort your judgment and eventually give us reason to think that wrong is all right. This is an age-old strategy of tyrants: demonize opponents and blame them for whatever problems arise.

Ahab had leadership potential, but his moral lens had become completely distorted. Wrong was right; right was whatever he wished. Elijah, the key person who could show Ahab his problem, was, in Ahab's mind, the nation's chief troublemaker. Ahab's lifeline to God was thin and fraying. By placing on Elijah the label "troubler," Ahab was cutting the cord altogether.

When friends confront us, we may call them disloyal. When parents urge us to mend a bad habit, we may call them conservative or out of touch. When a pastor counsels change, we may dismiss it with terms like *meddler* or *holier-than-thou*. These labels may be hatchets whacking at the lifeline — God's towrope to keep us from floating adrift.

We would be wise to put away the hatchet, quit labeling and start listening. Accept Christian counsel whenever it's given. Remain open to the corrective judgment of people who love you — you may be surprised by what you learn from them. And, of course, listen always to God's Word.                                     ❖

**PRAYER**

*Lord, I am listening...*

**READ**

Ahab's story is told in 1 Kings 16:28 — 22:40 and 2 Chronicles 18:1 — 19:3. He is also mentioned in Micah 6:16.

## AHAB
### *THE POUTING KING*

*So Ahab ... lay on his bed sulking and refused to eat.*                    1 KINGS 21:4

Do you sulk? When your plans are met with less than unanimous approval, when your preferences are rejected for other options, when promotions go to colleagues or dates to a roommate, do you pout?

Ahab failed to see setbacks as opportunities for toughness training. As a consequence, he was emotionally weak and easily manipulated by his aggressive, pagan wife, Jezebel. He acted like a baby his entire life.

When your plans hit a roadblock, do better than Ahab. First, trust God that the problem, rather than being a reason to sulk, is an opportunity for you to learn. Commit to solving the problem if it's important, abandoning it if it's trivial. Develop a plan, consult with trustworthy Christian mentors and pray. Forge ahead believing that God has good plans for you, and will bless or block your efforts accordingly.                                                                              ♣

**PRAYER**

*Lord, show me your way ...*

**READ**

Ahab's story is told in 1 Kings 16:28 — 22:40 and 2 Chronicles 18:1 — 19:3. He is also mentioned in Micah 6:16.

## AHASUERUS
### THE CENTER OF HIS UNIVERSE

*For any man or woman who approaches the king in the inner court without being sum-moned the king has but one law: that they be put to death unless the king extends the gold scepter to them.*                                                    ESTHER 4:11

Examples of human greatness throughout history seldom mirror God's definition. King Ahasuerus, also known as Xerxes the Great, may have ruled Persia in his day, but he must have been a minor figure in God's estimation. We know this to be true in part from the way he ruled. As God made clear at the anointing of another king, "The LORD does not look at the things people look at. People look at the outward appearance, but the LORD looks at the heart" (1 Samuel 16:7).

Like many leaders of his time, Ahasuerus indulged his desires for women. As king, he simply drafted them into his harem. Sometimes they were gifts that sealed political treaties. Ahasuerus's treatment of women reveals the king's prob-lem with royal self-centeredness. Most of us do not have the means to get all we want, but a king is able to spoil himself royally. Ahasuerus saw women, men and even nations almost entirely as things to be used or discarded depending on how they pleased him. At one point he casually approved a plan to annihilate the Jew-ish people. Devaluing persons was part of his daily routine.

Whether or not we have the means to gratify our every whim, we can be just as self-centered as Ahasuerus. The way we treat others can serve as a measurement of this self-centeredness. As you meet and work with people today, ask yourself how important they are apart from what they can do for you. Take some time to reflect on any insights you may discover. Are there any changes in your attitude you need to make?                                                                        ❖

**PRAYER**

*Lord, thank you for the value you place on each of us...*

**READ**

Ahasuerus appears throughout the book of Esther and is mentioned in Ezra 4:6.

## AHAZ
### THE ROOT OF SPIRITUAL ILLNESS

*In his time of trouble King Ahaz became even more unfaithful to the LORD.*

2 CHRONICLES 28:22

The circumstances describing the life of King Ahaz fall into the general categories of bad and much worse. When Judah suffered a debilitating attack from rival neighbors, his cry for help was answered by a foreign army, the Assyrians. Ahaz's cowardly leadership forced Judah into virtual slavery to Assyria.

Soon every piece of evidence that Judah had once been a God-fearing nation was smashed, defaced or tucked out of sight. Ahaz even presented his own children as an offering to the gods he hoped would rescue him and his nation from distruction.

Ahaz's life bears much similarity to our own potential to collapse spiritually beneath a load of failures and trials. Instead of repenting of any known sin and calling upon God for relief, we, like Ahaz, may entertain every other source of aid *but* God. Our abilities. Money. Harmful habits. The result is increased tragedy.

Difficulties and mistakes can and will devastate our faith, or they will stimulate growth and maturity. The difference is made when we choose to humbly seek God's help whatever the situation. ❖

**PRAYER**

*Help me, Lord ...*

**READ**

Read more about Ahaz's tragic life and reign in 2 Kings 16 and 2 Chronicles 28.

# day25

## AHAZIAH, KING OF ISRAEL
### A LEGACY OF SIN

*He served and worshiped Baal and aroused the anger of the LORD, the God of Israel, just as his father had done.*                                                      1 KINGS 22:53

Ahaziah's life demonstrates what can happen to children with dysfunctional families. He inherited from his father Ahab and his mother Jezebel the most evil reputation of any royal family in Israel. With his father's violent death, Ahaziah became king over a nation steeped in idolatry, dishonesty and blatant rebellion against God.

Ahaziah immediately began to add his own mistakes to his unholy heritage. The kingdom stumbled when Moab declared its independence from Israel, exposing Ahaziah's lack of power. Next, Ahaziah invested in a fleet of merchant ships hoping to create financial security. The fleet sank, along with the king's hopes. Then the king stumbled and fell from a palace porch, seriously injuring himself. Ahaziah added idolatry to injury by sending a servant to Ekron, a center for the worship of Baal-Zebub, to find out if he would recover. At this point, God decided Ahaziah had been given enough opportunities to repent. Elijah intercepted the messengers with the news that God had declared the end of Ahaziah's life. Even then, Ahaziah gave no sign of repentance.

Our past may handicap us, but our own decisions condemn us. Understanding family problems and dysfunctional relationships only becomes useful if we use the knowledge to make better choices. How often do you let your past influence your decisions? For better or for worse?                                                      ❖

**PRAYER**

*Let me not be shaped by my past, but be shaped by you, O God . . .*

**READ**

Ahaziah's story is found in 1 Kings 22:48—2 Kings 1:18 and 2 Chronicles 20:35–37.

## AHAZIAH, KING OF JUDAH
### *MOTHER DIDN'T KNOW BEST*

*He too followed the ways of the house of Ahab, for his mother encouraged him to act wickedly.*  2 CHRONICLES 22:3

Ahaziah definitely came from bad seed. Both his father (Jehoram) and mother (Athaliah) murdered members of their families. His grandfather, King Ahab, was considered one of the most evil kings in Israel's history. So when the people of Jerusalem enthroned him after Jehoram died, he had a choice. He could listen to the evil advice of his relatives or he could seek out the wisdom of God. Ahaziah chose to listen to his evil mother and her relatives in Israel for kingly advice. The consequences cost him his throne and his life. He was pierced by an arrow in a revolt and his evil mother greedily assumed his duties (see 2 Kings 11).

We all are in a position of responsibility over something, and it is wise to consider others' advice. However, it is equally wise to consider the source before we follow the advice. Think about what consequences have followed under the previous leadership of the advice-giver. God will supply his resources for godly persuasion, but the choice to take advantage of them is ours to make.  ✢

**PRAYER**

*Lord, please supply . . .*

**READ**

Insight into Ahaziah can be found in 2 Kings 8:25 — 9:29 and 2 Chronicles 22:1 – 9.

# day27

## AHIJAH
### SMALL ACTS OF FAITHFULNESS

*"Ahijah the prophet is there — the one who told me I would be king over this people."*
1 KINGS 14:2

Age was not a factor in Ahijah's usefulness to God. He spoke for God on two distinct occasions, illustrating a lifetime of faithfulness. First, Ahijah predicted that an aspiring common man named Jeroboam would become king over ten rebellious tribes of Israel. Apparently, Jeroboam saw this as little more than a confirmation of his own ambitions, for he did not pay attention to the warning included in Ahijah's prophecy. As king, he led the people into renewed idolatry.

Years later, faced with a sick child, Jeroboam recalled the truthfulness of Ahijah's prophecy. The aging prophet was pressed into service once again by the Lord. He informed Jeroboam that his sick child would die and his reign would come to a terrible end because of his disobedience to God. We know of only these two occasions when Ahijah carried out special duties, but each time he was faithful. The years that separated those assignments show that he was ready.

Today may or may not include a memorable event in your life. The hours may simply be filled with the small acts of obedience that make up a faithful lifestyle. But whether or not you are in the spotlight of special service, make this day another for which God can call you a good and faithful servant. ✤

**PRAYER**

*Lord, I long for you to call me faithful . . .*

**READ**

Ahijah's story is told in 1 Kings 11:26 – 40; 14:1 – 18.

## AHITHOPHEL
### *GOOD ADVICE AND GODLY ADVICE*

*So David prayed, "LORD, turn Ahithophel's counsel into foolishness."*     2 SAMUEL 15:31

Ahithophel was a trusted adviser of King David for many years. The qualities of his counsel, however, do not become apparent until the Bible records the details of Ahithophel's betrayal of David. Ahithophel's counsel always answered the question, "What's the shortest distance between two points?" He was a straight-line thinker whose suggestions were practical, efficient and direct. Once he switched loyalties from David to Absalom, his only concern was to guide his new king to success.

What mattered most to Ahithophel were his plans. He was used to being followed without question. Even his betrayal of David gives no evidence of personal conflict between them. Ahithophel simply decided David was no longer fit to be king and it was time to back Absalom. But when his counsel was rejected by Absalom in favor of Hushai's, Ahithophel could not handle the devastating loss of face or the prospects of punishment from a victorious David. He calmly returned home, ordered his affairs and hung himself. Ahithophel's practical thinking led him straight to the wrong side.

The most practical plans and effective efforts are pointless if they serve the wrong purpose. Unfortunately, we are capable of successful schemes while disobeying God. Target some areas concerning your family, vocation or ministry in which you may have settled into a compromising pattern of "what works." How can you invest the time and prayerful energy into God's plans of what could work better?                                        ♣

**PRAYER**

*May your will be done through me, Lord . . .*

**READ**

Ahithophel's story is told in 2 Samuel 15–17.

## AMASA
### *A REBEL IS RESTORED*

*Say to Amasa, "Are you not my own flesh and blood? May God deal with me, be it ever so severely, if you are not the commander of my army for life in place of Joab."*

2 SAMUEL 19:13

When we first meet Amasa, he has been chosen to replace Joab as the leader of Israel's army, then under the sway of the rebel Absalom. Amasa was no dark-horse candidate; he was a blood relative of David. Amasa chose poorly—his army was defeated by troops loyal to David. But instead of being executed, Amasa was named the commander in chief of the reunited army.

Some see Amasa's appointment as a shrewd political move on David's part to win over the rebellious faction of Israel's army, and perhaps it was. From Amasa's perspective, however, David's gesture must have seemed astounding and unbelievably kind. For here was a rebel, a trusted family member who had deserted his king in the hour of need, being welcomed back with all forgiven. Amasa and his troops responded gratefully; they were "of one mind" (2 Samuel 19:14).

In the same way, God astounds us daily with his marvelous grace. We are forgiven for all of our past rebellions and called "friends" of God (John 15:14). How do you respond to the grace God shows you every day? How can you thank him today for his tremendous mercy and kindness?    ❖

**PRAYER**

*Thank you, Lord, for . . .*

**READ**

Amasa's story can be found in 2 Samuel 17:24–26; 19:12–15; 20:4–13.

## AMAZIAH
### *HALFHEARTED OBEDIENCE*

*[Amaziah] did what was right in the eyes of the LORD, but not wholeheartedly.*

2 CHRONICLES 25:2

Young Amaziah grew up in a court setting illustrated by a brief appearance of righteousness in the midst of a host of idolatry and killing. He watched his father, Joash, do well under the godly influence of the old priest Jehoiada, only to resort to idolatry and murder after Jehoiada died.

When Amaziah became king, he also kept alive an appearance of attentiveness to God but his heart wasn't in it. He executed those who had assassinated his father. His early successes, which could have inspired humility, instead gave rise to arrogance. Furthermore, despite God's cautions, he challenged a reluctant Israel to a military confrontation and experienced the humiliating defeat God forewarned. The remainder of Amaziah's reign was desolate. As in the case of his father, his own people plotted and killed Amaziah.

The pattern surrounding Amaziah's life affirms that hoping to obey God without heartfelt motivation is wishful thinking. Unfortunately, we all do a little wishing now and then. Do you often know what the right thing is but sometimes resent having to do it? Life with Christ can be so much more than a series of duties or obligations. Let God transform you from the inside out so that your desire for him and his plans are not fleeting moments but the timeworn characteristic of your life. ♣

**PRAYER**

*Change me, Lord . . .*

**READ**

The story of Amaziah can be found in 2 Kings 14:1–23 and 2 Chronicles 25.

## AMNON
### *A CHAIN REACTION OF SIN*

*"You would be like one of the wicked fools in Israel."*          2 SAMUEL 13:13

Amnon was King David's firstborn son. He set in motion one of the most shameful and destructive series of actions in the royal family. He became sexually obsessed with his half-sister Tamar. When his attempt to seduce Tamar failed, he raped her. Then, his "desire" for her turned to loathing, and he humiliated her. He tried to make it look like the incest was his sister's fault. Tamar's brother Absalom later avenged her by killing Amnon. Tamar lived out the rest of her life alone, for after Amnon's attack, her chances for an honorable marriage ended.

Amnon, like most of his siblings, was a child out of control. He was frustrated when he couldn't have his way, and disgusted when he got his way. Without discretion, he acted upon the impulse of his own desires and brought tragedy to the lives of his family members. The Bible records that he did not have even a hint of remorse for what he had done to his own sister. Because of his uncontrolled impulses, his family was never the same again.

Family relationships can be systems of strength or systems of dysfunction. We can consider each of our individual acts of selfishness or selflessness as part of a chain reaction within the system. Many of the choices we make are laden with the potential to positively or negatively affect those we love. Can you think of any ways to begin a positive chain reaction of love and peace in your family?          ❖

**PRAYER**

*Let the chain of love start with me, O God . . .*

**READ**

Amnon's story is told in 2 Samuel 3:2; 13:1–39.

# day32

## ANANIAS OF DAMASCUS
### OBEDIENCE OVERCOMES FEAR

*In Damascus there was a disciple named Ananias.* ACTS 9:10

"Not him, Lord; that's impossible. He could never become a Christian!" That was the gist of Ananias's response when God told him of Saul's conversion. One moment Ananias was pondering the possibility of his own imprisonment and death; the next, God was telling him to go help the man who held the warrant for his arrest. Ananias must have felt like running, but he decided to obey God anyway.

Until God knocked him from his saddle, Saul of Tarsus had no mercy on Christians. Now, he was blind and at *their* mercy. Saul's first experience in his new life was a soft touch and a stranger's voice calling him "brother." Ananias left a lasting impression on Saul—later known as Paul. Many years later, when Paul told a crowd about his conversion, Ananias was the only person he mentioned by name.

Ananias was only in the spotlight for a moment. His role was small, but significant. Even though God told him of his plans for Saul, Ananias probably did not appreciate the scope of the events in which he was participating. We usually fail to see what God can accomplish through our "small efforts." Fortunately, we are not asked to understand the entire plan. We are simply asked to be faithful with our part. What "small" opportunities to practice obedience to God are before you today? ❖

### PRAYER

*Teach me how to obey you, Lord . . .*

### READ

The story of Ananias is told in Acts 9:10–19; 22:12–16.

# day33

## ANANIAS OF JERUSALEM
### GOD IS NOT DIVIDED

*Peter said, "Ananias, how is it that Satan has so filled your heart that you have lied to the Holy Spirit?"*                                                    ACTS 5:3

Almost any group will include those who want to belong without the trouble of real commitment. The early Christian church had its share of those who failed to count the cost. Ananias and his wife Sapphira preferred to appear committed rather than to be genuine in their faith. They were under the mistaken notion that appearances were just as good as the real thing, but cheaper. Caught in the act of dishonest giving, they lost everything.

When he confronted Ananias, Peter made the problem very clear. Ananias and his wife were not obliged to give to the church. That wasn't the problem. Ananias's sin came when he desired to gain prestige by making others think he had given the entire amount of the property sale when he had only given part of the money. Among those he intended to deceive was God. His punishment was quick—and fatal.

It's often tempting to bend the truth, but have you ever thought about who you're really trying to deceive? How often would we stop twisting the truth if we truly and fearfully realized that beyond those people we may fool is a God we cannot deceive? Ask God to help you be a person of truth today.                    ❖

### PRAYER

*Lord, please help me to be an honest person …*

### READ

The story of Ananias is told in Acts 5:1–6.

## ANDREW
### *A HOPEFUL DISCIPLE*

*The first thing Andrew did was to find his brother Simon and tell him, "We have found the Messiah" (that is, the Christ).* JOHN 1:41

Andrew knew a good thing when he saw it. He was one of the first people called in the Gospels to be a follower of Jesus. As soon as he met Jesus, he rushed to tell his brother Simon. Until that time, Andrew had been one of John the Baptist's disciples. But when John pointed out Jesus as the Savior, Andrew became a follower of Christ. Later, when Jesus invited him to become a fisher of men, Andrew dropped his nets without a backward glance.

Another glimpse of Andrew's positive outlook comes from an occasion when Jesus fed a multitude. Most of the disciples were initially stumped by the logistics. But Andrew, perhaps in jest, or in hope, tentatively said, "Here is a boy with five small barley loaves and two small fish, but how far will they go among so many?" (John 6:9). It turned out to be more than enough.

Andrew seized the most positive aspects of life with both hands. Even when the positive outlook seemed like a long shot, like the bread, Andrew took a chance on it. As Andrew's life affirms, one person bent on hopefulness can become a source of blessing for others. The world needs Andrews!

If you are not an Andrew yourself, try to spot one this week and give him or her a little encouragement. Being a hopeful person can sometimes be a lonely job. ✤

**PRAYER**

*Lord, for the "Andrews" in my life, I ...*

**READ**

Glimpses of Andrew are found in Matthew 4:18–20; Mark 3:18; John 1:35–45; 6:8–9; 12:21–22 and Acts 1:13.

## ANNA
### *THE REWARDS OF WAITING*

*She never left the temple but worshiped night and day, fasting and praying.*     Luke 2:37

Anna was a well-worn example of patient waiting. Her short marriage ended in widowhood. She spent the remainder of her 84-plus years serving in the temple as a prophet. She was there when Mary and Joseph brought the child Jesus to Jerusalem for the first time. That visit was probably one of Mary's indelible memories from her son's life that were shared with Luke. Anna overheard Simeon's prophecy about Jesus and immediately added her own excited words of praise for the Savior.

Anna made the temple her home. Though he was writing about widows in the church several decades later, Paul seemed to be describing Anna when he wrote, "The widow who is really in need and left all alone puts her hope in God and continues night and day to pray and to ask God for help" (1 Timothy 5:5). Anna discovered that God can make every passage of life meaningful and useful. The long years of widowhood were also effective years of worship and service.

Like Anna, you may patiently go about the daily routines of life. However, perhaps you feel you are waiting for God to reveal a more exciting plan for your life. Ask God to show you the potential for even this time of seeming insignificance to become meaningful and effective service for him.     ❖

**PRAYER**

*Lord, while I wait ...*

**READ**

Anna's story is told in Luke 2:36 – 38.

# day36 february 5

## APOLLOS
### *SERVING WITH HEART AND MIND*

*A Jew named Apollos, a native of Alexandria, came to Ephesus. He was a learned man, with a thorough knowledge of the Scriptures.*      Acts 18:24

The story of this brilliant public speaker and debater gives us some things to think about:

- The only public debate that some think is appropriate now is over policy, technology and money. To debate about the truth of Christ would offend too many people.
- Being "learned" is not so popular among some Christians today. Many think it is better to be "trained" or "called."
- Some think that learned people raise too many questions, and these questions can be troublesome and tiresome. Our church leaders and pastors are busy enough already.
- Some think that fervor seems out of line with our tendency to be respectable, mainstream citizens who are polite and tolerant.

When Apollos looked out at an audience, he could see a proud, even arrogant crowd of thoroughly secular skeptics on the one side—the Greeks and Romans—and on the other, deeply loyal Jews who, like himself, revered the Old Testament, but unlike himself, knew nothing of the Messiah and the new covenant. Those were tough crowds by any standards. Yet Apollos addressed them intelligently and passionately. He served the Lord with all his heart and mind.

Study widely and constantly, speak with conviction and urge all people to find the truth in Jesus Christ.                              ❖

### PRAYER

*Lord, I want to serve you...*

### READ

Apollos's story in found in Acts 18:24–28. He is also mentioned in 1 Corinthians 1:12; 3:4–6,22; 4:6; 16:12 and Titus 3:13.

## AQUILA AND PRISCILLA
### A FAITHFUL TEAM

*When Priscilla and Aquila heard him, they invited him to their home and explained to him the way of God more adequately.*      ACTS 18:26

This remarkable husband-and-wife team are remembered for their leadership in the early church. They assisted Paul, Apollos and many others unnamed. They were learners and teachers, passing on the great treasure of the gospel that had transformed their lives. They worked together in the tent-making business, helped Paul earn his living for a while, and befriended the talented evangelist Apollos, teaching him what they had learned about the Lord. The story of these two Christians is so full of hospitality, cooperation and excitement about the gospel that even a modern reader can feel the enthusiasm.

Aquila and Priscilla were faithful to each other, to the Lord and to Christian friends wherever their travels took them. We don't know many details about their ministry, but we have Paul's simple declaration of gratitude: "They risked their lives for me" (Romans 16:4). What a testimony of sacrifice, courage and love.

Do you see any ways you can emulate Priscilla and Aquila in your day-to-day life? What about in your ministry or outreach efforts? By finding these opportunities, you can also discover what an impact Christ can make through you.    ✤

**PRAYER**

*Lord, please show me avenues of ministry . . .*

**READ**

The story of Priscilla and Aquila is told in Acts 18. They are also mentioned in Romans 16:3–5; 1 Corinthians 16:19 and 2 Timothy 4:19.

# day38

## ARISTARCHUS
### *EXCEPTIONAL COMMITMENT*

*My fellow prisoner Aristarchus sends you his greetings.*　　　COLOSSIANS 4:10

Those who traveled with Paul did not paste on their luggage stickers from the exotic cities they visited; their only souvenirs were scars of suffering. In Ephesus, an angry mob couldn't find Paul immediately, so they vented their anger at Aristarchus and Gaius. Aristarchus, a Thessalonian native, accompanied Paul to Rome, where later he apparently spent time in chains with the apostle.

We have no record that Aristarchus was ever sent on any special missions by Paul. But he may have been the representative of the Thessalonian church in the team that took the collected money from the various Mediterranean churches back to Jerusalem to help the mother church. In any case, it appears that Aristarchus's main ministry was to Paul himself. The suggestion that he stayed in the background isn't as important as the fact that he was always there. He could be counted on without requiring special attention or grabbing the limelight.

Being a devoted servant such as Aristarchus takes more commitment than many disciples have been willing to give. Most of us would rather be in charge than in chains. Where in your church or circle of Christian friends can you do quiet supporting work like Aristarchus did in the early church?　　　✤

### PRAYER

*Heavenly Father, may my devotion be evident . . .*

### READ

Aristarchus is mentioned in each of the following contexts: Acts 19:29; 20:4; 27:2; Colossians 4:10 and Philemon 23–24.

## ASA
### *TAKING A TOUGH STAND*

*Asa called to the LORD his God and said, "LORD, there is no one like you to help the powerless against the mighty."*      2 CHRONICLES 14:11

The divided kingdom was still young when Solomon's great-grandson took the reins of Judah. Considerable pagan worship had crept into the culture, and Asa did his utmost to bring the country back to God. He was a courageous leader who stood up to fight the bully prince Zerah of Cush, despite overwhelming odds.

When faced with opposing numbers that would have brought goose bumps to Goliath, Asa knew the source of his strength: he asked God for help in a simple prayer and then moved forward. And when his scheming grandmother Maakah wanted to win points with a crowd of idol-worshipers (see 2 Chronicles 15:16), Asa made the decision to strip her of royal privilege, putting devotion to God above family loyalty.

Asa had a clear vision of the direction in which he was taking Judah and pursued his policy in the face of danger and family opposition.

We can learn from Asa's simple, take-charge attitude: There's no room for compromise when it comes to serving God. You can take a tough stand for what you know God wants, and you don't have do it alone—you can always ask God for help.       ❖

**PRAYER**

*Lord, grant me the courage to stand . . .*

**READ**

Asa's bravery is recounted in 1 Kings 15:8–24 and 2 Chronicles 14–16. He is also mentioned in Jeremiah 41:9 and Matthew 1:7–8.

# day40

## ASA
### *LOVE GROWN COLD*

*Asa was angry with the seer because of this; he was so enraged that he put him in prison.*
2 CHRONICLES 16:10

Something quite terrible but all too common happened to Asa in later life. He lost his heart for God.

Perhaps he let the prestige of his job go to his head. The job of being king tended to lead one to an exaggerated estimate of self-importance.

Perhaps the opposite occurred. Compared to David and Solomon, Asa was a minor-league ruler. Perhaps he could see his reign fading into history's backwater and grew cynical about religious devotion.

Whatever the problem, Asa's respectable and God-fearing career was hurt by an alliance with the pagan Ben-Hadad of Syria, jolted by his imprisoning of the prophet who dared to call him back to faith (see 2 Chronicles 16:7–10), then wrecked by a foot disease and his refusal to seek the Lord's healing strength. He died in the midst of war, a punishment from God.

We can guard each other from suffering a fate similar to Asa's. We need to support and encourage senior members of the church, and remember with prayer, visits, music and encouraging conversations those once-vital believers who now reside in nursing homes and convalescent centers, lest they forget in their ailment and loneliness the sure promises of the gospel. Christians approaching their golden years can still nurture their faith and trust always in the goodness of God. ✣

### PRAYER

*Lord, I offer my support to . . .*

### READ

Asa's story is told in 1 Kings 15:8–24 and 2 Chronicles 14–16. He is also mentioned in Jeremiah 41:9 and Matthew 1:7–8.

## ASAPH
### A MAN OF WORSHIP

*David left Asaph and his associates before the ark of the covenant of the LORD to minister there regularly, according to each day's requirements.* 1 CHRONICLES 16:37

Next to David, Asaph wrote more psalms than any other psalm writer. Eleven of Asaph's compositions appear in what is known as the third book of Psalms. We do not know much about his background or personality. We do know that Asaph was the father of several generations of worship leaders in the days of the tabernacle and temple. He and his fellow Levites were responsible for writing and performing music to praise God. Asaph was also the first to direct choirs. He led his fellow Levites in songs of thanksgiving.

A glance at Asaph's compositions tells us how seriously he took the task of worshiping God. His powerful psalms remind his readers of God's majesty and faithfulness, of his mercy and patience. They remind us too of our utter dependence on God. Asaph proclaims that God can be counted on to rescue and uphold his people.

Studying the works of Asaph and other psalmists takes us into the heart of worship. We need the daily refreshment of these words to bring perspective to our hurried lives, to remind us that we are meant to worship and love God with our whole being. Meditate on these words as often as you can. ❖

### PRAYER

*I praise you, Living God . . .*

### READ

Asaph is mentioned in the following passages: 1 Chronicles 15:19; 16:5,7,37; 25:1–9; 2 Chronicles 5:12; 20:14. In addition, he wrote Psalms 50; 73–83.

## ATHALIAH
### *KILLER QUEEN*

*When Athaliah the mother of Ahaziah saw that her son was dead, she proceeded to destroy the whole royal family.* 2 KINGS 11:1

The family of Queen Athaliah, the daughter of King Ahab, ranks as the most evil nuclear family in the Bible. King Ahab and Queen Jezebel established an alliance with Jehoshaphat, king of Judah, by giving Athaliah in marriage to Prince Jehoram. The Bible tells us she was a bad influence upon her son Ahaziah when he assumed the throne after his father's death.

The peak of Athaliah's wrongdoing came long after Jehoram's death when she received word that her son had been killed by Jehu in the same revolt that also saw the deaths of Athaliah's brother Joram, the former queen Jezebel, and at least 70 other half-brothers and half-sisters. Athaliah's appalling response was to put her own children and grandchildren to death. Not even her own flesh and blood would keep her from complete power.

For seven years, Athaliah ruled ruthlessly as the queen in Judah until she was overthrown and killed. The evil she caused was a shameful chapter in the story of God's people. Her story demonstrates that the family structure, a potential catalyst for great good, can also set into motion unspeakable evil. The natural love and respect that God intends for the family can turn into a destructive force, and the family community of love can become a community of hatred. As in the case of Athaliah, this hatred can have devastating consequences. Loving families are worth guarding. ♣

### PRAYER

*Father God, I pray for my family . . .*

### READ

Athaliah's story is told in 2 Kings 8:25 — 11:20 and 2 Chronicles 24:7.

# day43

## BALAAM
### *PROPHET FOR HIRE*

*They have left the straight way and wandered off to follow the way of Balaam son of Bezer, who loved the wages of wickedness.*                    2 PETER 2:15

Some craftsmen in the ancient world made tents, others forged tools, some built homes, but Balaam did sorcery. For a fee, you could hire Balaam to cast spells that would help your cause and hurt your opponents. That's how he made his living, and he made it quite well.

One day in the middle of his successful career, Balaam hit upon a problem. Asked by the Moabite king Balak to curse the Israelites, Balaam discovered the true God. He had invoked gods and spirits every working day, but on this day he hit a wall. God did not want him to curse the chosen people. To his credit, Balaam suppressed his greed and complied with God's instruction. (Choices were limited in this regard, since Balaam saw God's avenging angel, poised to strike him if he chose to disobey.) Balaam even confessed admiration for "the LORD" and taught the pagan Moabites about God's character (Numbers 23:18–24).

But in the end, Balaam's encounter with the true God did not change his greedy behavior. He went back to Moab during the Israelite attack and there met his end.                                                                    ❖

**PRAYER**

*Guard my heart, O Lord, against . . .*

**READ**

Balaam's story is told in Numbers 22–24. He is also mentioned in Numbers 31:7–8,16; Deuteronomy 23:3–5; Joshua 24:9–10; Nehemiah 13:1–2; Micah 6:5; 2 Peter 2:15–16; Jude 11 and Revelation 2:14.

# day44

## BARABBAS
### *THE UNEXPECTED REPRIEVE*

*Pilate asked them, "Which one do you want me to release to you: Jesus Barabbas, or Jesus who is called the Messiah?"*                                    MATTHEW 27:17

Did the echoes in the dungeon seem to emanate from hell? Did the convict shrink in terror at the sound of approaching feet? When they led him from his prison, did he follow quietly? Was he still mumbling excuses when they left him in the street? Was Barabbas at Golgotha, drawn by curiosity? Did he whisper his repentance, tears streaming down his face?

It's hard to know how Barabbas may have felt about his role in Jesus' trial. He knew he had been the unlikely beneficiary of a Passover custom. And Barabbas was indeed known as a hero among many Jews. Yet as the guards led him from his prison, perhaps he remembered that Jesus had once been popular with many in this same crowd. So what did he think when the people chanted his name as their choice for whom they wanted released? The Bible doesn't say, and the story ends with Barabbas's release. But was he really free?

Barabbas's small part in this story makes a big point. He represents us. Like him, sin has declared us guilty and worthy of death. The verdict has been rendered. Then, also like Barabbas, we hear the incredible news: Someone has taken our place. And yet, like Barabbas, we are not completely free until we respond to the one who offers total forgiveness. What is your response?                    ✤

**PRAYER**

*Lord, my response to the freedom you offer is . . .*

**READ**

Barabbas's story is found in Matthew 27:15–26. He is also mentioned in Mark 15:6–15; Luke 23:18–25 and John 18:39–40.

## BARAK
### *RELUCTANT WARRIOR*

*Barak said to [Deborah], "If you go with me, I will go; but if you don't go with me, I won't go."*  JUDGES 4:8

Barak stood before a once-in-a-lifetime opportunity and stepped forward—tentatively. He was summoned by Deborah, the current judge of Israel, and given a mission. Deborah informed Barak that God had chosen him to lead in the defeat of Sisera and his Canaanite forces. Although he had God's assurance about the outcome of his mission, Barak insisted on Deborah's presence throughout the operation. Chosen to be a leader, he settled for being a lieutenant. Deborah made all the command decisions. His request to keep Deborah by his side shows that he trusted more in human strength than in God's promise.

The New Testament lists Barak among the faithful of the past (see Hebrews 11:32). But the flaws in his faith also remind us that we seldom fully allow God to work through us. What might have happened if Barak had not insisted on altering the original plan?

We will not always have the luxury of others' company when we are carrying out God's plans. Our obedience must not depend on our companions of the moment. Trusting God will inevitably bring us to places where we have to stand alone. However, like he did for Barak, God can make our obedience result in a positive outcome. What will be your response if you find yourself in Barak's sandals today?  ❖

### PRAYER

*Lord, I offer to you my fear of . . .*

### READ

Barak's story is found in Judges 4–5. He is also mentioned in Hebrews 11:32.

## BARNABAS
### *THE ENCOURAGER*

*Barnabas took him and brought him to the apostles.*                    Acts 9:27

By any reasonable standard, it was a mismatch of wits that could have spelled disaster for the church. Saul (later Paul)—the urbane Greek intellectual, forceful Jewish Pharisee, privileged Roman citizen—now claimed to be a Christian and wanted to meet the leaders at Jerusalem. Everyone except Barnabas smelled a plot. If Saul was faking it, the heart of the church would be vulnerable.

Barnabas cast worry to the wind and went into the city to meet this new brother in Christ. It was Barnabas's faith in the power of God that sent him. His willingness to believe the best in each person won him a reputation as an encourager throughout the early church.

We need such people today. Many people who attend the same church do not know each other well and are unsure how to make friends. That's one of the reasons why so many church hallway conversations are about the weather and sports—very safe topics.

With a Barnabas in the church—an encourager of the saints—people begin to open up, conversation goes deeper, people begin to trust each other and the mission of the church is reinvigorated. What ailing brother or sister can you boost with a phone call or a gesture of acceptance, hospitality or help?                    ♣

**PRAYER**

*Lord, show me whom to serve today . . .*

**READ**

Barnabas's story is told in Acts 4:36–37; 9:27—15:39. He is also mentioned in 1 Corinthians 9:6; Galatians 2:1–13 and Colossians 4:10.

## BARNABAS
### *TAKING CRITICISM THE RIGHT WAY*

*The other Jews joined him in his hypocrisy, so that by their hypocrisy even Barnabas was led astray.* GALATIANS 2:13

The great encourager Barnabas, Paul's long-time friend and early mentor, had followed the belief that Gentiles could not be full-fledged Christians. That was not true, and Paul told him so. It must have been bitter medicine for Barnabas to realize that he had faltered at the point of his greatest strength.

In our areas of strength we expect only praise and admiration, yet we all need the corrective influence of a wider Christian community. Hard as it is to swallow—especially when it strikes so close to one's gifts—no Christian can live isolated from the church's discipline.

Barnabas survived and prospered because he admitted his mistake. He took correction and went on. Community was strengthened, ruffled feelings were soothed by grace and the church's mission was clarified. By any measure, the church would have been worse off had Barnabas stormed away to pout and sputter about ingrates and malcontents.

There is no virtue in defending our mistakes or in finding fault with those who spot them. It is far better to defer to the critics—or at least be open to what they have to say. We can learn from each other without taking offense. We cannot become so proud of our talents that we cannot hear the voice of an honest critic. ❖

**PRAYER**

*Lord, please grant me the humility to listen ...*

**READ**

Barnabas's story is told in Acts 4:36–37; 9:27—15:39. He is also mentioned in 1 Corinthians 9:6, Galatians 2:1–13 and Colossians 4:10.

## BARSABBAS
### *DISAPPOINTMENT IS NOT DOUBT*

*They nominated two men: Joseph called Barsabbas (also known as Justus) and Matthias.*
ACTS 1:23

Judas was gone, and the apostles decided he should be replaced. They narrowed their choices down to two men: Barsabbas (Justus) and Matthias. Each of them met an important qualification: they had been followers of Jesus from the beginning. When lots were drawn, Matthias was added to the apostolic band. From then on, Barsabbas must have been known as the "almost apostle." The prayer and the lots insured that the choice was not a popular or political one, but one in which God was involved.

Barsabbas may have been disappointed with the outcome, but he may just as well have been relieved. In order to be identified as a possible candidate, he must have already been active in ministry. Perhaps God honored his willingness to serve by permitting him to serve in some other way.

Keeping our lives available to God may not mean we will be able to do everything we would like to do, or even what others would like us to do. Jobs will come and go; doors will open and close; opportunities will be presented or withdrawn. God is neither surprised nor caught off guard by such situations. He will continue to honor our willingness to be used in other ways. For what recent disappointment do you need to be mindful that God is in complete control?                    ❖

**PRAYER**

*Help me, Father, to take to heart that you are in control . . .*

**READ**

Barsabbas's story is told in Acts 1:23–26.

# day49

## BARTIMAEUS
### *A DEMONSTRATION OF GRATITUDE*

*The blind man said, "Rabbi, I want to see."* MARK 10:51

Bartimaeus had one handicap and one strength: he was blind and he was bold. To the crowd pressing around Jesus, Bartimaeus was a nuisance. The roads were lined with other such "nuisances": the lame, the sick and the poor, begging for help. In this case, the blind man made sure he begged louder than most. They told him to be quiet, but the eyesore wouldn't cooperate. He kept shouting "Jesus, Son of David, have mercy on me!" (Mark 10:47).

When Jesus acknowledged Bartimaeus, the blind man leaped to his feet. In response to Jesus' question, Bartimaeus made his simple request, "Rabbi, I want to see." Jesus sent him on his way with the assurance that his faith had resulted in his healing. Sure enough, Bartimaeus gained his sight, but he didn't leave. Instead, he immediately followed Jesus.

The Lord did not make following him the prerequisite for mercy, but Bartimaeus realized that following Jesus was the best way to express his gratitude for what Jesus had done. How many examples of God's mercy in your life can you think of in fifteen seconds? How clearly have you expressed your gratitude to God recently? ❖

**PRAYER**

*Thank you, Lord . . .*

**READ**

The story of Bartimaeus is told in Matthew 20:29 – 34; Mark 10:46 – 52 and Luke 18:35 – 43.

## BARUCH
### *FAITHFUL SCRIBE*

*Jeremiah called Baruch son of Neriah, and while Jeremiah dictated all the words the LORD had spoken to him, Baruch wrote them on the scroll.*   JEREMIAH 36:4

Baruch was one of those unsung Biblical heroes—a scribe. Through the hands and pens of scribes like him, inspiration became Scripture. The Bible came about by God's inspiration to many different individuals, and some of those whom God inspired by his Spirit dictated to someone else what God moved them to communicate.

Not only did Baruch take dictation from Jeremiah, but he also acted as the prophet's spokesperson. As such, he put his own life in danger. The insults, threats and abuse heaped upon Jeremiah spilled over onto Baruch. Chapter 45 of the book of Jeremiah records a special memo to Baruch from God. Apparently, Baruch had been feeling sorry for himself. His future seemed in doubt. If Jeremiah's prophecies came true, he was equally at risk for being Jeremiah's secretary and for being a citizen of Israel. God's word to Baruch was very direct: "Wherever you go I will let you escape with your life" (Jeremiah 45:5).

Uncertainties in the world around us are frequently distressing. That is why certainties are important. Life may appear to be entirely chaotic, but we can remain calm in the knowledge of God's control. There will be times, maybe even today, when you will not be able to trust what you see, hear or feel. Remember God's memo to Baruch and trust only what you know.                                    ✤

### PRAYER

*Lord, I trust that . . .*

### READ

Baruch's life and ministry are outlined in Jeremiah 32:12–16; 36:1–32; 43:1–7; 45:1–5.

## BARZILLAI
### A FRIEND INDEED

*"Show kindness to the sons of Barzillai of Gilead and let them be among those who eat at your table."*

1 KINGS 2:7

Troubles and trials have a way of revealing who our friends are. When his son Absalom betrayed him, David barely had time to escape alive. Some of his closest advisers abandoned him. The kingdom seemed lost, and David was barely ahead of those pursuing him. Into this nightmare appeared Barzillai and several others with food and supplies. Their help was simple, timely and perfect.

Later, David tried to reward Barzillai by having him come back to Jerusalem with the king. But Barzillai was already 80 years old and too wise to make an unnecessary move. He was thankful he had been in a position to help the king. When David was giving Solomon counsel before handing over the throne, he made it a point to tell his son to treat the family of Barzillai with special honor. David did not forget those who proved themselves true friends in his time of trouble.

What people in your life have helped you most when you needed it? Perhaps your needs weren't material, but they gave you encouragement and understanding at the moment when you thought you were completely alone. They didn't substitute for God; they reminded you of God. What have you done lately to demonstrate you haven't forgotten the value of their gifts? ♣

### PRAYER

*For the encouragers in my life, Lord Jesus, I . . .*

### READ

Glimpses of Barzillai's life can be found in 2 Samuel 17:27–29; 19:31–39 and 1 Kings 2:7.

# day52

## BATHSHEBA
### GOD SEES IT ALL

*David sent messengers to get [Bathsheba]. She came to him.*        2 SAMUEL 11:4

The guilt was shared. David, who should have been with his army, was lounging in Jerusalem when sexual desire overcame him.

Bathsheba was not necessarily innocent in the matter. While it is uncertain whether her intent in bathing on the roof was simply to get some fresh air or whether she was doing it to get David's attention, it is clear that she went to be with David. When the invitation came to spend a night in the palace, did she hesitate, consider excuses or otherwise resist? Did she feel like she had a choice in the matter or did she jump at the chance? What motivated her to say yes? Was it the flattery of a king's invitation?

Two intelligent adults denied their separate responsibilities and gave in to lust. Dishonoring God, they suffered for it. Their child died, but in the end Bathsheba knew something more about her Lord.

Nothing escapes God's eyes. People cannot steal away at night as if God were asleep and morality on break. Sin has consequences. Bathsheba became pregnant and lost the child. She also lost her husband.

God can forgive and restore. A union that started out wrong produced an heir to the throne and a forefather of the Messiah. No matter how much you've sinned, never lose hope.                                                      ✣

**PRAYER**

*Forgive me, Lord ...*

**READ**

Bathsheba's story is told in 2 Samuel 11–12 and 1 Kings 1–2. A related passage is Psalm 51.

## BATHSHEBA
### *A PROMISE REMEMBERED*

*Bathsheba went to see the aged king in his room, where Abishag the Shunammite was attending him.* 1 KINGS 1:15

Many years earlier, Bathsheba and King David enjoyed one of the most infamous liaisons of all time. Following their sorrow and guilt, the loss of their baby and shame at David's plot against Uriah—after all that—David and Bathsheba had become the proud parents of a child they named Solomon.

Now Bathsheba, whose feelings are never revealed in Scripture, walked into David's room. With him is another beautiful young woman, and in her presence she spoke. "My lord, you yourself swore to me your servant by the LORD your God: 'Solomon your son shall be king after me, and he will sit on my throne'" (1 Kings 1:17).

David had many children, none of them successful, one a traitor. But Bathsheba wanted David to do what he promised. Then Nathan appeared to add his news, and David roused himself to perform one last kingly duty—the transfer of power.

We know little about Bathsheba, but at least we know this: she never stopped believing, and she wasn't afraid to confront the most powerful man in her world.

Faith means action based on your best sense of God's will, before it's too late. Let confidence in God drive you to do what must be done today. ❖

### PRAYER

*Lord, I am confident that you ...*

### READ

Bathsheba's story is told in 2 Samuel 11–12 and 1 Kings 1–2. A related passage is Psalm 51.

## BELSHAZZAR
### *WEIGHED AND FOUND WANTING*

*"You, Belshazzar, his son, have not humbled yourself, though you knew all this."*
                                                              DANIEL 5:22

Belshazzar was a man accustomed to pleasure. Living in a sumptuous palace that flowed with food and drinks and teemed with concubines, he was used to getting whatever he wanted, whenever he wanted. So when he recalled the cups that had been taken from the temple in Jerusalem, he demanded they be brought to his banquet so that he and his followers could drink to their idols.

Suddenly Belshazzar was confronted with a force he could not control: a hand writing strange words on the wall. After much anguish, he found Daniel, who interpreted the writing as a message of judgment. The prophet told the king that his empire would be torn apart and his life taken—all because he dishonored God and refused to humble himself. That very night, Belshazzar was assassinated.

Sooner or later, we will all come to the realization that terrified Belshazzar: We are powerless to control our own destiny. But will we shrink back as he did, reflecting on a life lived for self-gratification, or will we humbly turn to God and ask him to lead the way? Don't be lulled into a false security because of your power, wealth or status—give thanks to the God who shapes your destiny and lights your paths.                                                                  ❖

### PRAYER

*Lord, grant me a sense of your control . . .*

### READ

Belshazzar's tragic end can be found in Daniel 5.

# day55

## BENAIAH
### *A TRUSTWORTHY FOLLOWER*

*Benaiah son of Jehoiada, a valiant fighter from Kabzeel, performed great exploits.*

                                                              2 SAMUEL 23:20

David surrounded himself with powerful warriors whose personal accomplishments were remarkable. Besides their physical prowess, their most notable characteristic was their loyalty. Benaiah was an exceptional officer in David's army. The king demonstrated his trust in Benaiah by putting him in charge as his chief bodyguard. Benaiah never betrayed that confidence.

The roots of David and Benaiah's relationship probably began during the hectic days in the wilderness when David was trying to avoid Saul's attempts to kill him. Benaiah was part of a ragtag band of those who were in trouble or discontented for one reason or another (see 1 Samuel 22:2). David turned them into an effective fighting force. Benaiah watched his leader remain true to God, and he determined to be true to David. As a result, the Bible records the amazing, wholehearted efforts of Benaiah in his service to David.

Leaders depend on loyal and trustworthy friends and followers. The Bible says that we are to support and submit to the legitimate authorities with prayer and faithfulness. This is especially true for Christians in positions of leadership but also holds for other authorities (see Romans 13:1).                                    ♣

### PRAYER

*Lord, I support . . .*

### READ

The actions of Benaiah are recorded in 2 Samuel 8:18; 20:23; 23:20–23; 1 Kings 1–2 and 1 Chronicles 11:22–25; 27:5–6.

# day56 february 25

## BENJAMIN
### *A FAMILY MAN*

*As she breathed her last—for she was dying—she named her son Ben-Oni. But his father named him Benjamin.*                                                    GENESIS 35:18

Jacob had twelve sons by four different women. Benjamin was born last, the second son of Rachel. His older brother was Joseph. Benjamin grew up with the problems and privileges of a youngest child. He also lived with the knowledge that his mother died giving birth to him.

Benjamin was still young when a second tragedy shattered his life. His brother Joseph disappeared, presumed dead. His ten half-brothers returned home with Joseph's blood-soaked coat. Jacob concluded that his favorite son had been killed by wild animals. From then on, Benjamin became his father's main concern.

Meanwhile in Egypt, Joseph was riding a roller coaster of success and failure. A widespread famine eventually brought the family back together, but not before Benjamin was once again thrust into the center of a family crisis.

Perhaps because of all these events, Benjamin was a family man. The only word or action of Benjamin's recorded in the Scriptures occurs in Genesis 45:14: "[Joseph] threw his arms around his brother Benjamin and wept, and Benjamin embraced him, weeping." He also was the father of at least ten male children.

Tragedies often help us realize what's important in life. Benjamin's losses presumably made him deeply appreciate his loved ones. How can you take a few moments today to show your appreciation for those closest to you?                    ♣

**PRAYER**

*Lord, as I think of my family and friends, I . . .*

**READ**

Benjamin's story is told in Genesis 35:16—49:28.

# day57

## BERNICE
### *HEARING PROBLEM*

*After they left the room, they began saying to one another, "This man is not doing any-thing that deserves death or imprisonment."*  ACTS 26:31

The apostle Paul was a persuasive speaker, but he did not convince all his listeners. Bernice was part of the second-highest audience before whom Paul presented his defense. She was with her brother Herod Agrippa II when Festus invited them to evaluate this outspoken Jewish-Roman prisoner who had recently appealed his case to Caesar. Bernice was apparently convinced of Paul's innocence, but failed to apply his message to her own life.

We know from sources outside the Scriptures that Bernice led a shameful life. She lived with her brother in what appears to have been an incestuous relationship. She outlived one husband and abandoned another. Later she was the mistress of Titus, who eventually became Roman emperor. She moved in the highest social circles of her time, yet she rejected or ignored the opportunity to find the peace with God that came so close to her through Paul. We don't know if Bernice considered what Paul said, only that she did not respond to it.

God may well bring a life-changing opportunity into your life today, or he may simply nudge you toward a more honest, patient or self-controlled lifestyle. In either case, are you listening?  ❖

### PRAYER

*Lord, make me aware of your holy nudges . . .*

### READ

Bernice's story is told in Acts 25:13 — 26:32.

## BEZALEL
### *GOD'S CRAFTSMAN*

*"See, I have chosen Bezalel son of Uri, the son of Hur, of the tribe of Judah."*

EXODUS 31:2

What happens when God's Spirit fills a person? They receive special preparation to do God's work. But what God actually asks someone to do with his or her gifts varies greatly from person to person.

In Bezalel's case, God filled an artist with his Spirit in order to produce works of uncommon beauty and usefulness. For Bezalel, God said, "I have filled him with the Spirit of God, with wisdom, with understanding, with knowledge and with all kinds of skills—to make artistic designs for work in gold, silver and bronze, to cut and set stones, to work in wood, and to engage in all kinds of crafts" (Exodus 31:3–5). Elsewhere (see Exodus 35:34) we are told that Bezalel and Oholiab were also effective instructors in their crafts. Every object used in worshiping God, from the large movable tabernacle to the smallest utensil, was created by a person God had equipped for fine work.

When God's Spirit fills us, plain work takes on holy character. The medium may not be "spiritual" in the strictest sense (preaching, ministering, healing, praying), but it may be necessary, practical work (like building the acacia wood frames for the curtains in the tabernacle) done in such a way that the Mover behind the craftsman leaves his divine fingerprints on the product. Look for ways to see your tasks today as God's uniquely prepared jobs for you to perform to his glory. ♣

**PRAYER**

*Spirit of the Living God, fall afresh on me . . .*

**READ**

Bezalel's story is told in Exodus 31:1–11; 35:30—36:7.

## BOAZ
### *GIVER OF REFUGE*

*"May you be richly rewarded by the LORD, the God of Israel, under whose wings you have come to take refuge."*                                                    RUTH 2:12

The words spoken by Boaz to Ruth were her welcome to Israel. She was foreign, a young widow, without work and vulnerable. Boaz owned a lot of land and was related to Ruth's deceased husband. He understood the need to provide care for her. He also had a strong sense of God's providence and mercy. His estate would be the tangible expression of God's protection to Ruth.

What if Christians today understood their homes as God's pavilion for needy people? "Come," we might say, "take refuge under the wings of the Almighty." That very old way of talking would have to be modernized: "Here's the fridge; there's the shower. Clean up, let's eat and praise the Lord!"—or something like that.

We catch the tone and depth of Boaz's welcome only if we truly see that all we have is part of God's wonderful kingdom. When people enter our homes, they come under God's big umbrella.

Ruth would still spend days gleaning grain in the dirt and heat of Boaz's vast farm, but provision was now assured. Boaz did not hesitate to share with the foreigner a portion of all God had given to him.                                                    ❖

**PRAYER**

*I am grateful for your provision, Lord, to enable me to . . .*

**READ**

Boaz's story is told in the book of Ruth. He is also mentioned in Matthew 1:5.

# day60

## BOAZ
### *A HOLY REASON FOR HARD WORK*

*Naomi said, "Wait, my daughter, until you find out what happens. For the man will not rest until the matter is settled today."*                RUTH 3:18

Naomi assured Ruth that when Boaz put his mind to a task, things happened. Ruth could wait with high expectation; by evening her future would be clear.

Many of us could use Boaz's skill at getting things done. Work transforms the world. The architect shapes buildings from crude materials. The merchant matches customer needs with sensible prices and durable products. Good work brings order from chaos. It sorts priorities and establishes routes to meeting needs. It negotiates agreeable settlements. But why work hard?

Most people would say, "To enrich yourself." People work to achieve wealth and power. Is that all?

The Bible affirms that good work is motivated by love. God exerts himself because he loves us. Our work is first a loving response to God, and then a loving hand to others. No, not every transaction of every day is a gushy experience in handholding friendship. But the Bible's point is clear: The work you do counts for greatness only when it's done because you really care for others. And only God can give you that concern. Boaz experienced that concern and kept to the task until it was done.

Whatever your trade or profession, ask God to give you a new sense of love for the people you serve.                                                        ❧

**PRAYER**

*Lord, I need a sense of your love ...*

**READ**

Boaz's story is told in the book of Ruth. He is also mentioned in Matthew 1:5.

## CAIAPHAS
### *RECIPES FOR SUCCESS*

*Caiaphas, who was high priest that year, spoke up, "You know nothing at all! You do not realize that it is better for you that one man die for the people than that the whole nation perish."*        JOHN 11:49–50

No man was more bent on the arrest and execution of Jesus than Caiaphas. When the Sanhedrin seemed uncertain, Caiaphas rallied them. When Pilate wavered, Caiaphas insisted.

Caiaphas was an astute and savvy head of the Jewish state. He survived in that volatile job for 18 years, from AD 18 to 36. No one was better at placating the Romans and pacifying the Jews.

Caiaphas's big worry was that a Zealot uprising would bring the force of Rome crashing down on his people. He knew who held all the big sticks, and he also knew that his people, if stirred by revolutionaries, had the capacity to throw caution to the wind. That's why Caiaphas believed that executing one "troublemaker" was better than provoking Roman military action.

Pity Caiaphas. For all his learning, he failed to discern the truth. All the power of his personality and office was directed against God's Son, and he never saw it (or at least never admitted it). Politically and religiously he was a huge success, but spiritually he was bankrupt. He had it all, and it was nothing.

Seek God first, and your life will have the meaning and purpose God intended: fullness, joy, an eternal relationship of love and peace.      ❖

### PRAYER

*Lord, I seek your face . . .*

### READ

Caiaphas's story is told in Matthew 26:57–68 and John 18:12–28. He also is mentioned in Matthew 26:3; Luke 3:2; John 11:49–50 and Acts 4:6.

# day62

## CAIAPHAS
### CONFOUNDING THE WISE

*When they saw the courage of Peter and John and realized that they were unschooled, ordinary men, they were astonished and they took note that these men had been with Jesus.*
ACTS 4:13

Two of the disciples, not outstanding men by any measure, went before Caiaphas to face questioning related to the healing of a crippled beggar near the temple courts (see Acts 3). The people whom Caiaphas had sought to quiet down by Jesus' death were agitated again, carried away by "a miracle." How could this be? Who were these men?

Caiaphas got an earful that day from Peter and John. He had indicted and convicted their leader, yet these two disciples had the audacity to claim publicly that God had undone the Sanhedrin's plan, that Jesus was alive from the dead and directly responsible for the miracle healing. What arrogant blasphemy! Surely these two must also die.

But this time even Caiaphas was stymied. The people were too excited by the miracle. The Sanhedrin lacked consensus and thus had no legal basis for detaining Peter and John. Caiaphas was left with an empty court, stunned by a power he had never comprehended, bewildered that his carefully conceived plans were unraveling through the words of simple fishermen.

Today, the gospel still surprises powerful, intelligent people who thought they had life all boxed, wrapped and on the shelf. God's power stuns and stymies worldly wisdom. Be a student of God's wisdom. ✤

### PRAYER

*Lord, I need your wisdom . . .*

### READ

Caiaphas's story is told in Matthew 26:57–68 and John 18:12–28. He also is mentioned in Matthew 26:3; Luke 3:2; John 11:49–50 and Acts 4:6.

## CAIN
### *FULL PARDON IS AVAILABLE*

*The LORD said to Cain, "Where is your brother Abel?" "I don't know," he replied. "Am I my brother's keeper?"*                                                    GENESIS 4:9

Among other distinctions, Cain was the first to offer the world an unforgettable quotation. These famous words have come to stand for excuse making, disregard for loved ones and outright lying. A rough man, strong and impetuous, Cain despised weakness and had little patience for those whose work he judged inferior. He paid little heed to God. Independent and self-willed though he was, Cain was not above asking for a break when he knew he was beaten (see Genesis 4:13).

After Cain murdered Abel, God gave him a mark. It was a sign to keep hooligans away from him; it was also a reminder that God still cares for even the worst criminals.

Cain's story teaches us never to give up on anybody. God's love and mercy reaches people who do not deserve it, whose personalities are toughened and resistant. God never quits on anybody.

When you have opportunity to help toughened people, remember that God was merciful to Cain. If you are a prisoner or former offender, remember that the very first criminal was still a child of God. If you are a victim of crime, hard as it may be, let God do the judging and sentencing so that your heart is free to forgive and live again.                                                                                      ❖

### PRAYER

*Judge my heart, O Lord ...*

### READ

Cain's story is told in Genesis 4:1–17. Cain is also mentioned in Hebrews 11:4; 1 John 3:12 and Jude 11.

# day64

## CALEB
### *BOUNDLESS FAITH*

*Caleb silenced the people before Moses and said, "We should go up and take possession of the land, for we can certainly do it."* NUMBERS 13:30

Intelligence experts are masters at jigsaw puzzles. They piece together information until it makes a coherent picture. Rarely, however, do the pieces fit together neatly. More often huge gaps remain. Consequently, most intelligence reports depend on the grid upon which the pieces of information are laid. For Caleb that grid was faith in God; for the other spies, it was fear of the Canaanites.

Caleb was the Israelites' "can-do" person. Sure, he saw the fortified cities and sheer numbers of opposing forces. But doesn't faith mean moving out of your comfort zone and seeing what God can do?

That was Caleb's secret: he relied not on his own strength but on God's. Few people in the history of the Bible get the divine affirmation Caleb received in Numbers 14:24—he was a different spirit, a wholehearted follower. We can almost see God bursting with pride over this man.

Do you have a mission? Does your church? Is it big enough to stretch your faith? Do your planners and fundraisers and strategists agree that human will alone cannot make it happen? Take Caleb's "can-do" attitude to your church, to your home, to your job. Be prepared for "realists" who have no faith. Be prepared too for setbacks, delays and moments of discouragement. Trust God to help you reach the goals for which you're aiming. Help others grow in faith along the way. ❖

**PRAYER**

*Lord, I am trusting you to . . .*

**READ**

Caleb's story is told in Numbers 13–14 and Joshua 14–15.

# day65

## CALEB
### *READY AND HOPEFUL*

*"I am still as strong today as the day Moses sent me out; I'm just as vigorous to go out to battle now as I was then."* JOSHUA 14:11

Caleb had good reason to be depressed. He was at the prime of his life during the spy mission, but 45 years had passed because of others' failure of faith. At 40 he had counseled the people toward Canaan; now he was 85.

Were these words mere boasting, as men of all ages are inclined to do? Maybe not. Perhaps Caleb had set a path for his life that was as different from the mainstream as his faith had been different a generation earlier. Knowing his mission, frustrated at delay, he determined to keep himself in shape—and in full faith—for the day the Lord would say, "Go!"

Thus Caleb, courageous at 40, was ready for the most important work of his life at 85, brimming with faith and high expectation. Far from diminished or beaten, Caleb's confident attitude had survived the wilderness wanderings. He was ready to lead Judah into Hebron.

Does your life march along with dreams frustrated and goals unmet? Take a cue from Caleb—try to spend each day ready and hopeful. Of course, it isn't easy to remain strong all the time, but thankfully, you don't have to do it alone. ❖

### PRAYER

*Lord, I need your hope . . .*

### READ

Caleb's story is told in Numbers 13–14 and Joshua 14–15.

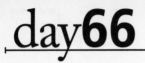 **day66**

## CLAUDIUS LYSIAS
### *EVERY DEED AN ACT OF SERVICE*

*Then the commander said, "I had to pay a lot of money for my citizenship." "But I was born a citizen," Paul replied.*                    ACTS 22:28

Paul owed his life three times over to a Roman soldier named Claudius Lysias. Twice in the temple grounds Claudius guarded him from the crowd. Later, when Claudius was told of a plot against the apostle, he arranged Paul's escort to Caesarea under military protection.

Roman officers in Judea did thankless work. They were hated by the local population and considered expendable by their superiors. They were expected to maintain order in a world they seldom understood. Claudius Lysias was not a Roman by birth, but he reached the rank of commander in the Roman army by sheer hard work and effective military discipline. He was a man who evidently took simple pride in doing his work well.

The Bible includes many examples of people God worked through, but whose eventual relationship with God we are not told. Claudius is one such person.

Remember in your dealings with others today that God might use you to touch someone else in ways you do not know. See everything you do as an act of service to him, and be grateful for the role he allows you to play.                    ✤

**PRAYER**

*Lord, thank you for allowing me to ...*

**READ**

Claudius's efficient work was recorded by Luke in Acts 21:27 — 23:35.

## CLEOPAS
### *KEEPING YOUR EYES OPEN*

*They asked each other, "Were not our hearts burning within us while he talked with us on the road and opened the Scriptures to us?"*      LUKE 24:32

If Jesus stepped into your life today without warning, how soon would you recognize him? What would give him away? Do you know him well enough to spot him undercover?

For Cleopas, it was the bread that gave Jesus away. God used that familiar way in which Jesus took the loaf, gave a prayer of thanks and then broke it to open his eyes. Unmistakable. Perhaps as he watched that simple liturgy Cleopas finally noticed Jesus' hands—the nail wounds. It was the Lord.

But Cleopas and his traveling companion failed to recognize Jesus right away. In fact, they had already spent several hours with Jesus, walking from Jerusalem to Emmaus. Neither Jesus' appearance nor the remarkable comments he made about himself tipped off the disciples. What would have happened if they hadn't extended simple hospitality to a fellow traveler at the end of the day?

Once they recognized Jesus, he disappeared. They rushed back to Jerusalem to add their report to the growing evidence that the Lord was no longer dead. As they were sharing their tale, Jesus appeared again. Cleopas saw Jesus twice on the day of the resurrection. How many clues about his presence will he place in your life today? Have you asked him yet to help you keep your eyes open?   ❖

**PRAYER**

*Open my eyes, Lord, to . . .*

**READ**

Cleopas's story is told in Luke 24:13–48.

## CORNELIUS
### *THE QUIET REVOLUTION*

*[Cornelius] and all his family were devout and God-fearing; he gave generously to those in need and prayed to God regularly.*                    ACTS 10:2

Beneath the surface, there's a revolution going on. You might not see it when you walk through the office or hear it when the swing shift gets onto the assembly line, but it's there. In every walk of life, in every place where people do business, a spiritual revolution is transforming lives.

Cornelius was an early part of it. He did his job, but he did it in a special way that told everyone he was different. He approached his men with discipline, but also with compassion. He imposed the power of Rome on the Jewish people around him, but with a keen eye toward fairness and reason. In Cornelius and among his family, the revolution was defining a new kind of person: a Christian.

Did Cornelius ever become a Roman general? Did his faith help or hurt his career? We do not know. But wherever Cornelius went, he was a witness to the revolution God started back in Genesis. He would never be just another centurion. His life had purpose that transcended rank and battle ribbon. His heart knew joy and peace in a new company of brothers and sisters, the church of Jesus Christ.

Be like Cornelius. Let God put his revolution in your heart.               ♣

**PRAYER**

*Lord, let change start with me . . .*

**READ**

Cornelius's part in the revolution is told in Acts 10–11.

## CORNELIUS
### GOD'S NEW COMMUNITY

*The circumcised believers who had come with Peter were astonished that the gift of the Holy Spirit had been poured out even on Gentiles.* ACTS 10:45

Cornelius's family was a test case of how far God was willing to go in changing peoples' hearts. Peter himself was unsure whether or not Gentiles had any share of God's attention. How could God give his blessings to someone so outside of the Jewish community—like a Roman army officer? Such a person represented everything offensive: a sharpened sword, emperor worship, foreign occupancy. But a strange thing happened. God sent the Holy Spirit on Cornelius and his family.

"Hey," they must have said, "God is blind to all those Gentile-Jewish distinctions that define one group as good and the other as bad. United in Christ and blessed by the Spirit, Gentile and Jewish believers are true brothers and sisters, however different their traditions and political bents." One in Christ! How surprising of God!

Today we know that other divisions are just as illusory in God's eyes: race and skin color, ethnic background, gender and social status. God has declared all people to be his people—none more than others by any measure of color or wealth. Still, many churches pretend as if God prefers one over another. So the revolution begun in Cornelius's home still goes on—proving God isn't finished with us yet. ❖

**PRAYER**

*Root out any unloving ways within me, Lord ...*

**READ**

Cornelius's story is told in Acts 10–11.

## CRISPUS
### LEADING BY EXAMPLE

*Crispus, the synagogue leader, and his entire household believed in the Lord; and many of the Corinthians who heard Paul believed and were baptized.* ACTS 18:8

Paul first visited Corinth during his second missionary journey. As was his practice, he began his ministry in that city by making contact with the local Jewish synagogue. He obviously created a stir, showing up on the Sabbath with a fresh dose of the gospel. Eventually some of the Jewish leaders banded in opposition to Paul and a confrontation occurred. Their rejection left Paul free to turn his attention to the Gentiles.

One person caught in the middle of the conflict was Crispus, a leader of the synagogue. Paul's message had reached him. But when Paul was forced out of the synagogue, Crispus was faced with a choice: He could remain in the safety of his religious role or openly declare his belief in Jesus. His choice became a family decision. He and his household became believers. Paul baptized him. Luke attributes to Crispus's public faith the rapid growth of the church in Corinth. His decision opened a way for others to trust Christ. People who step out in faith are rarely alone for long. ❖

### PRAYER

*Lord, here I stand, ready to . . .*

### READ

Crispus appears in the events of the early church in Acts 18:1–17.

# day71

## DAMARIS
### *RESPONDING TO THE TRUTH*

*Some of the people became followers of Paul and believed. Among them was Dionysius, a member of the Areopagus, also a woman named Damaris, and a number of others.*
ACTS 17:34

Centuries after Socrates and Plato, Athens continued as a center of philosophy. Alone in that great marketplace of ideas, Paul began to preach the gospel. Paul was eventually invited to present his case for Christianity in the official forum. Among the people who heard the apostle that day was a woman named Damaris.

Paul achieved two results with his message: a strong reaction and a small response. The majority of his listeners reacted to his call for repentance and his claim that God had raised Jesus from the dead. Some sneered and others decided to think about it another day. We don't know Damaris's reason for being part of the Areopagus audience, but she believed Paul's message. The fact that Luke mentioned her name probably means she became a faithful follower of Christ. She was also a charter member of the local church in Athens.

God's truth requires a response. Damaris was one of those who responded to the truth rather than reacting from her prejudices and preconceptions about the way the world works. Instead of postponing it until another time, her commitment was prompt and wholehearted. How would you describe your usual pattern of response to God's truth? ❖

### PRAYER

*Lord, in regard to truth, I . . .*

### READ

Damaris's story is told in Acts 17:16–34.

## DANIEL
### *FIT FOR GOD'S SERVICE*

*Daniel resolved not to defile himself with the royal food and wine, and he asked the chief official for permission not to defile himself this way.* DANIEL 1:8

Best known for surviving the lions' den (see the devotion at March 14), Daniel was a remarkable young adult whose faith gave him unusual composure and personal discipline. He was the type of guy who would honor God in public and in private, and mean it—a rare person with a gifted mind and a firm heart for God.

Daniel was also something of a scientist. His approach to finding an amiable way to decline the royal food and wine took involved observation and experimentation (see Daniel 1:8–15). Daniel proved his point not by sophistry or debate but by simple evidence.

Daniel lived faithfully in an environment opposed to faith in God. Yet he won the respect of the non-believers around him and never flinched from his duty to obey God first. Daniel's obedience in a hostile situation began with his diet, extended through to his education and finished with his constant practice of prayer.

If you have ever wondered where to start in being a witness for God, follow Daniel's example. ❖

**PRAYER**

*Lord, make me an example . . .*

**READ**

Daniel's story is told in the book of Daniel. He is also mentioned in Matthew 24:15.

## DANIEL
### *TRUSTING IN GOD'S GOODNESS*

*When Daniel was lifted from the den, no wound was found on him, because he had trusted in his God.*                                          DANIEL 6:23

Most living lions seen by people today are restrained by cages in zoos. Babylon had its cage too, and in the scariest experience of his life Daniel was condemned to enter it. He did so with a prayer. God kept the lions pacified, and Daniel was freed the next morning.

Sometimes Christians do not get the rescue Daniel received. Cancer strikes with fatal results. A car accident claims a life. Prayers for healing or safety do not result in healing or safety. Is the difference a measure of Daniel's faith and ours?

No. God hears prayers from even those with faith the size of a mustard seed. Throughout the Bible, we see that God grants mercy, but people still die. Tragedy and deliverance are both common themes. Daniel could not have presumed that his prayers or his faith obligated God to rescue him. Rather, whether hurt or spared, Daniel would trust in God's goodness every moment of his desperate night, just as he trusted in God every other night. In life or death, Daniel's Savior was the Lord God.

When frightened or threatened, pray, then trust in God and his goodness.  ✣

**PRAYER**

*Lord, I fear that ...*

**READ**

Daniel's story is told in the book of Daniel. He is also mentioned in Matthew 24:15.

# day74

## DAVID
### *TRAINING FOR OUR MISSION*

*David said to the Philistine, "You come against me with sword and spear and javelin, but I come against you in the name of the LORD Almighty, the God of the armies of Israel, whom you have defied."*                                           1 SAMUEL 17:45

In history's most famous fight, David made his mission plain. This was to be a showdown between the power of God and the power of this world, winner take all.

Everything would have changed if David had misunderstood his mission. "Golly, Goliath, my scaredy-cat brothers put me up to this!" or "We're filming an ad for this new sling" or "It's national stardom if I hit the first shot" all miss the mark.

To understand his mission, David needed a personal history of prayer, worship and faith. He needed prayer for the courage to challenge the giant. He needed worship to know he was engaged in a spiritual battle. And he needed a well-practiced faith to believe he could succeed. Then, and only then, he stepped out of the trench onto the plain.

Believe it or not, we all carry on David's torch in the fight against evil. Our adversary is the lie that will increase sales, the kiss that will violate vows, the compromise that makes all claims of truth one jumbled stew. David knew perhaps better than anyone else that a decisive spiritual battle must be engaged that day and that he must fight. He was ready.

Are you?                                                                                          ❖

### PRAYER

*Lord, make me ready for the challenge . . .*

### READ

David's story is told in 1 Samuel 16:1 — 1 Kings 2:46. David is also mentioned in Amos 6:5; Matthew 1:1,6; 22:42 – 45; Luke 1:32; Acts 13:22; Romans 1:3 and Hebrews 11:32.

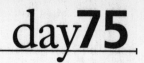
## DAVID
### *A CHERISHED FRIENDSHIP*

*Jonathan said to David, "Go in peace, for we have sworn friendship with each other in the name of the LORD."*                          I SAMUEL 20:42

David and Jonathan had a friendship that made each a stronger person. They trusted each other completely and were loyal to each above anyone else.

How does such friendship develop? Surely, some of it has to do with attractions that are deeply personal, as hard to explain as a preference for red over blue. But "chemistry" does not sustain these bonds. They come from a common faith, a shared mission and the practice of *agape*, the New Testament word for other-minded love, which harbors no jealousies and seeks the good of the other above all.

Such friends are few and far between. Sadly, many people have no one like this in their lives.

Among the many descriptions of God throughout the Bible, his friendship with us is portrayed as steady and strong, the *agape* kind. God seeks our best; God loves us deeply.

One of God's great gifts to us is friendship with him and other people. We should strive to develop deep and meaningful friendships and stay loyal to our friends. We should also know God as a friend. He stays with us when all others leave.

How can you develop, protect and nurture your friendships today? What about your friendship with God?                                                             ❖

*Father, I am grateful for these friends ...*

**READ**

David's story is told in 1 Samuel 16:1 — 1 Kings 2:46. David is also mentioned in Amos 6:5; Matthew 1:1,6; 22:42–45; Luke 1:32; Acts 13:22; Roman    3 and Hebrews 11:32.

# day76

## DAVID
### *ONE SIN LEADS TO ANOTHER*

*At David's invitation, he ate and drank with him, and David made him drunk. But in the evening Uriah went out to sleep on his mat among his master's servants; he did not go home.* 2 SAMUEL 11:13

In committing adultery with Bathsheba, David allowed himself to fall deeper and deeper into sin. He let lust take over and ran toward temptation instead of away from it. He deliberately sinned, focusing on his own desires. He also tried to cover up his own sin by deceiving others. David's first moral compromise led him into one sin after another. Had he tried to make things right after his first misstep, he and others would have been spared the pain of further compromises.

David's mistakes serve as a vivid example to us today. No good comes from trying to cover up sin; instead, it is crucial to stop and confess our sins. David's venture down the road of adultery led him (and others) to pay heavy tolls. What was he thinking? Perhaps he reasoned to himself, "I've already done this, so I may as well do that." He may have thought he had no choice, but clearly he was wrong.

Whenever you sin, don't think, "I may as well go even further" or think, "I can fix this myself." God prefers—and enables, if you're willing—you to turn back before things get out of hand. ❖

### PRAYER

*Lord, I want to turn back . . .*

### READ

David's story is told in 1 Samuel 16:1—1 Kings 2:46. David is also mentioned in Amos 6:5; Matthew 1:1,6; 22:42–45; Luke 1:32; Acts 13:22; Romans 1:3 and Hebrews 11:32.

## DAVID'S MIGHTY WARRIORS
### *ALL FOR ONE AND ONE FOR ALL*

*All those who were in distress or in debt or discontented gathered around [David], and he became their commander. About four hundred men were with him.*     1 SAMUEL 22:2

David's brigade of fugitives, mercenaries and renegades must have enjoyed a fearsome reputation during Saul's reign, for the king could not capture them, and neighboring Philistine rulers tolerated them. They were usually described as intensely loyal to David. Actually, like most people, their loyalty depended on their leader's success. After the sacking of their city, Ziklag, they talked openly of mutiny (see 1 Samuel 30:6), but David's leadership prevailed.

They certainly performed with valor and were known for their ferocity and fearlessness. The elite units were known as the Thirty and the Three. The final name on the list in 2 Samuel 23 is of one who refused to betray his leader even while his leader betrayed him. These men were not mere military robots who did David's bidding.

We could learn from the loyalty and camaraderie these men enjoyed, given our penchant for individualism and our tendency to cut ties with a church if things aren't to our liking. The mighty warriors stuck together, followed their leader and pulled their weight. They were no sluggards.

We would do well to imitate their example. With God's help, consider how you might be like them today.                                                                  ✤

**PRAYER**

*Lord, make me like . . .*

**READ**

The mighty warriors are mentioned in 1 Samuel 22:1—2 Samuel 23:39 and 1 Chronicles 11–12.

# day78

## DEBORAH
### *A SONG FOR GOD'S PEOPLE*

*"So may all your enemies perish, LORD! But may all who love you be like the sun when it rises in its strength."*                    JUDGES 5:31

What song do you sing? This verse is the last stanza in the famous song of Deborah, the fourth (and only female) leader of Israel during the long and difficult period following Joshua's death. She organized a military response to the aggression of Jabin, a Canaanite kingpin, whose army included a fearsome 900 iron chariots. Foot soldiers facing this armada would be like modern infantry advancing against tanks and artillery.

In Israel's army, the determining factor was never the order of battle, but always the faith of its leaders. In an ugly, evil era, Deborah called the nation to its mission. For 40 years the people prospered under her leadership. In one decisive moment, she did not flinch at Sisera's overwhelming military advantage, but pressed her countrymen to victory—by prayer, words of encouragement and her presence. In the end, her bully adversary lost his army, his life and his honor.

What song do you sing? Deborah took the noonday sun as her symbol of God's strength—too bright for direct view but its heat and light everywhere evident. She found a song that encouraged her faith and gave that song to the nation.    ♣

### PRAYER

*Here is my song to you, O God . . .*

### READ

Deborah's story is told in Judges 4–5.

## DELILAH
### *HOW TO LOSE FRIENDS THE FAST WAY*

*With such nagging she prodded [Samson] day after day until he was sick to death of it. So he told her everything.*      JUDGES 16:16–17

Delilah's name is synonymous with treachery and attractiveness. We know the first quality to be true because of her infamous treatment of Samson. We infer the second because this world-class strongman could not resist her. In one important way, she was the stronger of the two.

Her relationship with Samson seemed like such a game. This physical behemoth, so much stronger than she, would be putty in her hands. When the deed was done, she taunted him, "Samson, the Philistines are upon you!" (Judges 16:20). Wasn't she surprised to discover that with his hair clipped, she was his equal in physical strength too?

Delilah is a study in how not to treat people, how not to develop friends, how not to nurture intimacy. Do the opposite of Delilah, and you're probably on the right track.

Are you the listener people need? Are you the steady friend few people have? Delilah treated people like sport. We need to relate to others as ambassadors of God's love. In order to develop stronger friendships, try concentrating less on your troubles and more on the potential of each day to reveal God's blessing to you. ✤

**PRAYER**

*Lord, I want to be loyal . . .*

**READ**

Delilah's story is told in Judges 16.

## DEMAS
### *LOVING THE WORLD*

*Demas, because he loved this world, has deserted me and has gone to Thessalonica.*

2 TIMOTHY 4:10

Jesus described four different responses to the gospel in the parable of the sower (see Mark 4:1–20). Demas was among those represented by the third kind of soil: "Still others, like seed sown among thorns, hear the word; but the worries of this life, the deceitfulness of wealth and the desires for other things come in and choke the word, making it unfruitful" (Mark 4:18–19). Demas chose the world and may have lost his soul.

Our picture of Demas emerges in brief glimpses. He joined Paul sometime before the apostle's first visit to a Roman dungeon. The letters to the Colossians and to Philemon included his name among Paul's companions. But his role and character were not described. Only the length or difficulties of Paul's second imprisonment revealed the depth of Demas's commitment. When the going got tough, he quit. Hardship eventually did for Demas what it does for every believer—it forced him to make a choice. When following Christ seems easy, the world has little to offer us. But when difficulties come along, life away from Christ takes on a whole new attraction. Part of the tragedy in Demas's case was that he lost himself and deserted others he could have helped. They could have helped him too. ♣

**PRAYER**

*Guard me, Lord, from the love of the world . . .*

**READ**

Demas is mentioned three times: Colossians 4:14; 2 Timothy 4:10 and Philemon 24.

## DEMETRIUS
### *THE GODS OF OUR MAKING*

*[Demetrius] called them together, along with the workers in related trades, and said: "You know, my friends, that we receive a good income from this business."*   ACTS 19:25

The idol business in Ephesus found itself in a slump. Silver symbols of the goddess Artemis were not selling. Demetrius, a well-known local silversmith, traced the economic downturn to a traveling evangelist named Paul, who was convincing people that silver idols were just silver. Demetrius disagreed. Silver idols weren't just silver; they were also his livelihood. Besides, he argued to his fellow businessmen, their great goddess might be threatened if people came to believe that "gods made by human hands are no gods at all" (Acts 19:26).

The anger and arguments of the craftsmen revealed who their god really was — their own self-interest. Their religion was a profit motive. Interestingly enough, a non-Christian city clerk demolished their case by calling their bluff. If Artemis was really a goddess, she could certainly take care of herself!

The lesson to us is clear: If we find the focus of our faith threatened, we may be trusting in something less than God. We may have substituted ourselves, another person or some *thing* for the one true God. The God who revealed himself in Jesus Christ doesn't need to be defended. Invest your faith in him alone.   ✤

**PRAYER**

*Lord, you alone are God . . .*

**READ**

Demetrius's attempt to corner the silver market is recorded in Acts 19:23–41.

# day82

## A DEMON-POSSESSED MAN
### *RELEASED TO TELL HIS STORY*

*He shouted at the top of his voice, "What do you want with me, Jesus, Son of the Most High God? In God's name don't torture me!"*　　　MARK 5:7

Jesus brought out the best and worst in people. One of his most vivid encounters was with an unnamed man who lived among the tombs near the Sea of Galilee. Others had long since given up on helping him. They hadn't even been able to control him, so they isolated him where he could only hurt himself. The demonic gang in him had almost accomplished its mission of destruction—until Jesus arrived unexpectedly.

Speaking through the man, the demons immediately panicked at having to face the Son of God. The tormentors found themselves suddenly in danger of torment. In a frenzy, they pleaded to be sent into a herd of pigs grazing nearby.

We may not understand entirely why Jesus agreed to destroy the animals, but we can appreciate in that action the value Jesus placed on the life of that one human being.

Jesus didn't let the healed man accompany him into the boat; rather, he told the man to return to the man's hometown to share the good news of his healing. Those who knew the man when he was possessed needed to see the change in him. They also needed to hear who had caused the change. Our last glimpse of the rescued man shows him amazing people of his hometown with his story.　　♣

**PRAYER**

*Show me how to use my story for your glory, Lord...*

**READ**

This story can be found in Matthew 8:28–34; Mark 5:1–20 and Luke 8:26–39.

# day83

## DINAH
### *SHAMED AND FORGOTTEN*

*Some time later she gave birth to a daughter and named her Dinah.*     GENESIS 30:21

As far as we know, Dinah was an only daughter. She had ten older brothers and two younger ones. Eventually, when Dinah was probably a teenager, she and her family moved to Shechem. Jacob, her father, bought a piece of land outside of town, and they pitched their tents. Jacob was actually procrastinating about fulfilling a promise to God to return to Bethel and worship. Jacob's delay proved disastrous for his family.

Apparently no one really paid much attention to Dinah until she went out for a walk one day in the city of Shechem. During her visit to town she was raped by Shechem, the son of the ruler of the city. Violated and shamed, Dinah found herself in the center of a family crisis. Shechem asked his father to arrange a marriage with Dinah. But in the eyes of Jacob and his sons, Dinah had been damaged, and their family had been insulted. Jacob failed to provide any fatherly leadership in this situation, and his sons took matters into their own hands. The results were treacherous and bloody.

In all of this the victim was overlooked. Dinah was neither comforted nor consulted. Instead, she was treated with almost as much disrespect by her family as she was originally by Shechem. Dinah's brothers profited from the massacre of Shechem. Jacob was angry at his sons for their actions, but he hadn't given them any direction. Meanwhile, Dinah slipped back into oblivion and was never mentioned again. Her story reminds us of the tragedies that occur when family members are careless with each other. Someone ends up paying a high price.    ❖

### PRAYER

*Lord, please help my family...*

### READ

Dinah's sad moment in the spotlight is recounted in Genesis 34.

## DIOTREPHES
### *AUTHORITY PROBLEM*

*I wrote to the church, but Diotrephes, who loves to be first, will not welcome us.*

3 JOHN 9

The explosion of Christianity within the Roman world swept many different kinds of people into the church. Some arrived with their own plans. Some even tried to make a personal kingdom out of those who had been called into God's kingdom. Diotrephes and others had to be identified and confronted by the true leaders within the church. John had to deal with Diotrephes.

All we know about Diotrephes is that he wanted to control the local church in which he was a leader. His rise to leadership has not been recorded, but we do know he enjoyed being in charge. He slandered his fellow leaders and refused to recognize their God-granted authority. He also set a bad example in refusing to welcome traveling Christians. Reveling in his own dictatorship, he even excommunicated those who opposed his control and offered hospitality.

Sins such as pride, jealousy and slander are still present in the church, although they may not be as blatant as in the case of Diotrephes. Well-intended concern can easily slip into subtleties of slander, and resentment can simmer unrecognized. Unchecked, such sin continues to grow. Ask God to help you search for the seeds of self-centeredness within your own heart. ❖

**PRAYER**

*Search my heart, Lord . . .*

**READ**

The record of John's confrontation of Diotrephes is found in 3 John 9–11.

## DOEG
### *THE (TEMPORARY) TRIUMPH OF EVIL*

*Why do you boast of evil, you mighty hero? Why do you boast all day long, you who are a disgrace in the eyes of God?*                    PSALM 52:1

Being the inspiration for one of David's psalms would seem like an honor, but in Doeg's case, it was a harsh judgment. Even though David was familiar with the violence and bloodshed of war, he was horrified by the news that Doeg had slaughtered the priests of God and their families. David felt responsible because a lie he told (see 1 Samuel 21:1–3) made it possible for Doeg to betray the entire town of Nob.

Doeg fits the description of a ruthless killer. His false testimony about the priests of Nob conspiring with David against Saul made the king furious. Saul ordered his guards to kill 85 priests in spite of their claim of innocence. When the guards refused, Doeg readily stepped in to commit the atrocities. Then he attacked the priest's families without mercy. Only one person from Nob, Abiathar, lived to tell David the sad news.

Doeg reminds us that people can become committed to evil. Their actions may hurt and even kill others. Even though it may seem like godly people have been unfairly treated, God has promised that evil people and their plans are only temporarily successful. God remains in control. Our challenge remains to follow God's guidance even in the face of evil opposition.                    ❖

**PRAYER**

*Lord, I need your guidance . . .*

**READ**

Doeg's story is told in 1 Samuel 21–22.

## DORCAS
### *DEVOTED TO GOOD WORKS*

*In Joppa there was a disciple named Tabitha (in Greek her name is Dorcas); she was always doing good and helping the poor.*                                    ACTS 9:36

Who makes a local church function well? We can usually think of several personality types that can regularly make life in the local church miserable. But what kind of person provides necessary balance? Leaders are needed, but their energies can be consumed by those who want to bend the church their way. The heartbeat of the church can most often be found among a tiny band of people who resemble a woman named Dorcas.

Dorcas (also known as Tabitha) only appears briefly in the New Testament. She was a disciple of Jesus in Joppa. She was too busy to sit still in the spotlight very long. In fact, she probably didn't plan to get sick and found it a nuisance to discover she was dying. There was too much to get done to leave any time for illness.

When Dorcas died, Peter happened to be visiting in nearby Lydda. The Christians in Joppa sent him a message to come. Since they had prepared her body for burial, it isn't likely that they were expecting a miracle. They simply wanted to honor Dorcas by having Peter present at the funeral. When Peter arrived, Dorcas's wake turned into a wake-up call. How amazed the believers must have been to see back alive someone they were going to miss so badly.

Luke tells us many people came to believe because of what God did through Dorcas. Do you know someone in your church like Dorcas to whom you could show appreciation in some special way today?                                              ♣

**PRAYER**

*Lord, give me the words to encourage ...*

**READ**

Dorcas's story is briefly told in Acts 9:32–42.

## EHUD
### *FAITH AND PREPARATION*

*Again the Israelites cried out to the LORD, and he gave them a deliverer—Ehud, a left-handed man, the son of Gera the Benjamite.*      JUDGES 3:15

Ehud's career as a judge in Israel was highlighted by a violent deed that freed his people from the oppressive Moabites. His story reads much like a modern adventure movie script. The hero carefully plots an attack and fashions the weapon to accomplish his task. A bold and shocking murder of a king is carried out in an isolated upstairs room, followed by a fast getaway. In the ensuing war with Moab, Ehud led God's people to a swift and decisive victory.

We may feel that Ehud's life is difficult to relate to. However, we must not ignore the life lesson of this leader. Ehud demonstrated intentional and resourceful obedience. He invested much energy in designing a plan to obey God and relied on God's help to carry through with that plan. How often do we to tell God of our intentions to honor him but falter when we attempt to follow through on our promises? Ehud demonstrated unwavering determination to not only listen to God, but to obey him, whatever the cost. To follow his example, you can begin by asking God to show you how he can use one of your unique qualities or abilities (like Ehud's left-handedness) for his purposes.     ❖

**PRAYER**

*Lord, please show me how I can serve . . .*

**READ**

Ehud's adventure is told in Judges 3:12–31.

# day88

## ELEAZAR
### *THE VALUE OF GODLY ROLE MODELS*

*The LORD said to Moses and Aaron, "... Get Aaron and his son Eleazar and take them up Mount Hor. Remove Aaron's garments and put them on his son Eleazar, for Aaron will be gathered to his people; he will die there."*  NUMBERS 20:23–26

Eleazar, son of Aaron, was an excellent understudy, well trained for his eventual leading role as the high priest of Israel. In order to assume such a responsible and potentially stressful undertaking, Eleazar had to be thoroughly prepared. An understudy benefits from having both the script and a human model of the role. Ever since childhood, Eleazar had been able to observe Moses and Aaron. Now he could help Joshua, with whom he was paired to lead the people into the promised land. Eleazar served as a trusted advisor to Joshua and supervised everything in the tabernacle.

An understudy must know the lead role completely and be willing to step into it at a moment's notice. What life lessons are you learning from those around you? God may have put certain people in your life in order to prepare you for future positions of leadership and responsibility. If you are single, seek counsel from married couples you respect. If you are planning to have children one day, observe the model of godly parents. Learning from those around us is an effective way to prepare for what God has planned for our future. ❖

**PRAYER**

*Point out my teachers, Lord ...*

**READ**

Eleazar is mentioned in Leviticus 10:16–20; Numbers 3:1–4; 4:16; 20:25–29; 26:1–3; 27:15–23 and Joshua 14:1; 24:33.

# day89

## ELI
### *BACKING DOWN FROM CONFRONTATION*

*"Therefore I [the Lord] swore to the house of Eli, 'The guilt of Eli's house will never be atoned for by sacrifice or offering.'"*                          1 SAMUEL 3:14

Eli was an Old Testament person with a very modern problem—he ignored difficult situations rather than resolving them. Eli's sons, both temple priests, brought him grief and ruin with their disrespectful behavior. God had pointed out their errors, but Eli's attempts to reprove them were halfhearted at best.

Because he was the high priest, Eli's reluctance to discipline his sons brought disastrous consequences. Eli's sons were making a mockery of their solemn priestly responsibilities. Eli invited God's judgment by refusing to put an end to the sin that was poisoning the worship of Israel. The consequences of his failure as priest and parent affected every succeeding generation in his family.

Like Eli, we often want to avoid becoming involved in situations where confrontation is unavoidable. Is there something in your life, family or work that you allow to continue even though you know it is wrong? When faced with a moral issue that requires decisive action, do you react hesitantly or with resolve?     ✤

### PRAYER

*Help me, Lord, to act with resolve . . .*

### READ

You can read about Eli's priestly reign in 1 Samuel 1–4. He is also mentioned in 1 Kings 2:26–27.

# day90

## ELI
### *THE SOURCE OF OUR POWER*

*When he mentioned the ark of God, Eli fell backward off his chair by the side of the gate.*
1 SAMUEL 4:18

The Israelites, under Eli's leadership, thought of the ark of the covenant as their lucky charm. They carried it into battle with them, believing that the ark itself—the wood and metal box—was their source of power. Consequently, Eli was devastated when he was told the Philistines had captured the ark during a battle.

Eli had become more concerned with the symbols of his religion than with the God they represented. The ark of the covenant had become a relic to be protected rather than a reminder of the Protector. Eli's faith shifted from the Creator to the created.

It may be easier to worship things we can see, whether buildings, people or Scripture itself, but such tangible things have no power in themselves. The Bible can be merely a respectable religious relic or it can be the sharp and effective Word of God. Your attitude toward it is largely shaped by your relationship to the God from whom it comes. A relic or antique has to be carefully stored away; God's Word has to be used and obeyed. Which attitude accurately describes your approach to the Word of God? ❖

### PRAYER

*Lord, in regard to your Word, I . . .*

### READ

You can read about Eli's priestly reign in 1 Samuel 1–4. He is also mentioned in 1 Kings 2:26–27.

## ELIEZER
### *THE HONOR OF SERVICE*

*Whoever wants to become great among you must be your servant.*   MARK 10:43

Eliezer was a friend and servant of Abraham. To describe him that way both tells all and tells too little, for we know little about him except that he was perhaps the most exemplary servant in the Bible besides Jesus.

Here's his simple story. Abraham wanted to find a wife for Isaac, Abraham's only son. So Abraham called in his trusted Eliezer and gave him the outline.

Eliezer clarified what he was being asked to do. After considering and ruling out the alternatives with Abraham, he gave his word to do his best. He designed a careful plan, keeping in mind that he should leave room for God to work. As he traveled and searched, he practiced patience in his task and thankfully accepted God's guidance. And he respectfully followed his plan through to completion, bringing Rebekah to Isaac as Abraham had requested.

The word *serve* carries a vaguely derogatory meaning these days. Eliezer's attitude and actions in carrying out his mission embody the honor and importance of service. He was what God wants us all to be first and above all: friend and servant.

Consider the variety of people you will rub shoulders with today. Will they receive service from you?                                                                                   ❧

**PRAYER**

*Lord, make me a servant...*

**READ**

Eliezer's story of service can be found in Genesis 24. See also Genesis 15:2–3.

## ELIJAH
### *KNOWING GOD ABOVE ALL*

*The prophet Elijah stepped forward and prayed: "LORD, the God of Abraham, Isaac and Israel, let it be known today that you are God in Israel and that I am your servant and have done all these things at your command."*                                  1 KINGS 18:36

Elijah may be the most well-known and dramatic of all the prophets in the Bible. His spiritual resume includes remarkably accurate predictions, raising the dead and a single-handed showdown with idolatrous priests. Add to that an astonishing ride to heaven via a fiery chariot and an appearance with Moses during Christ's transfiguration (see Matthew 17).

The amazing miracles God accomplished through Elijah may dazzle us, but we would do well to focus on the relationship he and God shared. All that happened in Elijah's life began with the same relationship that is available to us — Elijah knew God. How else could he have put himself in a life-threatening position with the prophets of Baal if he had not come to know God was trustworthy? How could he have been God's messenger without having spent time listening to God for the message?

Sure, performing amazing miracles for God is admirable, but what we learn from Elijah is that our goal should be on developing a relationship with God. The time we spend with God is far more precious to him than the things we do for him. The real miracle of Elijah's life was his very personal relationship with God. And that relationship is available to us.                                                              ✣

### PRAYER

*Heavenly Father, I value the time we ...*

### READ

Elijah's story is told in 1 Kings 17:1 — 2 Kings 2:11. He is also mentioned in 2 Chronicles 21:12–15.

## ELIJAH
### *THE ANXIOUS PROPHET*

*Elijah was afraid and ran for his life.*      1 KINGS 19:3

Elijah reminds us of the fickleness of human emotions. After God worked an overwhelming miracle through him in defeating the prophets of Baal, Elijah panicked and fled because of one woman's threat on his life. As if he were struck with a sudden case of amnesia, Elijah felt afraid, depressed and abandoned by God. He wanted to die. God bolstered Elijah with an audiovisual display of his power and revealed his presence to the troubled prophet in a gentle whisper.

Elijah, like us, struggled with his feelings even after receiving God's comfort. So God confronted Elijah and revealed a plan for action. He told Elijah what to do next. God also informed him that his loneliness was based in part on ignorance, for 7,000 others in Israel were still faithful to God.

God has given us a capacity for faith. Although it will still be a struggle, our faith can keep us from being controlled by self-defeating thoughts and irrational feelings. A strong faith in God can encourage us to continue in his work for us even when we are fearful.      ✛

**PRAYER**

*Lord, today I struggle with ...*

**READ**

Elijah's story is told in 1 Kings 17:1—2 Kings 2:11. He is also mentioned in 2 Chronicles 21:12–15.

# day94

## ELIPHAZ, BILDAD AND ZOPHAR
### *FRIENDLY ADVICE WORTH FORGETTING*

*When Job's three friends, Eliphaz the Temanite, Bildad the Shuhite and Zophar the Naamathite, heard about all the troubles that had come upon him, they set out from their homes and met together by agreement to go and sympathize with him and comfort him.*

JOB 2:11

Few people in history have experienced the kind of tragedy that crushed Job. He lost everything. His children were killed, his possessions and wealth were taken, his wife turned her back on him and his health became very poor — all in a matter of days.

Upon learning of Job's difficulties, his friends Eliphaz, Bildad and Zophar came to comfort him. Shocked by Job's appearance, they wept for him and sat in silence for seven days.

Why did his friends remain silent for so long? One ancient Jewish tradition teaches that people who come to comfort someone in mourning should not speak until the mourner speaks. Job's friends were either demonstrating wisdom or were simply too stunned to speak.

The problem came when they opened their mouths. The more they tried to explain Job's suffering, the less they helped. God didn't want these men offering their well-meaning but misguided advice. God himself never answered Job's questions, but instead challenged Job to trust, even beyond understanding.

Got a hurting friend? Avoid the mistake Job's friends made and resist the temptation to explain the suffering, to put a theological spin on it, to demonstrate the logic of it. Simply sit there. Show affection. Weep with those who weep.       ♣

**PRAYER**

*Lord, help me to be there for ...*

**READ**

The story of Job and his conversations with his friends is told in the Old Testament book of Job.

## ELISHA
### *A DOUBLE PORTION OF SERVICE*

*Elijah said to Elisha, "Tell me, what can I do for you before I am taken from you?" "Let me inherit a double portion of your spirit," Elisha replied.*      2 KINGS 2:9

Few replacements in Scripture were as effective as Elisha. Elisha had a great example to follow in the prophet Elijah, even though each was called to a different role. The fiery Elijah confronted and exposed idolatry, while his counterpart Elisha quietly served the poor. Elisha spent less time in dramatic conflict with evil and more time caring compassionately for the suffering and sick. The Bible records 18 encounters between Elisha and needy people.

Elisha's ministry reminds us that God does not call all believers to high-profile, headline-grabbing work. How easy it might have been for Elisha to downplay his contribution simply because he did not command the presence that Elijah did! He knew, however, that God counted the work of both men as equally and invaluably important. God has created you with specific gifts and abilities in order to serve him well. Are you comparing your abilities with others or are you committing what you have to God's service?      ❧

**PRAYER**

*Lord, I commit to …*

**READ**

Elisha's story is found in 1 Kings 19:16 — 2 Kings 13:20.

## ELISHA
### *FAITH IN A TIGHT SPOT*

*The officer on whose arm the king was leaning said to the man of God, "Look, even if the LORD should open the floodgates of the heavens, could this happen?" "You will see it with your own eyes," answered Elisha.*                                            2 KINGS 7:2

Elisha seemed to place the people he encountered in a tight spot. Possessing the brash ways of a prophet speaking on God's authority, he tested the faith of those he encountered. He offered a starving city hope, assured a lone servant victory over an army and promised an aged woman that she would mother a son. But Elisha knew that God's power relied on the faithfulness of those whose faith was being tested. They would be called upon to believe and see the unseen.

Elisha's service reminds us of the importance of trusting God's provision for the future. We may encounter Elishas in our everyday circumstances. God may use such people to put us in a tight spot—a place where our faith is challenged. Perhaps an employer's unexpected notice of pending cutbacks will challenge your belief in God's promises to care for you. Or maybe a loved one has become ill, and you wonder where God has gone. Your response during these difficult times will either boost or stunt your spiritual growth. Ask God for the faith to respond in complete trust concerning every aspect of your future.                              ❖

### PRAYER

*Grant me, Lord, the faith to . . .*

### READ

Read about Elisha's interactions in 1 Kings 19:16—2 Kings 13:20.

## ELIZABETH
### *GOD'S PERFECT TIMING*

*They were childless because Elizabeth was not able to conceive, and they were both very old.* LUKE 1:7

In societies like ancient Israel's in which a woman's value was largely measured by her ability to bear children, an aging couple without children often faced personal hardship and public shame. Elizabeth's childless plight was a painful and lonely time, yet she remained faithful to God.

Life had probably settled into a well-worn routine when Zechariah silently announced the good news. What had been a faded dream would become an exciting reality: Elizabeth would bear a son. She knew God had given her a gift she had not dared to hope for at her age.

The pieces of God's once puzzling plan began to fall into place. In another town, Elizabeth's niece, Mary, also unexpectedly became pregnant. Mary soon came to visit Elizabeth, and the women instantly bonded over the unique gifts God had given them. Knowing about Mary must have made Elizabeth marvel at God's timing. Things had worked out even better than she could have planned.

In our own lives, we can remember that God is in control of every situation. Beyond any fevered planning and rushed efforts of our own, God's timing and plans are perfect. While it may not seem so according to our self-made arrangements, God knows what he's doing. When did you last pause to recognize God's timing in the events of your life? ❖

**PRAYER**

*Your timing, Lord, means . . .*

**READ**

Elizabeth's story is told in Luke 1:5 – 80.

## ELIZABETH
### *REJOICING WITH GOD'S PEOPLE*

*When Elizabeth heard Mary's greeting, the baby leaped in her womb, and Elizabeth was filled with the Holy Spirit.*　　　　　　　　　　　　　　　　　　LUKE 1:41

An angel sent out the birth announcements: Elizabeth was expecting a baby! The exciting news overwhelmed her family and friends, initiating a series of delightful surprises. As Elizabeth whispered her praise to God for the baby she felt so strong and alive inside of her, the Holy Spirit revealed to her the biggest surprise yet: Mary would give birth to God's Son.

Thus when she saw Mary standing at her doorstep, beaming with excitement, Elizabeth exclaimed, "Why am I so favored, that the mother of my Lord should come to me?" (Luke 1:43). Elizabeth was by now no stranger to the wonder of the impossible, so she rejoiced.

Even though she herself was pregnant with a long-awaited son, Elizabeth could have envied Mary, whose son would be even greater than her own. Instead she was filled with joy that the mother of the Lord would visit her. Have you ever envied people whom God has apparently singled out for special blessing? A cure for jealousy is to rejoice with them, realizing that God uses his people in ways best suited to his purpose. The next time you feel a twinge of envy toward someone, remember how Elizabeth rejoiced. Make it your aim to enjoy that person's blessing.    ❖

### PRAYER

*Lord, I confess my envy of . . .*

### READ

Read about Elizabeth's unexpected surprises in Luke 1:5 – 80.

# day99

## ELKANAH
### *REASON TO OBEY*

*Her husband Elkanah would say to her, "Hannah, why are you weeping? Why don't you eat? Why are you downhearted? Don't I mean more to you than ten sons?"* 1 SAMUEL 1:8

Some husbands are insensitive by nature; others are insensitive out of ignorance. Elkanah loved his wife Hannah. She was deeply troubled about being childless, but Elkanah didn't know how to comfort her. He had another wife, Peninnah, who was fertile. Why didn't Hannah understand that he loved her just as she was? Elkanah didn't know that the more he expressed his love to Hannah, the more Peninnah taunted her for her inability to bear children.

When God honored Hannah's prayer by giving her a child, Samuel, Elkanah seemed to realize he was only a small part of a much larger plan. He demonstrated his love for his wife by allowing her to follow through on her vow to dedicate Samuel to the Lord. He may not have understood his wife's deed, but he knew enough to support her actions. Besides his consistent love for Hannah, Elkanah made a steady effort to respond reverently to God. Their later fruitfulness in having five other children bears witness to the way in which their relationship was strengthened by their obedience. ✤

**PRAYER**

*Lord, I bring before you this challenge to my obedience ...*

**READ**

The record of Elkanah's life can be found in 1 Samuel 1–2.

# day100

## ELYMAS
### *BLINDED BY SIN*

*"You are a child of the devil and an enemy of everything that is right! You are full of all kinds of deceit and trickery. Will you never stop perverting the right ways of the Lord?"*
ACTS 13:10

Luke wrote that Elymas was the Greek name of a Jewish false prophet and magician called Bar-Jesus. A person sold out to evil, Elymas acted as an adviser to Sergius Paulus, the local Roman ruler in Cyprus. Paul and Barnabas ran into him on their first missionary journey.

When Sergius Paulus heard Paul and Barnabas and expressed an interest in the gospel, Elymas publicly tried to distort the message. Under the influence of the Holy Spirit, Paul exposed Elymas's evil character and predicted an immediate punishment from God. Elymas lost his sight in that moment.

We don't know if Elymas recognized his spiritual condition while he was blind. But the clear demonstration of God's power certainly opened Sergius Paulus's eyes of faith. As we strive to spread the gospel, we ought not to be surprised when we experience opposition to our message. We may not have to confront someone as Paul did, but we can trust God to ensure that his message reaches those ears for which it's intended. ♣

### PRAYER

*Lord, I sense that you want me to confront...*

### READ

Elymas's showdown with Paul and Barnabas is recorded in Acts 13:6–12.

## ENOCH
### *LONG-TERM FAITHFULNESS*

*By faith Enoch was taken from this life, so that he did not experience death: "He could not be found, because God had taken him away." For before he was taken, he was commended as one who pleased God.* HEBREWS 11:5

When Jude reviewed the history of human rebellion against God, he mentioned the warnings of Enoch the preacher (see Jude 14–15), a man best known for being one of two Old Testament people who never experienced death.

The epistle to the Hebrews lists Enoch as the second figure inducted into the "Hall of Faith." By faith, Enoch pleased God. Enoch was a person who believed God "exists and that he rewards those who earnestly seek him" (Hebrews 11:6). The book of Jude informs us that Enoch told others about the God in whom he believed. He warned them that God was to be worshiped and obeyed.

Genesis gives us the simplest description of Enoch's life—he "walked faithfully with God" (Genesis 5:24). God was as real, immediate and apparent in Enoch's life as taking a walk.

We who measure faithfulness to God in terms of weeks and days can look to the example of Enoch's life. His faithfulness stretched out three hundred years. If your life were to be summarized at the close of this day, what three- or four-word description would fit best? ❖

**PRAYER**

*Lord, I want to walk faithfully with you . . .*

**READ**

Enoch's life is recorded in Genesis 5:18–24. He is also mentioned in Hebrews 11:5 and Jude 14–15.

## EPAPHRAS
### HOMETOWN HERO

*You learned it from Epaphras, our dear fellow servant, who is a faithful minister of Christ on our behalf.*  COLOSSIANS 1:7

During his third missionary journey, Paul made a significant visit to Ephesus. There he found a group of disciples who were living by the message of John the Baptist. They had repented and been baptized, but had not yet heard about Jesus or the promised Holy Spirit. As soon as they did hear, they believed. Likely among those twelve men was Epaphras.

Though Epaphras may have been converted in Ephesus, he returned to Colossae, his hometown. Paul credits him with founding the church that eventually met in Philemon's house. Epaphras later visited Rome and told Paul about the problems in the Colossian church. This prompted Paul to write his letter to them.

Paul was impressed by Epaphras's deep concern for the Christians in Colossae. He described that concern as "wrestling in prayer" (Colossians 4:12). Epaphras's faith was others-centered. He carried the gospel to his hometown and then committed himself to a long-term, caring relationship with those people. Even when he wasn't with them, his care continued.

What contacts have you maintained with other Christians over the years? Today, make it a point to pray for those several Christians you know but don't necessarily see in person very often.  ♣

**PRAYER**

*Lord, today I pray for . . .*

**READ**

Epaphras is mentioned in Colossians 1:7; 4:12 and Philemon 23.

# day103

## EPAPHRODITUS
### OUR EXPECTATIONS AND GOD'S PLANS

*[Epaphroditus] almost died for the work of Christ. He risked his life to make up for the help you yourselves could not give me.*                    PHILIPPIANS 2:30

When the Christians in Philippi heard about Paul's imprisonment, the news must have been especially significant to them. They surely remembered Paul's brief stay in their own city jail, when a midnight songfest concluded with an earthquake that cracked the prison open (see Acts 16:11–40). They decided to support their former teacher and encourager by sending Epaphroditus to help Paul.

Epaphroditus arrived in Rome bringing gifts from the Philippians. Unfortunately, he soon became very sick and almost died. Word got back to Philippi of his illness, and that fact distressed Epaphroditus. He may have felt his mission had failed. But Paul saw matters differently. He was deeply thankful for Epaphroditus's visit and urged the Philippians to welcome him home with joy.

Our plans don't always match God's objectives. Epaphroditus wasn't able to accomplish all he set out to do. But his effort had cheered Paul, who described the gifts he received as "a fragrant offering" (Philippians 4:18).          ❖

**PRAYER**

*Lord, please reveal the way that I can be of service . . .*

**READ**

Epaphroditus and his ministry were mentioned by Paul in Philippians 2:25–30; 4:14–19.

## ESAU
### *RUINED BY AN IMPULSE*

*See that no one is sexually immoral, or is godless like Esau, who for a single meal sold his inheritance rights as the oldest son.*                    HEBREWS 12:16

Esau made several choices in life that he must have regretted bitterly. He appears to have been a person who found it hard to consider consequences, reacting to the need of the moment without realizing what he was giving up to meet that need. Trading his birthright for a bowl of stew is the clearest example of this weakness. He acted on impulse, satisfying his immediate desires without pausing to consider the long-term consequences.

We too can fall into the same trap. When we see something we want, our first impulse is to get it. At first we feel intensely satisfied and sometimes even powerful because we have obtained what we set out to get. Immediate pleasure often clouds our sight of the future. We may feel so much pressure to indulge our appetites that nothing else seems to matter.

What are you willing to trade for the things you want? Do you find yourself, at times, willing to negotiate anything for what you feel you need now? Does your family, spouse, integrity, body or soul get included in these deals? Be mindful of asking God to help you clearly see the long-term effects of your choices.          ♣

PRAYER

*Lord, help me make the right choices . . .*

READ

Esau's story is told in Genesis 25–36. He also is mentioned in Malachi 1:2–3 (which is quoted in Romans 9:13) and Hebrews 11:20; 12:16–17.

## ESAU
### *REDIRECTING ANGER*

*Esau held a grudge against Jacob because of the blessing his father had given him.*

GENESIS 27:41

Common sense isn't all that common. In fact, the common thread in many decisions is that they don't make sense. Such was the case with Esau's resolution to kill his brother Jacob for receiving the blessings of their father. In his bitter anger, Esau overlooked the fact that it was his foolish mistake to forfeit his birthright to his brother in the first place. Esau's vengeful decision, girded by anger, sent him barreling toward the destruction of both brothers' lives. Fortunately, Esau eventually worked through his anger, forgave his brother and dispelled the bitterness between them.

When we lose something of great value or when others conspire against us and succeed, anger may be our first and most natural reaction. In itself, feeling anger is not wrong as long as we direct the energy of that anger toward a solution and not toward ourselves or others. The alternative is to let anger critically impair our ability to make right decisions.

As Esau's life testifies, effectively dealing with anger is beneficial. Think about some anger hot spots you may have concerning your past, your spouse, your workplace or your friends. Where are you channeling your energy: toward yourself, the problem or a solution?     ❖

**PRAYER**

*Lord, I offer you my anger . . .*

**READ**

Esau's story is told in Genesis 25–36. He also is mentioned in Malachi 1:2–3 (which is quoted in Romans 9:13) and Hebrews 11:20; 12:16–17.

## ESTHER
### *NOT JUST A COINCIDENCE*

*"If you remain silent at this time, relief and deliverance for the Jews will arise from another place, but you and your father's family will perish. And who knows but that you have come to your royal position for such a time as this?"* ESTHER 4:14

What others may call coincidence, wise believers know as providence. Esther could have rationalized her unique position in the palace as simply happenstance or a roll of the dice. In fact, it seems she was initially tempted to downplay her role altogether, which became evident when she brought up the fact that those who approached the king without being summoned would be put to death (see Esther 4:10–11). Mordecai, Esther's cousin and adviser, responded by reminding her of her particular place in the larger picture of God's plan. Esther realized that her beauty, nationality, relatives and influence in the palace could be used in service to God.

Have you considered lately how the people around you and the circumstances you face figure into God's design for your life? Are you aware of your untapped resources, past experiences and personal contacts that could be used for God's purposes? Nothing about you is a coincidence; in fact, everything about you is useful for accomplishing God's work. Set aside time this week to take stock of the potential assets you have yet to use in service to God. ✤

### PRAYER

*All I have is yours, Lord . . .*

### READ

Read about Esther in the book named after her.

## ESTHER
### *FAITH AND TRUE SECURITY*

*"I will go to the king, even though it is against the law. And if I perish, I perish."*

ESTHER 4:16

We treasure security, even though we know that security in this life carries no guarantees—possessions can be destroyed, beauty fades, relationships are broken, death is inevitable. Real security, then, must rest on God and his unchanging nature.

Even though Esther had won King Xerxes' heart, she risked her life by attempting to see the king when he had not requested her presence. There was no guarantee that the king would even see her. Although she was queen, she was still not secure. But, cautiously and courageously, Esther decided to risk not only her honor, wealth and prestige but also her life by approaching the king on behalf of her people. When she went before him, he asked her to come forward and speak. Esther's risk confirmed that God was the source of her security.

How much of your security rests on your possessions, position or reputation? God does not intend for you to use such gifts for your own benefit. He asks you to serve him. Like Esther, you may risk your security to please God, but such risks will detach you from the false hope this world offers. Today, think of practical ways you can rely exclusively on the security only God can offer. ✣

### PRAYER

*Help me truly see you as my refuge, Lord . . .*

### READ

Esther's story is told in the book of Esther.

# day108

## THE ETHIOPIAN EUNUCH
### *A RESPONSIVE HEART*

*This man had gone to Jerusalem to worship, and on his way home was sitting in his chariot reading the Book of Isaiah the prophet.* ACTS 8:27–28

The Ethiopian eunuch had more to think about than most people. An official of the Kandake, he had charge of the entire Ethiopian treasury. But his stopover this day came about on a trip from Jerusalem, where he had visited not to negotiate a deal or to broker a settlement but to worship the God of Israel. During the trip back he had a little free time on his hands, and he decided to use it reading the Scriptures.

The eunuch focused his attention on the passage in Isaiah that foretells the suffering of Christ. He read even though he did not really understand it. When the opportunity (Philip) came to have it explained to him, he jumped at it. No wonder this Ethiopian official became a Christian that day.

A man caught up in the political realm would not have had time for Scripture reading. A man concerned with power and selfish interest would not have invested in personal reflection. A man too calloused to hear the words of Isaiah 53 would not have cared about the suffering servant. But this man's heart responded when he heard about Christ. How often do you listen with your heart as you read the Scriptures, hear a sermon or seek advice? Be like the eunuch. Try always to keep you mind open and your heart soft. Let the truth of what you hear capture your attention. ❖

**PRAYER**

*Lord, reveal your truth to me ...*

**READ**

The Ethiopian eunuch's story is told in Acts 8:26–40.

## EUNICE
### *PASSING ON OUR FAITH*

*I am reminded of your sincere faith, which first lived in your grandmother Lois and in your mother Eunice and, I am persuaded, now lives in you also.*      2 TIMOTHY 1:5

Some of us grew up in families that instilled values and behavior that benefitted us greatly as we developed into mature men and women. One of Paul's disciples, Timothy, received such an upbringing. He received the gift of life twice from his mother. She gave birth to him and then showed him what a life of faith could be.

Timothy's mother and grandmother, Eunice and Lois, were early Christian converts, possibly through Paul's ministry in their home city, Lystra (see Acts 16:1). They had communicated their strong Christian faith to Timothy, even though his father was probably not a believer. Despite this division within his home, his mother instilled in him a character of faithfulness that carried into adulthood. Eunice was one of those behind-the-scenes saints who will eventually be recognized in heaven as one of the true heroes of the faith.

Don't hide your light at home: Our families are fertile fields for receiving gospel seeds. It is the most difficult land to work, but it yields the greatest harvests. Let your parents, children, spouse, brothers and sisters know of your faith in Jesus, and be sure they see Christ's love, helpfulness and joy in you.      ✤

**PRAYER**

*Make me a witness for you, Lord . . .*

**READ**

Eunice was mentioned by Paul in 2 Timothy 1:5.

# day110

## EUTYCHUS
### A SOUND SLEEPER

*"Watch and pray so that you will not fall into temptation. The spirit is willing, but the flesh is weak."*             MARK 14:38

Every Christian, sometime in their life, ought to stand behind the pulpit during a worship service. The perspective is unforgettable. Inevitably, at some point in every service, at least one listener falls asleep. Watching them struggle to stay awake can actually distract a preacher. Poor Eutychus! We've all been in his seat.

It was Paul's last night in Troas, and the believers gathered in an upper room. The apostle had a lot to say. Midnight passed and the oil lamps probably flickered in a hypnotic way. Eutychus likely wasn't bored; he was just tired. Because the room was packed, he had chosen to sit on the windowsill. He drifted off to sleep and tumbled from his precarious perch. Luke notes that he fell three stories and was shortly declared dead.

Fortunately for Eutychus, Paul was not a person to accept death lightly. He took the young man into his arms. "'Don't be alarmed,' he said. 'He's alive!'" (Acts 20:10). The believers may have awakened Eutychus to make sure he was all right, then let him go back to sleep. They all took a break for a snack and then Paul continued to speak until dawn. Eutychus's narrow escape left a lasting impression on the believers in Troas.      ♣

### PRAYER

*Make me watchful, Lord . . .*

### READ

Eutychus's unexpected adventure is recorded in Acts 20:7–12.

# day111

## EVE
### FOLLOWING DANGEROUS DESIRES

*When the woman saw that the fruit of the tree was good for food and pleasing to the eye, and also desirable for gaining wisdom, she took some and ate it.*          GENESIS 3:6

We know very little about Eve, the first woman in the world, yet she is the mother of us all. She was the final piece in the intricate and amazing puzzle of God's creation. As her descendants, we have inherited her propensity for sin, particularly when it comes to questioning God's sufficiency in our lives.

Eve was vulnerable to Satan's line of attack, for he knew her weakness: lack of contentment. How could she be happy when she was not allowed to eat from one of the fruit trees? Eve fell for the idea that the one item that was not within her reach would make her happy. And Eve was deceived, willing to accept Satan's insinuations without checking with God.

Sound familiar? How often is our attention drawn from the much we possess to the little that we don't? We get that I've-got-to-have-it-feeling. We open ourselves to envy, greed and all kinds to selfish behavior in order to satisfy our longings. And when we follow through on our impulses, the satisfaction we find is hollow and vanishes quickly.

God has given us all we need to be happy. Why waste time pursuing something that's second rate?                                                                    ❖

### PRAYER

*Lord, help me find my satisfaction in you alone . . .*

### READ

Eve's story is told in Genesis 2:19 — 4:2.

# day112

## EVE
### *PASSING THE BUCK*

*The LORD God said to the woman, "What is this you have done?" The woman said, "The serpent deceived me, and I ate."*                GENESIS 3:13

Adam and Eve's fall into sin provides the first instance in history of people who passed the buck. When God asked Adam about his sin, he blamed Eve. Eve said, in effect, "Don't look at me—it was the serpent's fault." And if God had inquired of the serpent, he certainly would have passed the blame back to Adam and Eve. How relieved Eve must have been when God turned to the serpent and announced his punishment! Her relief was short-lived, however. God refused to accept her rationalization and held her responsible for her wrongdoing.

The consequences of Eve's rebellion are well-known, but humans have followed her example ever since. It is so easy to excuse our sin by blaming someone else. It is a way of avoiding the pain of getting right with God and other people. But God knows the truth. He also holds each of us responsible for our decisions. Admit your sin and confess it to God. Blaming someone else only makes matters worse.    ♣

### PRAYER

*Lord, I confess that ...*

### READ

Eve's story is told in Genesis 2:19—4:2.

# day113

## EZEKIEL
### OUR RESPONSIBILITY TO OTHERS

*"Go now to your people in exile and speak to them. Say to them, 'This is what the Sovereign LORD says,' whether they listen or fail to listen."*       EZEKIEL 3:11

During Israel's exile in Babylon, God called Ezekiel to be his prophet. God described Ezekiel as "a watchman for the people of Israel" (Ezekiel 3:17), which was a fitting metaphor for his ministry. A watchman's job required unceasing vigilance. If he failed at his post, he and the entire city might be destroyed.

As spiritual watchman, Ezekiel warned the people of coming judgment. If the people in Judah continued in their sins, they and their land and cities would be swallowed up by Nebuchadnezzar's armies. If they turned to God, however, they would be spared. God would hold Ezekiel responsible for his fellow Jews if he failed to warn them of the consequences of their sins.

Every man and woman is responsible to God, but believers often have a responsibility to warn others of the consequences of wrong living. If we are faithful, we may lead others to repentance and restored relationship with God. This should motivate us to begin sharing our faith with others—by both word and deed—and to stop living calloused, unconcerned lives. Are you ready today to keep watch? ✣

### PRAYER

*Show me those I need to warn, Lord . . .*

### READ

Ezekiel's story is told in the book of Ezekiel.

# day114

## EZRA
### *GROWING IN GOD'S WORD*

*Ezra had devoted himself to the study and observance of the Law of the LORD, and to teaching its decrees and laws in Israel.*                    EZRA 7:10

The most effective leaders in the Bible likely had little awareness of the impact their lives had on others. They were too busy obeying God to keep track of their successes. Ezra fits that description.

About 80 years after the rebuilding of the temple under Zerubbabel, Ezra returned to Judah. He was given a letter from Artaxerxes instructing him to carry out a program of religious education. As part of his prestigious assignment, Ezra pioneered the last spiritual awakening in the Old Testament. He may have even authored two other books in the Bible—1 and 2 Chronicles.

Ezra's accomplishments can be attributed to his diligent obedience to God's Word. He studied it seriously and applied it faithfully. Ezra affirms for us that personal achievement should be secondary to a personal commitment to live for God. Your growing relationship with God is always more profitable for you and your family than any pay raise, promotion or position in social standing. What does your lifestyle reveal about your priorities? What changes could you incorporate, beginning today, to guard your time alone with God?                    ✤

### PRAYER

*Lord, these are my priorities . . .*

### READ

Ezra's story is told in Ezra 7:1—10:17 and Nehemiah 8:1—12:36.

# day115

## FELIX
### *AVOIDING THE GOOD NEWS*

*Felix was afraid and said, "That's enough for now! You may leave. When I find it con-*
*venient, I will send for you."*                                    ACTS 24:25

Felix had been the Roman governor of Judea for six years when Paul appeared
before him. He certainly would have known about the Christians (then sometimes
called "the people of the Way"), a topic of conversation among the Roman leaders.

Felix announced he would wait to pass judgment, but within days, he apparently became curious to hear more from Paul. Rather than defend himself again,
the apostle instead preached forcefully to the governor. Paul's words fascinated
the governor until they turned to "righteousness, self-control and the judgment to
come" (Acts 24:25). Whether he knew it or not, Paul had exposed a very tender
spot in Felix's conscience, for the governor had taken another man's wife. Felix
abruptly ended the interview and kept Paul under guard. Instead of repenting,
Felix brushed off Paul's troubling words in the hope that the apostle would offer
a bribe for his release.

Many people will be glad to discuss the gospel with you as long as it doesn't
involve them personally. When it does, some will resist or run. Don't assume you
have failed in your witness if a person's conversion isn't immediately evident. Continue to spread God's Good News regardless of the response you receive.      ❖

### PRAYER

*Lord, make me a partner in the spread of your Good News ...*

### READ

Paul's encounters with Felix are recorded in Acts 23:23—24:27.

# day116

## FESTUS
### *THE HOPE WITHIN US*

*"I was at a loss how to investigate such matters."*                    ACTS 25:20

Festus found himself in the middle of a legal firestorm. He replaced Felix as the Roman governor of Judea in AD 59 or 60. Festus practiced a more fair-minded version of Roman law and treated Paul more justly than Felix had.

Shortly after Festus arrived, he was confronted by Jewish leaders anxious to bring Paul to trial. The new governor stalled them until he could hear from Paul. Upon arriving in Caesarea, Festus immediately ordered Paul's trial to resume. As soon as Festus gave Paul the opportunity, he made a formal appeal to be heard by Caesar. It was Paul's right as a Roman citizen. Festus was required to send him on to Rome.

Festus was unclear about the difficulties surrounding Paul. The charges against him sounded like religious hairsplitting. Paul seemed to be babbling about someone named Jesus who had died then come back to life. To Festus, Paul seemed like a reasonable man until it came to this Jesus. He certainly wasn't the first to find the Christian way puzzling and farfetched. Jesus still gets the same reception today. Christianity offers a startling contrast to the struggle for power, success and wealth that consumes the world. But, like Paul, we should be ready at any time to give an account of the hope within us.                                        ❖

### PRAYER

*Lord, please show me who needs your hope today...*

### READ

Festus's dealings with Paul are recorded in Acts 24:27—26:32.

# day117

## GAD
### TELLING THE TRUTH WHEN IT HURTS

*The LORD said to Gad, David's seer, "Go and tell David, 'This is what the LORD says: I am giving you three options. Choose one of them for me to carry out against you.'"*

1 CHRONICLES 21:9–10

The prophet Gad faithfully gave King David wise counsel on several occasions.

First, the prophet tracked down David when he was hiding from Saul and instructed him to return to Judah. Second, after David disobeyed God's long-standing order against taking a census, Gad arrived to deliver the consequences. The king had to choose between a three-year famine, a three-month military defeat or a three-day plague. Gad must have been grimly pleased that his king placed himself at God's mercy by choosing the third alternative.

When David expressed overwhelming remorse over the suffering caused by his sin, Gad stepped in a third time with direction for the king. He instructed David to buy a certain piece of land and erect an altar there so that he might ask for relief from the plague.

Our best friends save their influence for times that really matter. Gad was interested not in controlling David but in serving him for God's sake. A friend who will tell us the truth we don't want to hear will be of greater value than a dozen friends who fill our ears with false comfort. Do others know you as a friend who speaks the truth? ❖

**PRAYER**

*Make me the kind of friend, Lord, who speaks truth . . .*

**READ**

Gad's ministry to David is recorded in 1 Samuel 22:5; 2 Samuel 24:10–25; 1 Chronicles 21; 29:26–30 and 2 Chronicles 29:25.

# day118

## GAIUS, FRIEND OF JOHN
### THE MINISTRY OF HOSPITALITY

*Dear friend, you are faithful in what you are doing for the brothers and sisters, e̱  ̱n*
*though they are strangers to you.*                                            3 JOHN 5

One day Gaius received a letter from John the apostle. We now know the letter
as John's third epistle. The scroll was probably handed to Gaius by a man named
Demetrius, a highly respected Christian. John's brief letter contains what little we
know about Gaius's leadership in the early church.

John prayed for Gaius's physical and spiritual well-being. He also noted Gaius's
hospitality. Apparently Gaius's church was located in a town along a trade route.
Members of the church often hosted traveling teachers and missionaries. John
remarked about the reputation that Gaius was gaining as a generous and hospitable host. People who stayed in his home left feeling rested and equipped to do
their work. The apostle clearly wanted to encourage someone who was such an
example of faith in action.

Hospitality is a ministry all believers should practice (see Romans 12:13). We
may not be particularly comfortable in that role, but we will surely improve with
practice. Make it a point to identify in your church someone who already demonstrates great hospitality as Gaius did and spend some time with that person. Take
advantage of all that you could learn!                                    ❖

### PRAYER

*Make my home a place of healing, Lord . . .*

### READ

Gaius's ministry of hospitality is recorded in 3 John.

# day119

## GAIUS, FRIEND OF PAUL
### FRIENDSHIPS ROOTED IN FAITH

*Gaius, whose hospitality I and the whole church here enjoy, sends you his greetings.*

ROMANS 16:23

Gaius was Paul's companion. Although many people became Christians while Paul was in Corinth, Gaius was one of the few he baptized personally (see 1 Corinthians 1:14). Later, just before his final trip to Jerusalem, Paul wrote the Roman church a letter while he was staying in Gaius's house in Corinth. When he left Corinth that time, Gaius probably traveled with him.

Luke notes that Paul's companions were believers from many of the places where Paul had planted churches (see Acts 20:4). They were going with Paul to deliver a large gift to the church in Jerusalem from many of the younger churches in Asia Minor. Paul and Gaius must have enjoyed a close relationship. Gaius undoubtedly looked for ways to serve Paul and other Christians.

We are deeply indebted to those who introduce us to Jesus Christ. Sometimes we should express our thanks with more than just words. We can serve those who have helped us as well as seek to pass on the Good News to others. In what ways have you thanked those who have had the greatest influence on your faith?   ✣

**PRAYER**

*Lord, thank you for ...*

**READ**

Gaius is mentioned in Acts 19:29; 20:4; Romans 16:23 and 1 Corinthians 1:14.

## GAMALIEL
### AN UNLIKELY ADVOCATE

*"If it is from God, you will not be able to stop these men; you will only find yourselves fighting against God."* ACTS 5:39

Christians owe a lot to Gamaliel. He trained one of the greatest defenders of the faith—a young man he knew as Saul of Tarsus who later become the apostle Paul. He equipped Saul with a thorough understanding of the Hebrew Scriptures. Paul later spoke of Gamaliel humbly and with respect (see Acts 22:3).

Gamaliel may have been present at the trials of Jesus. He was not consulted, apparently, nor was he mentioned by name. Later, during the explosive times following Jesus' resurrection and the birth of the Christian church, Gamaliel became a voice of reason. By that time, Peter and most of the apostles had been arrested. The Jewish council was intent on killing them as they had Jesus. But the previously timid disciples now refused to be cowed.

Gamaliel astutely observed that the popularity of the apostles would only be enhanced if they were martyred. He understood that fanaticism burns itself out, while the truth becomes stronger under pressure. He also considered the possibility that the apostles were speaking the truth and warned of the consequences of opposing God. His reasoning won the release of the Christian leaders. Perhaps he understood more about Jesus than he revealed. ❖

**PRAYER**

*Lord, I understand that you . . .*

**READ**

Gamaliel's wisdom can be found in Acts 5:33–42 and 22:1–5.

## GEDALIAH
### *RESTING IN A FALSE SECURITY*

*Jeremiah went to Gedaliah son of Ahikam at Mizpah and stayed with him among the people who were left behind in the land.* JEREMIAH 40:6

Power, prestige and popularity can come or go overnight. Gedaliah, the son of a court secretary, found himself appointed as the largest fish in a very small pond. His sudden rise was due to Babylon's defeat and destruction of Judah. Jerusalem had been torn down to its foundations. Most of the people were deported to Babylon, except for a handful who were left behind as caretakers of the land. Gedaliah was appointed as their governor.

Apparently Gedaliah felt secure as the highest officeholder in the land. Instead of seeking God's direction, he trusted in the goodwill of Judah's conquerors to keep him safe. Yet Judah's enemies remained determined to wipe out God's people. Others, like Ishmael, one of the surviving military leaders, resented Gedaliah for selling out to the Babylonians. The governor was aware of these threats, but he ignored them. The oversight cost him his life.

Depending on God's protection doesn't mean that bad things can't happen to us. But being under God's care ensures that even suffering, failure and death will fit into his purpose for us. Jeremiah reminded us of this truth: "'For I know the plans I have for you,' declares the LORD, 'plans to prosper you and not to harm you, plans to give you hope and a future'" (Jeremiah 29:11).                    ❖

### PRAYER

*Thank you for your good plans, Lord . . .*

### READ

Gedaliah's brief career is recorded in 2 Kings 25:22–26 and Jeremiah 39:11—41:10.

# day122

## GEHAZI
### *DECEPTION'S REWARD*

*Gehazi... said to himself, "My master was too easy on Naaman, this Aramean, by not accepting from him what he brought. As surely as the LORD lives, I will run after him and get something from him."*
2 KINGS 5:20

Some people live so close to the truth that they have to stumble over it before they really notice it. Gehazi, Elisha's servant, witnessed the fulfillment of one of Elisha's prophecies and saw him perform miracles and even raise the dead. However, we suspect that Gehazi did not appreciate the privilege of seeing God's amazing work.

When Elijah healed Naaman the leper, Gehazi saw a perfect opportunity to get rich by selfishly asking for the reward Elisha had refused. He even lied and tried to cover up his motives for accepting the money. What Gehazi received from Naaman was leprosy, not the payoff he had hoped for. He had to live with this illness as a permanent reminder of his deception before he finally took God seriously.

Most of us have daily opportunities to recognize God's power, mercy and faithfulness. When God uses painful measures to get our attention, it can be because we have turned a blind eye to the obvious signs he gives us. We can decide to notice and express our gratitude for God's "fingerprints" in our world today. Our eyes may be opened because of it. ♣

### PRAYER

*Lord, I see that you ...*

### READ

Gehazi's life is recorded in 2 Kings 4:11 — 8:6.

# day123

## GESHEM
### AN UNHOLY ALLIANCE

*"I [Nehemiah] am carrying on a great project and cannot go down. Why should the work stop while I leave it and go down to you?"* NEHEMIAH 6:3

Nehemiah faced a huge logistical problem in rebuilding the walls of Jerusalem. But that wasn't his only concern. He also faced great opposition from Sanballat and Tobiah, two Canaanite leaders, and Geshem, an Arab with clout. These men are remembered in Scripture primarily for their evil motives and unsavory tactics: intimidation, ridicule and threats of physical attack.

Whenever we set out to follow God's directions, we can expect to deal with reactions similar to the ones Nehemiah faced. Although the names and circumstances involved in our situations will be different, God's opponents always share the same objective: to keep us from doing what God wants us to do.

We need to remember how Nehemiah countered his opposition: He prayed, planned and kept on working. Even the threat of death did not keep him from carrying out what he knew God wanted him to do. How often do we give up before much weaker opposition? Sure, it's not fun to be challenged and can at times be frightening, but we gain much strength when we rely on God and the resources he has provided for us. ♣

### PRAYER

*Almighty God, I rely on you to . . .*

### READ

Geshem, Sanballat and Tobiah's infamous deeds are recorded in Nehemiah 2:17—6:14.

## GIDEON
### *PREPARING FOR GOD'S WORK*

*When the angel of the LORD appeared to Gideon, he said, "The LORD is with you, mighty warrior."*                                                                 JUDGES 6:12

Gideon had a limited vision, but he was committed to it. His challenge was to obtain food for his family even though hostile invaders were making it almost impossible. But Gideon was resourceful. He put a winepress to double duty by using it to hide from the enemy the grain he was threshing. An angel appeared one day to give him a different challenge: God wanted Gideon to lead Israel against the Midianites.

Most of us want to know God's plan for our lives. And many of us falsely assume God's guidance has nothing to do with what we're currently involved in. Between deadlines at work, hectic carpool schedules and a marathon of social phone calls, we often think God's call will have to come "when all of this is over." However, God's call to Gideon came when he was completely immersed in the task at hand. Looking back, he must have realized that many of the qualities he developed during the threshing-floor days served to prepare him for the next step in God's plan. We can remember Gideon as a man who obeyed God by giving his attention to whatever he was currently working on. Then we can trust God to use each of today's tasks to prepare us for tomorrow.                                     ❖

**PRAYER**

*Prepare me, Lord, for ...*

**READ**

Gideon's story is told in Judges 6–8. He is also mentioned in Hebrews 11:32.

## GIDEON
### *GOD'S STRENGTH, NOT OUR WEAKNESS*

*The LORD turned to him and said, "Go in the strength you have and save Israel out of Midian's hand. Am I not sending you?"*   JUDGES 6:14

When we first encounter Gideon in the Bible, he appears as the type who is full of excuses. His response to God's call to lead the Israelites into battle was a barrage of reasons not to. First, he hinted that God had abandoned the Israelites. Second, he reminded God of the lowly status of his extended family, whom he claimed to be the poorest of the poor. Third, he asked for a sign to prove that God was sending him. Blinded by his limitations, Gideon didn't believe God could use him at all. But God could, and he did.

Like Gideon, we are sometimes our own worst critic, especially as we try to discern God's plan for our lives. Every phobia, excuse and failure immediately comes to mind. However, reminding God of our limitations implies that he does not know everything about us or that he has failed to evaluate our character. In response to our excuses, God says, as he said to Gideon, "Go in the strength you have" (Judges 6:14). His grace and provision are more than enough to make up for what we may lack. We shouldn't spend time making excuses. Instead, we should spend it serving God.   ❖

**PRAYER**

*Lord, help me want to do your will ...*

**READ**

Read more about Gideon and his excuses in Judges 6–8. He is also mentioned in Hebrews 11:32.

## GIDEON
### *WAITING FOR ANOTHER SIGN*

*Gideon said to God, "... Look, I will place a wool fleece on the threshing floor. If there is dew only on the fleece and all the ground is dry, then I will know that you will save Israel by my hand, as you said."*                    JUDGES 6:36–37

"Prove it!" is a cherished phrase in the evolving language of a child. Gideon's request that God fulfill a series of experiments with a wool fleece may seem to resemble the same childish desire for hard evidence. Was Gideon really testing God or was he simply seeking assurance?

In either case, it is clear that Gideon's motive was right (to obey God and defeat the enemy), but his particular method was flawed. After asking for a miracle and receiving it, he still did not believe. He delayed his obedience because he wanted another miracle to confirm his calling. Gideon's demand for extra signs was an indication of unbelief.

Today, the greatest source of God's guidance is his Word. Unlike Gideon, we have God's complete revealed message to humankind. Unfortunately, we share Gideon's tendency to wait for more confirmation when we should be obedient. If we want to experience more deeply God's guidance, we should not ask for signs but study God's Word.                                                              ♣

**PRAYER**

*Lord, I need your wisdom ...*

**READ**

Gideon's story is recorded in Judges 6–8. He is also mentioned in Hebrews 11:32.

## GOLIATH
### *FIGHTING AGAINST GOD*

*"Who is this uncircumcised Philistine that he should defy the armies of the living God?"*
1 SAMUEL 17:26

Goliath was a giant with an attitude. In modern times, this Old Testament character might have been called "The Intimidator." He immobilized an entire army of Israelites by challenging one of them to duel with him. He made them forget they had a champion mightier than any human. It took a bold shepherd boy to remind them all that they were the army of the living God.

Goliath's strengths were obvious: size, armor, confidence. But no one is invincible, and Goliath's vulnerability became apparent when David's stone struck him down. When David was given Goliath's kind of weapons he quickly concluded that he couldn't even function, much less fight, with those tools. David instead chose the two weapons he knew he could rely on: his trust in God and his shepherd's sling.

David had armor to match Goliath's, but it was invisible. In Ephesians 6:10–18, Paul describes in detail the resources God places at our disposal. How unfortunate that we face our world each day on its terms, too often trying to match its weapons. God's weapons are not as obvious, but they never fail us! How much of your spiritual armor are you wearing today?    ❖

**PRAYER**

*Lord, today, I know I'm wearing...*

**READ**

Goliath's rise and fall are recorded in 1 Samuel 17.

## GOMER
### *LOVE WITHOUT CONDITIONS*

*[Hosea] married Gomer daughter of Diblaim, and she conceived and bore him a son.*

HOSEA 1:3

Hosea knew ahead of time that his wife, Gomer, would be unfaithful and that their married life would parallel God's relationship with the wayward nation of Israel. However, Gomer didn't have this insider's perspective. So what did she think and feel? What was her reaction when a holy man plucked her out of a life of prostitution and made her his wife?

She certainly tested the limits of Hosea's love. She bore three children, but perhaps she couldn't say with certainty they were his. During her infidelity, she apparently either sold herself into slavery or became another man's mistress in order to survive. But Hosea brought her back from her situation. Did this second chance mean anything to Gomer? We don't know. She must have been surprised by Hosea's relentless love for someone with her track record.

Probably the closest we come to feeling what Gomer felt are those times when we act unfaithfully toward God. Yet he continues to faithfully lavish his love on us. We know Gomer better than we might think, for she was what we are—sinners offered overwhelming grace! In what ways does this extravagant love and grace affect the way you look at yourself?    ✤

### PRAYER

*Jesus, lover of my soul, thank you for ...*

### READ

Gomer's relationship with Hosea is found in Hosea 1–3.

## HABAKKUK
### *THE TIMETABLE OF HEAVEN*

*"The righteous person will live by his faithfulness."*      HABAKKUK 2:4

Like many of the Old Testament prophets, the power of Habakkuk's message outlived the memory of his life. But we can draw at least one conclusion from Habakkuk's writing: He was like us. Hard times forced him to ask God hard questions. Why isn't life fair? Why do evil people succeed while the innocent suffer? Why does God put up with so much mockery? Why does God seem so distant? Habakkuk expressed the same doubts we often feel; he also received answers from God.

What were God's answers to Habakkuk's questions? Similar to how the Lord answered Job, God insisted on being trusted as God, not as the one we can compel to answer our every question. God will not be held hostage by our doubts. God pointed out to Habakkuk that when we take the larger view of history and the world, we are more likely to see God in control. And when we experience the confusion and pain of daily living, we need to cling more tightly to God.

Habakkuk ended his prophecy with a prayer in which he stated his intention to trust in God. He realized that there would be times when the immediate evidence would challenge the presence of God. In those times of darkness he would remember the God he had met in the light.      ❖

**PRAYER**

*Lord, I need your light . . .*

**READ**

What little we know of Habakkuk is found in the book that bears his name.

## HAGAR
### *RUNNING AWAY FROM PROBLEMS*

*The angel of the LORD told [Hagar], "Go back to your mistress and submit to her."*

GENESIS 16:9

Escape can be the most tempting solution to our problems. In fact, it can also become a habit. Hagar, the servant-wife of Abraham, used that approach. When the going got tough, she often got going—in the other direction.

Hagar's pregnancy caused her to look down on Sarah, who consequently mistreated her. Hagar ran away. When she returned to the family and gave birth to Ishmael, Sarah looked for any excuse to have Hagar and Ishmael sent away for good. In the desert, out of water and facing the death of her son, Hagar once again tried to escape. She left Ishmael under a bush and walked away so she wouldn't have to watch him die. Once again, God graciously intervened.

Have you noticed how God sometimes blocks our exits for our own good? He wants us to face our problems with his help. We see his provision most clearly in times of conflict and difficulty. Are there problems in your life for which you've been using the "Hagar solution"? Choose one of those problems, ask for God's help and begin to face it today. ✛

**PRAYER**

*Lord, I need your help with this problem ...*

**READ**

Hagar's story is told in Genesis 16–21.

## HAGGAI
### THE ONE-YEAR PROPHET

*"Is it a time for you yourselves to be living in your paneled houses, while this house remains a ruin?"*                                             HAGGAI 1:4

Haggai could well be called the "One-Year Prophet." God gave him a very specific mission that required him to deliver four messages over the course of a single year. In 520 BC, Haggai spoke to Jews who had been home from their Babylonian exile for nearly 20 years. He criticized them for looking after their own comfort while leaving the rebuilding of the temple unfinished.

Haggai used the condition of the temple as a metaphor to describe the spiritual lives of the people. Their relationship with God was in shambles and needed to be restored from the bottom up. Haggai assured the people that a healed relationship with God would result in wonderful benefits that had been forgotten in the years of neglect.

Haggai's message reminds us how the daily habits of our relationship with God (for example, our involvement in church fellowship and service, consistency in prayer and Bible study) need continual attention. If you've been letting slide some of the disciplines of your faith, ask the Lord to show you what effect this has had on your relationship with him.                                             ♣

**PRAYER**

*Lord, I'm sorry that I stopped . . .*

**READ**

The book of Haggai and Ezra 5:1; 6:14 give us glimpses of Haggai's ministry.

## HAMAN
### *PRIDE AND DESTRUCTION*

*When Haman saw that Mordecai would not kneel down or pay him honor, he was enraged.*                    ESTHER 3:5

The most arrogant people are often those who must measure their self-worth by the power or influence they have over others. Haman was an extremely arrogant leader. An Amalekite, he hated all Jews because of their long-standing enmity with his people. So when Mordecai refused to bow in submission to him, Haman wanted to destroy him. Mordecai's dedication to God and refusal to pay homage to any man challenged Haman's self-centered religion. He became consumed with plotting Mordecai's arrest. But like others who opposed God, Haman's scheme led to his downfall.

Our initial response to the story about Haman might be to say that he got what he deserved. But the Bible leads us to ask deeper questions: "Do I share some of Haman's traits?" "Do I desire to control others?" "Am I threatened when others don't appreciate me as I think they should?" "Do I want revenge when my pride is attacked?" Haman's treachery should remind us that power corrupts. Christians are not exempt from its temptations. Ask God to create in you an attitude of mercy and humility.                                                             ❖

**PRAYER**

*Lord, give me an attitude of mercy and humility . . .*

**READ**

Haman's story is told in the book of Esther.

## HANANIAH
### *SWEET-SOUNDING LIES*

*The prophet Jeremiah said to Hananiah the prophet, "Listen, Hananiah! The LORD has not sent you, yet you have persuaded this nation to trust in lies."*     JEREMIAH 28:15

False prophets draw a crowd because they tell people what they want to hear. God's prophets unswervingly speak the truth. Hananiah, a false prophet, consoled his countrymen with sweet-sounding lies. In contrast, Jeremiah had long warned that punishment for the sins of the nation was coming in the form of a conqueror. Now he urged the nation to prepare for its fate.

Hananiah was sure he had it right. Perhaps he thought he could change God's mind by announcing publicly a better plan to save Judah. Surely God wouldn't pass up the opportunity to endorse a last-minute, stunning defeat of the Babylonians. So Hananiah contradicted Jeremiah's prophecy of humiliation and broke the yoke Jeremiah had been wearing. Jeremiah responded by reminding Hananiah what happened to false prophets. Within a year Hananiah was dead.

Because we have good intentions, we sometimes assume that God will bless our plans. We know from experience, however, that God does not always behave the way we want. God is not bound by our plans or by our limited understanding. He gives us specific promises in his Word, but he also wants us to humbly rely on his goodness to supply our needs.     ❖

### PRAYER

*Lord, I submit my will to you ...*

### READ

The rise and fall of Hananiah is recorded in Jeremiah 28.

## HANNAH
### ON LOAN FROM GOD

*"I [Hannah] prayed for this child, and the LORD has granted me what I asked of him. So now I give him to the LORD."* 1 SAMUEL 1:27–28

Hannah might have had many excuses for being a possessive mother. After all, she had spent many years yearning for children she could not bear. Now she was given a gift from God—a son. When God answered her prayer, she followed through on her promise to dedicate Samuel to God's service.

Her prayer of thanks shows us that all we have and receive is on loan from God. She discovered that the greatest joy in having a child was to give that child fully and freely back to God. She entered motherhood prepared to do what all mothers (and fathers) must do eventually—let go of their children.

When children are born, they are completely dependent on their parents for all their basic needs. Those same children will grow toward independence within the span of a few short years. Being sensitive to the different stages of that healthy process can greatly strengthen family relationships; resisting or denying that process can cause great pain. We will all learn to gradually let go of our children in order to allow them to become independent. While it may be difficult to let go, the gratification that comes from watching them grow into mature adults is well worth the difficulty. ♣

**PRAYER**

*Lord, I am praying for ...*

**READ**

Hannah's story is told in 1 Samuel 1–2.

## HANUN
### *DEFENDING A MISTAKE*

*David thought, "I will show kindness to Hanun son of Nahash, because his father showed kindness to me."*      I CHRONICLES 19:2

David's relationship with Hanun began with the best intentions. Hanun's father, king of Ammon, had been on cordial terms with David. When Hanun succeeded to the throne, David sent a welcoming party to the new king. But Hanun was led to believe the worst about David. Instead of being received with diplomatic courtesy, David's envoys were humiliated and treated as spies. Hanun shaved their beards, cut their robes and sent them home.

Hanun and his counselors belatedly realized they had provoked David's anger. Instead of humbly admitting their mistake, they compounded their problems by hiring allies to defend themselves against David. A gesture of peace had unexpectedly become a prelude to a war in which Hanun was soundly defeated. Former neighbors became enemies.

Defending what we know to be wrong is a costly and futile effort. Jumping to false conclusions, responding to others with prejudice and misunderstanding other people's intentions are all familiar mistakes we make. But we can make things right by putting aside our pride and seeking reconciliation, even if we feel like we are the offended party. Is there currently a conflict in your life that was caused by misunderstood intentions? What steps can you take to resolve the conflict?   ✤

**PRAYER**

*Lord God, you know the issues I have with . . .*

**READ**

David's dealings with Hanun are recounted twice in the Old Testament: 2 Samuel 10:1–19 and 1 Chronicles 19:1—20:3.

## HAZAEL
### DECEIVING OURSELVES

*Hazael said, "How could your servant, a mere dog, accomplish such a feat?"*

2 KINGS 8:13

When Elisha told Hazael, a servant to the king of Syria, of the terrible things he would do the people of Israel, Hazael reacted indignantly. He was a decent man, he thought; he wouldn't be the sort to commit such deeds. Yet the day after Elisha predicted that Hazael would become king of Syria, the servant shamefully murdered King Ben-Hadad and replaced him on the throne. In the following years, Hazael was a constant threat to Israel and Judah during his reign. God allowed Hazael success in order to humble his own people. He also held Hazael responsible for his sins, and his own family suffered for them.

Like Hazael, we can deceive ourselves into thinking we are incapable of blatant sin. We think we have the self-control to prevent us from sinking so low. But often we are kept from sin by a lack of opportunity rather than by our strength of character. God protects us from countless temptations that we are too weak to handle on our own. Instead of patting ourselves on the back for our goodness, we should take an honest look at ourselves and admit our sinful potential. We need to be reminded often that only God is capable of delivering us from evil.  ❖

> **PRAYER**

*Lord, deliver me from ...*

> **READ**

Hazael's rise and fall is mentioned in the following passages: 1 Kings 19:15–18; 2 Kings 8:8–15,28–29; 9:14–15; 10:32; 12:17–18; 13:3–25; 2 Chronicles 22:5–7 and Amos 1:4.

# day137

## HEROD AGRIPPA I
### *GIVING CREDIT WHERE IT IS DUE*

*Immediately, because Herod did not give praise to God, an angel of the Lord struck him down.*                                                                    ACTS 12:23

Early in his reign, Herod Agrippa I traveled on the fast track to fame among the Jews. His popularity proved to be deadly.

An unexpected opportunity for Herod to gain new favor with the Jews was created by the growth of the Christian movement. Eager to solidify his position and popularity, Herod initiated the revival of the persecution of Christians. He pleased the Jewish leaders with his clever arrangement for the murder of James and the arrest of Peter. However, Herod made a fatal error while visiting Caesarea, where he gave a moving speech. Inspired, the citizens proclaimed Herod to be a god, and he willfully accepted their praise. He was immediately struck with a painful disease and, according to other sources, died within a week.

Herod may have been uncommonly evil, but his prideful disposition is universal. Most of us know what it's like for others to offer us recognition for our accomplishments. And we must admit—the affirmation makes us feel good. But Herod's story reminds us of the foolishness of wanting to receive the credit for our achievements. When others acknowledge our abilities, it is best to use it as an opportunity to acknowledge God as the source of our success.                    ✣

**PRAYER**

*Lord, you are the source of...*

**READ**

Herod Agrippa I's story is told in Acts 12:1–23.

## HEROD AGRIPPA II
### BAD BLOOD

*King Agrippa and Bernice arrived at Caesarea to pay their respects to Festus.*

ACTS 25:13

Like great-grandfather, like grandfather; like father, like son—this tells the story of Herod Agrippa II. His life is an insightful study in family dynamics and dysfunction. This is most evident in Agrippa II's interpersonal relationships. He emulated the moral weaknesses of his great-grandfather (who murdered his own wife and children) and his great-uncle (who committed adultery with his brother's wife). It was the choice of the youngest Herod to become involved in an incestuous relationship with his sister, Bernice.

While he was not responsible for the bad decisions of his predecessors, he was undoubtedly influenced by this heritage of evil. Regardless, his ultimate destiny and course in life was never beyond his control. He could have broken the cycle of abuse and shame that pervaded his family.

Many people, like Herod Agrippa II, inherit the effects of harmful familial influence—whether it is abuse, alcoholism, greed or a quick temper. But it is our willful choice to allow ourselves to become the next link. Remember, you can take a stand against any family pattern of behavior you do not want to perpetuate. Ask God that a new and hopeful family heritage begin with your life. ✤

### PRAYER

*Lord, please break this pattern of ...*

### READ

The Herod family history is recorded in the Gospels and Acts. Herod Agrippa II's story is told in Acts 25:13—26:32.

# day139

## HEROD AGRIPPA II
### *MISSED OPPORTUNITY*

*Agrippa said to Paul, "Do you think that in such a short time you can persuade me to be a Christian?"*
ACTS 26:28

Each generation of the powerful Herods had a confrontation with God, but each failed to realize the importance of their decisions. Herod Agrippa II's opportunity came during his official visit to Jerusalem to meet with Festus, the Roman governor. Paul, who was imprisoned, was allowed by Festus to present his case before the king. Herod heard the prisoner's animated testimony but considered the message mild entertainment. He found it humorous that Paul actually tried to convince him to become a Christian.

Like so many before and after him, Agrippa II stopped within hearing distance of the kingdom of God. He listened to the gospel but decided it wasn't worth responding to. Unfortunately, his mistake isn't uncommon. Many who read his story also will not believe. Their problem is not that the gospel isn't convincing or that they don't need to know God. It is that they willfully choose not to respond, showing little concern for the eternal consequences of such a decision.

How have you responded to the gospel throughout your life? Did you always welcome it, taking comfort in the hope of eternal life? Or was it ever a message you resisted and rejected? How do you respond now? ❖

**PRAYER**

*Lord, this is my response ...*

**READ**

Herod Agrippa II's story is told in Acts 25:13—26:32.

# day140

may 20

## HEROD ANTIPAS
### *HEARING WITHOUT LISTENING*

*Herod feared John and protected him, knowing him to be a righteous and holy man.*
MARK 6:20

Herod's illegal marriage to his brother's wife, Herodias, was public knowledge. One man—John the Baptist—made Herod's sin a public issue.

Herod respected John, but the truth about his sin was a bitter pill to swallow. Herod wavered at the point of conflict: He couldn't afford to have John constantly reminding the people of their leader's sinfulness, but he was afraid to have John killed. Eventually Herodias forced Herod's hand, and John was executed. Of course, this only increased Herod's guilt.

When Herod and Jesus met briefly during Jesus' trial, Jesus would not speak to Herod. Herod had proved himself a poor listener to John, and Jesus had nothing to add to John's words. Herod responded with spite and mocking. Having rejected the messenger, he found it easy to reject the Messiah.

For each person, God chooses the best possible ways to reveal himself. He uses his Word, our various circumstances, our minds or other people to get our attention. He is persuasive and persistent, but he never forces us. To miss or resist God's message, as Herod did, is tragic. How aware are you of God's attempts to enter your life? How have you welcomed him? ❖

### PRAYER

*Lord, I welcome you...*

### READ

Herod Antipas's story is told in the Gospels. He is also mentioned in Acts 4:27 and 13:1.

## HEROD THE GREAT
### *THE DISEASE OF SELF-CENTEREDNESS*

*When King Herod heard this he was disturbed, and all Jerusalem with him.*
MATTHEW 2:3

Herod the Great is remembered for his enormous building projects, including the reconstruction of the temple in Jerusalem. He is also remembered for his destruction of people. Herod's title, king of the Jews, was granted by Rome but never accepted by the Jewish people. Therefore, his constant concern was to hold on to his ill-fitting crown at any price. When Herod heard a new king was born in Bethlehem, he ordered the murder of all the male infants in the town in an attempt to abolish the threat to his throne. His suspicions and jealousy eventually led to the murder of his wife and several of his children.

Herod's appalling behavior reveals a full-blown case of self-centeredness. It is a disease that infects us all. In its initial stages, it seriously impairs one's ability to make wise decisions and can cause extensive damage to the family. Left untreated, the human heart is soon ravaged with corroded desires, resulting in a tragic prognosis for everyone involved. The antidote for this universal malady is a commitment to live for Christ and his ideals—to be renewed daily. The recovery rate is slow but certain. Have you renewed your commitment to him today? ❖

**PRAYER**

*Lord, I am committed to . . .*

**READ**

Herod the Great is mentioned in Matthew 2:1–22 and Luke 1:5.

## HERODIAS
### *TURNING TOWARD THE DARKNESS*

*Herodias nursed a grudge against John and wanted to kill him.*       MARK 6:19

Herodias appeared on the stage of history as the wife of Herod Philip I, who was actually her uncle. Later she exchanged one incestuous relationship for another when she left Philip to marry his brother Herod Antipas. When John confronted the two for committing adultery, Herodias formulated a plot to kill him. Instead of correcting her sin, Herodias aimed to get rid of the one who called attention to it.

Herod arrested John the Baptist under pressure from his wife and advisers. Though Herod didn't want to kill John, he was no match for his wife's ingenuity. Herodias arranged John's death by using her daughter, Salome, when she danced for Herod and his guests during Herod's birthday party. The king made her a thoughtless promise to grant her any request. With the pressure of the public moment on her side, Herodias had Salome ask for John's head on a platter. Herod had to keep his vow.

Herodias chose a pathway of evil. We have no evidence that she ever veered toward the truth. But she had at least one crystal-clear moment to change her sinful ways. John showed her the light, but she turned toward the darkness. Herodias's life was an example of our human tendency to defend ourselves and our actions when confronted with our failings.                                              ❖

**PRAYER**

*Lord, when I hear hard truths, I...*

**READ**

Herodias's part in history is recorded in Matthew 14:1–12 and Mark 6:14–29.

## HEZEKIAH
### *THE COURAGE TO RESIST SIN*

*"Remember, LORD, how I have walked before you faithfully and with wholehearted devotion and have done what is good in your eyes."*        2 KINGS 20:3

"No more excuses; the time has come for change." Such was the resolution of King Hezekiah, who wanted to stamp out the idolatry running rampant in Judah. Hezekiah boldly cleaned house. Altars, idols and pagan temples were destroyed. Even the bronze snake Moses had made in the desert was not spared, for it had diverted people from worshiping God. The temple, the doors of which Hezekiah's own father had nailed shut, was cleaned out and reopened. The Passover was reinstituted as a national holiday. Revival came to Judah.

Hezekiah may have felt overwhelmed by the task of such a drastic religious reformation. Few would have blamed him if he had deferred the call for awakening to another king and another time. Yet he acted boldly, knowing that God was entrusting him with this kingly responsibility.

We may feel powerless as we consider the problems of our communities. *Crime. Prejudice. Homelessness.* We may be tempted to excuse our responsibility and "let someone else do it" in light of the magnitude of the problems. We need Hezekiah's resolve if we want the kind of society we pray for to become reality. What idols need to be torn down? Look for ways you can breathe God's life-giving Word into our dying world.       ❖

### PRAYER

*Lord, today I will . . .*

### READ

Hezekiah's story is told in 2 Kings 16:20 — 20:21; 2 Chronicles 28:27 — 32:33 and Isaiah 36:1 — 39:8.

## HEZEKIAH
### *NO REGARD FOR THE FUTURE*

*"The word of the LORD you have spoken is good," Hezekiah replied. For he thought, "Will there not be peace and security in my lifetime?"*     2 KINGS 20:19

The past is an important part of today's actions and tomorrow's plans. The people and kings of Judah brought sorrow and ruin upon themselves when they forgot that their God, who had cared for them in the past, also cared about the present and the future. He still demanded their continued obedience.

Although Hezekiah responded admirably to contemporary problems, he did little to ensure his reforms would last. His foolish display of wealth to a Babylonian delegation made Judah a likely target for aggression. When Isaiah criticized Hezekiah for his lack of prudence, the king was merely relieved that any evil consequences would be delayed until after he died. The lives of kings who followed him were deeply affected by both Hezekiah's accomplishments and weaknesses. As Isaiah prophesied, "The time will surely come when everything in your palace, and all that your predecessors have stored up until this day, will be carried off to Babylon. Nothing will be left, says the LORD. And some of your descendants, your own flesh and blood who will be born to you, will be taken away, and they will become eunuchs in the palace of the king of Babylon" (2 Kings 20:17–18).

The past affects your decisions and actions today, and these, in turn, affect the future. There are lessons to learn and errors to avoid repeating. Today, reflect on a past shortcoming and consider how the lessons you've learned from that experience will benefit you today and tomorrow.     ♣

### PRAYER

*Lord, based on my past, I've learned . . .*

### READ

Hezekiah's story is told in 2 Kings 16:20—20:21; 2 Chronicles 28:27—32:33 and Isaiah 36:1—39:8.

## HILKIAH
### *EXPERIENCING REVIVAL*

*Hilkiah the high priest said to Shaphan the secretary, "I have found the Book of the Law in the temple of the LORD."*        2 KINGS 22:8

Hilkiah served as high priest under Josiah, one of the few godly kings of Judah. The young king initiated a sweeping reform of the nation's religious life. Idols and pagan temples were torn down. Eventually, Hilkiah received orders to oversee the restoration of Solomon's temple, which had fallen into disrepair.

Buried in the trash, Hilkiah found a treasure—a scroll containing the Mosaic Law. Misplaced for years, the discovery was indicative of the spiritual condition of the people. They had lost God's Word. An entire generation, including the king, was largely ignorant of God's commands. Josiah tore his clothing in deep concern after hearing the Scriptures.

Hilkiah experienced the privilege of guiding a revival. Under his leadership a great Passover was celebrated. This reintroduced the people to vital worship. In his lifetime Hilkiah witnessed the restoration of the law and temple to their previous place of respect.

We still find it easy today to drift from the input of God's Word and the expression of worship. The emphasis we put on the Bible and worship in our lives is still a good indication of the state of our relationship with God.      ❖

**PRAYER**

*Your Word, O Lord . . .*

**READ**

Parallel accounts of Hilkiah's ministry are recorded in 2 Kings 22:1—23:24 and 2 Chronicles 34:1—35:19.

## HIRAM
### PURSUING EXCELLENCE

*"I am sending you Huram-Abi, a man of great skill."*            2 CHRONICLES 2:13

One of the most remarkable buildings in all of history was the temple of the Lord built by Solomon in Jerusalem. The architect and on-site builder was Hiram (also known as Huram or Huram-Abi). Hiram transformed ideas, metals, stones and wood into a structure of beauty.

Hiram's mother was from the tribe of Naphtali. His father was a metalworker from Tyre. Perhaps his father sharpened his work skills while his mother trained him in the faith of Israel. We can only guess that the quality of his work was a tribute to the God whose temple he was building.

Hiram apparently was not intimidated by his formidable undertaking, though some of the individual pieces he cast for the temple were immense. Large or small, the descriptions of his work convey a tone of admiration for his skill. From pillars to pomegranates, from bowls to bulls, from pots to shovels, Hiram produced articles of beauty.

We honor God not only by allowing him to develop our character but also by making the best use of the skills he has given to us. The pursuit of excellence can be an eloquent tribute to our Creator. How can your efforts today make a statement to others about your relationship with God?            ❖

**PRAYER**

*Lord, I want to honor you by ...*

**READ**

Hiram's work is recorded in 1 Kings 7:13–45 and 2 Chronicles 2:13—4:16.

## HIRAM, KING OF TYRE
### *MAKING FRIENDSHIPS THAT COUNT*

*When Hiram king of Tyre heard that Solomon had been anointed king to succeed his father David, he sent his envoys to Solomon, because he had always been on friendly terms with David.*                                                   1 KINGS 5:1

Hiram of Tyre befriended two kings: David and Solomon. He became their helpful and loyal neighbor. Their friendship stretched over many years, mutually benefiting Israel and Tyre. With both father and son, Hiram was the friend who took the initiative.

When David conquered Jerusalem and was crowned king of Israel, Scripture tells us Hiram was the first ruler who established diplomatic relations with David. He immediately offered his best materials and skilled workers to build a suitable palace for the new king.

No sooner had Solomon taken the throne than he heard the knock of Hiram's messengers on the diplomatic door. David had already stockpiled much of the material needed to build the great temple to God in Jerusalem, but Hiram provided the design and building experts who made the project a reality. Solomon's own palace was built the same way. And Solomon provided the capital for a shipping venture with Hiram in which the crews of the vessels were sailors from Tyre and Sidon. The collaboration between the two rulers made them both very wealthy.                                                                       ✤

**PRAYER**

*Lord, I am grateful for the influence of . . .*

**READ**

Hiram's story is recorded in 2 Samuel 5:11; 1 Kings 5; 9:10–28 and 2 Chronicles 2.

## HOBAB
### *A TRUSTWORTHY GUIDE*

*Moses said, "Please do not leave us. You know where we should camp in the wilderness, and you can be our eyes."*　　　　　　　　　　　　　　NUMBERS 10:31

Moses married into a family who gave him several priceless relationships: His wife, Zipporah; his wise father-in-law, Jethro (also called Reuel); and a brother-in-law named Hobab who knew the Sinai desert like the back of his hand. Hobab guided the people of Israel as they traveled in the wilderness.

Hobab grew up with Moses during those 40 years the future leader spent away from Egypt. Shepherds who didn't learn their way around the Sinai Peninsula didn't survive. A seasoned guide with 30 years of experience, Hobab was an ideal choice to lead the people as they traveled.

By complimenting Hobab's skills, Moses let him know he was needed. People cannot know you appreciate them if you do not tell them they are important to you. Complimenting those who deserve it builds lasting relationships and helps people know they are valued. Think about those who have helped you this month. What can you do to let them know how much you need and appreciate them? ❖

**PRAYER**

*Lord, please help me to offer my appreciation for . . .*

**READ**

Hobab's quiet but necessary role is recorded in Numbers 10:29–32.

## HOSEA
### *EXTRAORDINARY OBEDIENCE*

*"I will betroth you in faithfulness, and you will acknowledge the LORD."*     HOSEA 2:20

God told Hosea to marry a prostitute as a vivid illustration of God's love for a consistently unfaithful Israel. Hosea chose Gomer. Hosea's marriage itself was an act of obedience, but God allowed Hosea to decide which woman he would marry. Why did he choose Gomer? He certainly knew her past. But did he know she would be unfaithful? Or was Hosea's challenge to accept as his wife a woman he knew had already been intimate with many other men?

Hosea and Gomer had three children, though because of her unfaithfulness, the children may not have been his. Later Gomer apparently returned to prostitution, for God then gave Hosea a different command: He was to love this woman who had deserted him. Her behavior had landed her in trouble, and Hosea had to purchase her freedom.

God often required extraordinary obedience from his prophets. God may ask you to do something difficult and extraordinary too. If he does, how will you respond? Will you obey him, trusting that he who knows everything has a special purpose for his request?     ❖

**PRAYER**

*Make me ready, Lord, for when you call me to obey . . .*

**READ**

Hosea tells his own story in the Old Testament book named after him.

## HULDAH
### *PREPARING FOR THE RIGHT MOMENT*

*Hilkiah and those the king had sent with him went to speak to the prophet Huldah, who was the wife of Shallum son of Tokhath.*      2 CHRONICLES 34:22

King Josiah was stunned when his crackdown on Judah's idolatry led to the discovery of a scroll containing the Mosaic Law. He decided to consult with a prophet because there were dreaded consequences described in the law for those who failed to obey. Although other, better-known prophets could have been consulted, Josiah turned to the prophet Huldah. Even though his written Word had disappeared from Judah, God made sure that a person who could profess his wisdom was available at this critical time.

Huldah was the wife of the king's valet, or "keeper of the wardrobe." She confirmed the truth of the scroll: The idolatry of the people would bring painful consequences. She also added a note of grace for Josiah. His personal repentance and humble work of reformation had afforded the people extra time for peace during his reign.

This story contains the only mention of Huldah's life. She had a key opportunity to testify to God's truth, and she didn't miss it. Huldah's secret was simply quiet preparation and obedience to God's way. The most basic spiritual successes start with this formula.      ✤

**PRAYER**

*Open my eyes, Lord, to the opportunities to testify to your truth . . .*

**READ**

Huldah's brief appearance is recorded in 2 Kings 22:14–20 and 2 Chronicles 34:19–28.

## HUSHAI
### *LOYAL IN ALL CIRCUMSTANCES*

*Ahithophel was the king's counselor. Hushai the Arkite was the king's confidant.*

1 CHRONICLES 27:33

Ahithophel's counsel could be trusted, but his loyalty was suspect. Hushai proved himself loyal to the point of death. When Absalom usurped the throne from David, Hushai was willing to follow his king into exile. Ahithophel followed Absalom. Hushai must have been quite old, for David frankly told him he would slow down the escape if he insisted on going along. So, David sent Hushai back to the palace to do what he could to complicate Absalom's plans.

Hushai was able to convince Absalom that he had switched loyalties. He was then able to challenge Ahithophel's counsel in such a way that he allowed time for David to accomplish his escape and organize his forces. He didn't try to stop Absalom—only delay him. His advice was reasonable and acceptable. Absalom didn't realize, however, that Hushai's advice helped David more than it helped him.

Hushai's service reminds us the importance of loyalty. Ahithophel's loyalty was fickle; it was determined solely by who held power. Hushai's loyalty was to David, and changing circumstances did not weaken it. To what degree can others depend on you? How many people would trust you with their lives?          ❖

**PRAYER**

*Lord, I appreciate the loyalty of . . .*

**READ**

Hushai's loyal actions are recorded in 2 Samuel 15:32—17:22 and 1 Chronicles 27:33.

## HYMENAEUS
### *SHIPWRECKED FAITH*

*You may fight the battle well, holding on to faith and a good conscience, which some have rejected and so have suffered shipwreck with regard to the faith.*     1 TIMOTHY 1:18 – 19

Several leaders of the church in Ephesus had been seduced by false teaching. Among these leaders, Paul specifically mentioned Hymenaeus.

According to Paul, Hymenaeus made two mistakes that shipwrecked his faith: He rejected both the faith itself as well as the need for a good conscience. Apparently, Hymenaeus wasn't bothered by what his teaching was doing to his own life or to the lives of others. The results were so disastrous that Paul had been forced to take drastic action. He told Timothy he had handed Hymenaeus "over to Satan to be taught not to blaspheme" (1 Timothy 1:20). Paul hoped Hymenaeus would come to his senses by experiencing the consequences of his mistakes.

Two or three years later, when Paul again wrote to Timothy, Hymenaeus was still spreading falsehoods. No wonder his efforts were destroying the faith of others.

Today many people treat the teachings of Christ lightly. To them, faith boils down to little more than personal preference. But a faith that has no conscience or that is not anchored to the truth is a ship sailing to disaster. How would you describe the seaworthiness of your ship of faith? Can it handle the rough seas of temptation, or does it need to return to port for repairs?                                   ✤

### PRAYER

*Lord, I am tempted to . . .*

### READ

Hymenaeus was mentioned by Paul in 1 Timothy 1:18 – 20 and 2 Timothy 2:14 – 19.

# day153

## ISAAC
### *THE IMPORTANCE OF A NAME*

*God said, "Yes, but your wife Sarah will bear you a son, and you will call him Isaac. I will establish my covenant with him as an everlasting covenant for his descendants after him."*
GENESIS 17:19

A name can do a lot of things. It sets you apart. It triggers memories. The sound of it calls you to attention anywhere.

Many Biblical names accomplished even more. They often described important facts about one's past and hopes for the future. Abraham and Sarah's name for their son Isaac—meaning "he laughs"—must have created a variety of feelings each time it was spoken. It surely recalled the laughter of Abraham and Sarah at God's announcement that they would be parents in their old age. At other times, Isaac must have reflected on the joyful laughter he brought his parents as their long-awaited answer to prayer.

Most important, Isaac's name testified to God's power. Perhaps Abraham and Sarah had assumed that God had forgotten his promise to give them a son of their own. But God overcame the barriers of old age and surprised the couple with a long-awaited child. Isaac thus became a reminder of the holy laughter that God delights in giving his children who obey him. ❖

### PRAYER

*Heavenly Father, for the gift of laughter, I . . .*

### READ

Isaac's story is told in Genesis 17:15—35:29. He also is mentioned in Romans 9:7–10; Hebrews 11:17–20 and James 2:21–24.

## ISAAC
### *KEEPING THE PEACE*

*[Isaac] moved on from there and dug another well, and no one quarreled over it.*

GENESIS 26:22

Although we don't know much about Isaac's personality, we see he was capable of resolute action when it was needed. His jealous neighbors, the Philistines, once crafted a malicious plot against him. In an area where water was as precious as gold, Isaac's hostile neighbors plugged up his wells two separate times and threatened to drive him away. Even though plugging another landowner's well was a serious crime, Isaac refused to let the incident provoke him to rash action. Instead, he and his men simply dug another well. Finally, there was enough room for everyone, and the dispute settled down. Isaac's willingness to compromise for the sake of peace headed off a bloody showdown.

Would you be willing to forsake an important position or valuable possession to keep the peace? In some situations, you may have a good reason to be angry. But what else might be at stake? You may face conflict with your friends, family or co-workers this week. Ask God for the wisdom to know when to withdraw and when to stand your ground.    ❖

**PRAYER**

*Lord, I need wisdom to . . .*

**READ**

Isaac's story is told in Genesis 17:15 — 35:29. He also is mentioned in Romans 9:7 – 10; Hebrews 11:17 – 20 and James 2:21 – 24.

# day155

## ISAIAH
### A LIFE-CHANGING EVENT

*In the year that King Uzziah died, I saw the Lord, high and exalted, seated on a throne; and the train of his robe filled the temple.* ISAIAH 6:1

Certain experiences have the capacity to alter our entire life. Those who have had a brush with death, such as a close call in a traffic accident, often resolve to live with renewed appreciation and vigor. Isaiah's encounter with God, gloriously exalted in his temple, was one such life-changing experience. His message would flow from the vision that affected him so profoundly.

The book of Isaiah is a message of contrasts. The prophet's remarks are sometimes comforting, sometimes confronting. He feverishly details God's abandonment of Israel in one paragraph and lovingly consoles God's people in the next—all within the same passage.

Isaiah's intent was to point his people to the only One capable of exercising perfect justice and perfect mercy—God himself. Sin separates us from God and brings us pain and suffering. But if we confess our sin and repent, God willingly forgives us. If your heart is heavy with sin you have yet to confess, a joyful reunion awaits you if you will ask God's forgiveness and return to him. ♣

**PRAYER**

*Lord, I confess that . . .*

**READ**

Read about Isaiah's encounter with God in Isaiah 6. He is also mentioned in 2 Kings 19:2—20:19.

## ISAIAH
### *PLANTING THE SEEDS*

*[Isaiah] said, "Here am I. Send me!"*       ISAIAH 6:8

Trees and prophets share at least one important characteristic—both are planted for the future. Yet seedlings are often overlooked and prophets often ignored. Isaiah belonged in the latter category. Had they listened, the people of Judah could have saved themselves from misery to come. Instead, they refused to believe Isaiah. Kings ignored his warnings, and the government accused him of treason because he disapproved of many national policies.

When he called Isaiah as a prophet, God did not encourage him with predictions of great success. In fact, God told Isaiah that the people would not listen. He was to speak his messages anyway because eventually some *would* listen. God compared his people to a tree that would have to be cut down so that a new tree could grow from the old roots.

We who are part of that future can see that many of the promises God gave through Isaiah have been fulfilled in Jesus Christ. We also gain the hope of knowing that God is active in all of history, including our own lives. Therefore, be mindful of God's timetable as you patiently watch and pray.      ✤

PRAYER

*Lord, I am waiting for . . .*

READ

Isaiah's story is told in 2 Kings 19:2—20:19. His prophetic ministry is recorded in the Old Testament book that bears his name.

## ISH-BOSHETH
### AN UNLIKELY KING

*When Ish-Bosheth son of Saul heard that Abner had died in Hebron, he lost courage, and all Israel became alarmed.*     2 SAMUEL 4:1

Ish-Bosheth probably never planned to be king. His older brother Jonathan was the obvious choice to replace their father, King Saul. Then, in a single day, Saul, Jonathan and two other brothers were killed in battle. Ish-Bosheth's absence from the battle might have indicated a lack of heart for fighting or leading.

Much like his father, Saul, Ish-Bosheth was a hesitant and ineffective king. He was put on the throne by Abner, the commander of Saul's army. Though Ish-Bosheth was a surviving son of the king, he owed his position to Abner. Yet Ish-Bosheth, whose reign lasted only two years, was also afraid of Abner's power. When Abner was killed, Ish-Bosheth must have realized the weakness of his position. The king was soon murdered by two of his own officers.

Ish-Bosheth mistook an opportunity for a responsibility. Like him, we are often compelled to fill a need, regardless of its incompatibility with our gifts and strengths. When Abner offered the throne to Ish-Bosheth, he could have declined, knowing he wasn't suited for the job. He certainly did not ask for God's counsel. Even when the door before us seems open wide, we would be wise to pray before we go inside.     ❖

**PRAYER**

*Lord, help me discern the opportunities and responsibilities before me ...*

**READ**

Ish-Bosheth's short reign is recorded in 2 Samuel 2:8—4:13.

# day158

## ISHMAEL
### *DISCOVERING GOD'S FAITHFULNESS*

*Sarah saw that the son whom Hagar the Egyptian had borne to Abraham was mocking.*
GENESIS 21:9

Have you ever wondered if you were born into the wrong family? That question must have haunted Ishmael at times. Sarah's pregnancy and Isaac's birth must have had a devastating impact on Ishmael. Until then he had been treated as a son and heir, but this late arrival made his future uncertain. During Isaac's weaning celebration, Sarah caught Ishmael teasing his half-brother. As a result, Hagar and Ishmael were permanently expelled from Abraham's family.

Much of what happened to Ishmael was not his fault. He was caught in circumstances he had little power to control. Yet God made sure he was cared for. For instance, he provided refreshment when Hagar and Ishmael were in the desert. Later, God would make Ishmael's descendants into a great nation.

Ishmael's rescue testifies to God's faithfulness. Earlier Abraham learned that Ishmael would inherit blessings. The fulfillment of that promise looked doubtful, however, after Hagar was abruptly sent packing. But in his timing, God unfolded his promise for Ishmael, which included a long life and many descendants.

Have you thought about God's faithfulness today? Take some time to thank God for the ways he has cared for you and provided for you. ❖

**PRAYER**

*Lord, you have been faithful ...*

**READ**

Ishmael's story is told in Genesis 16–17; 21:8–21; 25:12–18.

## ITHAMAR
### ATTENTION TO SMALL DETAILS

*These are the amounts of the materials used for the tabernacle, the tabernacle of the covenant law, which were recorded at Moses' command by the Levites under the direction of Ithamar son of Aaron, the priest.* EXODUS 38:21

God chose Aaron's sons to be responsible for the care of the tabernacle—the huge worship-tent that Israel used during its years in the wilderness. God gave careful, detailed instructions for the orderly dismantling, transporting and setting up of the tabernacle each time Israel moved (see Exodus 25–40). Ithamar, the youngest of Aaron's four sons, got the detail work. He had to make sure everything was in its proper place.

Ithamar's older brothers Nadab and Abihu apparently decided that details could be overlooked. They treated God's directions in a disrespectful way and were killed for their insolence (see Leviticus 10:1–2). But Ithamar took pains to be obedient to God. Considering the many detailed lists found in the law, Ithamar performed a remarkable feat. He knew what God wanted and how he wanted it done. Ithamar served God with a proper attitude.

Ithamar reminds us how carefully we ought to obey God. God wants us to be thoroughly holy people, not a rough approximation of the way his followers should be. This week, assess your life and see where you have failed to heed God's instructions. Then resolve to let the Holy Spirit bring those areas into alignment with God's will. ❖

### PRAYER

*Please look at my life, Lord . . .*

### READ

The life and ministry of Ithamar are recorded in Exodus 6:23; 28:1; 38:21.

## JACOB
### *UNIQUELY BLESSED*

*"I am with you and will watch over you wherever you go, and I will bring you back to this land. I will not leave you until I have done what I have promised you."*

GENESIS 28:15

If there was a "most blessed" list in the Old Testament, Jacob would be one of the top candidates. God named Jacob as the third male in the Abrahamic line of promise. Wealth and an abundance of servants and livestock were a sign of God's favor upon Jacob. He was granted the woman he loved in marriage, and she bore him two sons. His other wives bore him several other sons, and God bestowed on Jacob the fatherhood of the twelve tribes of Israel.

It is important to realize that God gave his blessings with full knowledge of Jacob's shortcomings. Although Jacob was uniquely blessed by God, he also proved to be not-so-unique in his ability to lie, deceive and assert his independent nature. He was not the perfect hero. Instead, he was just like us: trying to please God, yet often falling short.

The Christian life is often an awkward dance of two steps forward and three steps back; the key is that God honors our efforts in spite of our errors. As you pray, put into words your desire to be available to God. You will discover that his willingness to use you is even greater than your desire to be used.    ✤

**PRAYER**

*I am available, O God . . .*

**READ**

Read about Jacob's life in Genesis 25–50.

## JACOB
### *CLINGING TO GOD*

*Then the man said, "Your name will no longer be Jacob, but Israel, because you have struggled with God and with humans and have overcome."*      Genesis 32:28

During the early years of Jacob's life, he lived up to his name, which means *grasper* or *grabber*. He stormed through life, grabbing every desire that lured his greedy heart. He grabbed Esau's heel at birth, and by the time he fled from home, he had also grabbed his brother's birthright and blessing.

When we read about Jacob again, many years have passed. He returned to his homeland in the prime of his life, having accumulated many wives and a stockpile of wealth, servants and animals. Soon, however, Jacob was grabbing again. This time, by the Jordan River, he grabbed onto God and would not let go. He realized his dependence on the God who had continued to bless him. No longer known as Jacob, who ambitiously adhered to his possessions, he became Israel, the one who clings to God.

Contrary to contemporary wisdom, the one who grabs the most toys in this life does not come out the winner. All of our assets become liabilities if we have not gained the most important possession: a relationship with the living God. Which personality characterizes your life right now: Jacob grabbing all he can in life or Israel claiming God as his greatest gain?      ❖

**PRAYER**

*Lord, I cling to you . . .*

**READ**

Jacob's story is told in Genesis 25–50.

## JAEL
### *READY TO OBEY*

*"Certainly I will go with you," said Deborah. "But because of the course you are taking, the honor will not be yours, for the LORD will deliver Sisera into the hands of a woman."*

JUDGES 4:9

Sometimes people in the same family choose opposite sides of a war to support. Israel declared war with Canaan. "There was an alliance" (Judges 4:17) between Heber the Kenite, a descendant of Moses' father-in-law, and the Canaanites. But Heber's wife, Jael, decided to become an ally of Israel.

During the decisive battle of the war, Sisera, the Canaanite commander, sought refuge in Heber's camp, and Jael invited him into her tent. Sisera let down his guard and went to sleep, trusting Jael to keep watch. Instead, she drove a tent peg through his temple and killed him. When Barak, the leader of Israel's forces, came looking for Sisera, Jael presented him with the body.

Jael's rather gruesome act is an important illustration of the decisiveness needed in a believer. Not only did Jael's obedience cause her to break from her husband's values, it also put her in danger. Although we may never be brought to such a precarious position, there will be many occasions that call for the same resolute determination Jael displayed in order to demonstrate our allegiance to God. Make it your resolve to obey.

Are you prepared to show immediate obedience to God in any situation?  ♣

### PRAYER

*Lord, I resolve to obey ...*

### READ

Jael's actions are recorded in Judges 4:11 — 5:31.

# day163

## JAIRUS
### TIME FOR TRUST

*Overhearing what they said, Jesus told him, "Don't be afraid; just believe."*  Mark 5:36

We don't know how many remedies Jairus tried in attempting to help his young daughter, but he was convinced that Jesus was his last hope. His little girl was dying. Jairus desperately threw himself at Jesus' feet and begged for help. To his relief, Jesus agreed to see his child.

The next several minutes must have been agonizing for Jairus. The pressing crowds made progress difficult. Jesus stopped to heal a woman. Then Jairus heard his name being called. Someone arrived from his house with the crushing news—his little girl was dead. The messenger's well-meaning but misguided advice was to accept the facts and get on with life. Jesus was no longer needed.

Fortunately, Jesus overheard the news. His words to Jairus must have encouraged and bewildered him simultaneously: "Don't be afraid; just believe" (Mark 5:36). Jairus, Jesus and three of Jesus' disciples found a grieving and unbelieving group of people who derided Jesus for saying the girl was only sleeping. After escorting the mourners outside, Jesus spoke to the child and she got up.

The words Jesus spoke to Jairus—"Don't be afraid; just believe"—ought to echo frequently in our hearts. Fear can make for a hopeless outlook, but trust in God keeps hope alive. Those who trust in God often find they get back what they thought they had lost.  ❖

### PRAYER

*Lord, I trust in . . .*

### READ

Jairus's story is told in Mark 5:21–43 and Luke 8:40–56.

# day164

## JAMES, BROTHER OF JESUS
### *FAITH LEADS TO ACTION*

*I saw none of the other apostles—only James, the Lord's brother.*    GALATIANS 1:19

James was one of Jesus' siblings who found it difficult to accept the identity of his brother. In fact, he did not believe until Jesus went to the cross. When Jesus rose from the grave, one of those he singled out to see was James.

James won a reputation in the early church for his wisdom. He was a practical man. The gift of discernment that drove his need to be convinced of the resurrection became a powerful asset in the young church, and James quickly became recognized as a leader. He chaired the first church council mentioned in Acts 15 that settled the crucial issue of how Gentiles would be treated in the church. James reminded the group that God was clearly working among non-Jewish believers and that Scripture supported their inclusion. His advice won the day.

Later, James demonstrated the extent of his wisdom in the short New Testament letter that bears his name. Those with any doubts about the practicality of Christianity need look no further than James. For James, faith was action. Browse through this letter, keeping in mind that it was written by someone who watched Jesus closely for almost 30 years.

What about you? To what degree would you be called a "doer" of the word (see James 1:22)?                                                                    ✤

### PRAYER

*Lord, make me a doer and not just a hearer of your Word . . .*

### READ

Our picture of James comes from the following passages: Matthew 13:55; John 7:3–8; Acts 15:1–21; 21:17–18; 1 Corinthians 15:7 and the epistle of James.

## JAMES, BROTHER OF JOHN
### *A HEAVENLY PERSPECTIVE*

*[James and John] replied, "Let one of us sit at your right and the other at your left in your glory."*
         MARK 10:37

Jesus singled out three of his twelve disciples for special training. Peter, James and his brother John made up this inner circle. James enjoyed being in this elite group, but he misunderstood Jesus' purpose. He and his brother even tried to secure their role in the kingdom to come by asking Jesus to promise them each a special position. James had not yet grasped the nature of Jesus' mission; he could see only an earthly kingdom that would overthrow Rome and restore Israel's former glory. His understanding of God's kingdom would be transformed by Jesus' death and resurrection.

Like James, our expectations about life will be limited if this life is all we can see. And like him, we too must admit we can become consumed with securing a personal kingdom on earth. How long has it been since you withdrew from the distractions of this world, even for a moment, to think about heaven and your future life there? Take advantage of the opportunity to do so throughout this day and let a heavenly perspective guide you in all your actions and decisions.    ✤

**PRAYER**

*Show me your perspective, Lord . . .*

**READ**

James's story is told in the Gospels. He is also mentioned in Acts 1:13; 12:2.

## JAMES, BROTHER OF JOHN
### SUFFERING AND ENDURANCE

*[Herod] had James, the brother of John, put to death with the sword.*　　ACTS 12:2

James was among the first of many to die for the sake of the gospel. His martyrdom was not an isolated event, but the culmination of other related sufferings he endured as Christ's disciple. When James was called to follow Christ, he forfeited the opportunity to work in his father's fishing business. He was separated from his parents and would never enjoy a settled life with his family.

As a disciple, James's life was marked by inconvenience and difficulty. Without a place he could call home, he followed Jesus from town to town, carrying only the clothes he wore on his back. Sometimes he endured swollen feet and an empty stomach. But James's joy outweighed his sorrow because he grew closer to Christ through suffering.

It is easy to say we are willing to suffer anything for Christ, yet most of us complain when even little irritations come. If we say we are willing to suffer on a grand scale for Christ, we must also be willing to endure in little ways. Begin now to pray that God may use your suffering to strengthen you and glorify him.　　✤

**PRAYER**

*Use my hurts to your glory, Lord...*

**READ**

James's martyrdom is mentioned in Acts 12:2. His story is told in the Gospels.

## JASON
### *A COSTLY INVESTMENT*

*"These men who have caused trouble all over the world have now come here, and Jason has welcomed them into his house."*                                    ACTS 17:6–7

Jason found out quickly that being a Christian can be costly. He lived in Thessalonica and met Paul and Silas when they passed through on their second missionary journey. Within a matter of weeks the gospel took root among the Jews and Greeks in town. The number of believers began to grow rapidly. Among them was Jason.

When a riot started over Paul's preaching, an angry mob showed up on Jason's doorstep. Paul and Silas were out, so they took Jason and some other new believers into custody. Jason was accused of aiding and harboring men who were challenging the authority of Rome. The charges had little truth to them, but they stuck. Jason and the others had to post bond before they could go home.

Jason is one of many unsung heroes who faithfully played their part to help spread the gospel. When Jason opened his home to Paul and Silas, he couldn't have known what that gesture would cost. You may not receive much attention for your service for Christ (in fact, you may receive only grief). But God wants to include you in his work. Lives can be changed because of your courage and faithfulness.    ❖

**PRAYER**

*Lord, show me the work you have for me . . .*

**READ**

Jason's part in the gospel's advance is recorded in Acts 17:1–9.

## JEDUTHUN
### MINISTER OF THANKSGIVING

*With them were Heman and Jeduthun and the rest of those chosen and designated by name to give thanks to the LORD, "for his love endures forever."*   1 CHRONICLES 16:41

Although David was not allowed to build the temple in Jerusalem, he organized the people who would carry on worship there. Among those chosen for special duty were a group of men designated as ministers of thanksgiving. One of them was Jeduthun.

We know practically nothing about Jeduthun's life. He had six sons who also served in the temple. Jeduthun's family apparently specialized in music with the lyre, a small harp. Jeduthun also had the gift of prophecy. His understanding of God added insight to his thanksgiving, just as his thanksgiving heightened his understanding of God.

Jeduthun participated in the great dedication of Solomon's temple. He is associated in Scripture with Psalms 39, 62 and 77 and very likely composed music for them. These psalms demonstrate Jeduthun's familiarity with the big questions of life and his utter dependence on God.

What comes to mind when you think about God? Awe? Praise? Thanksgiving? Contemplation? Understanding? Intimacy? Fellowship? Obedience? Humility? Ask God to show you a new aspect of his character today.                    ❖

### PRAYER

*That I might see your face, Lord...*

### READ

Jeduthun is mentioned in the following places: 1 Chronicles 16:37–43; 25:1–8 and 2 Chronicles 5:11–14.

## JEHOIACHIN
### *GOING WITH THE FLOW*

*"Record this man as if childless, a man who will not prosper in his lifetime."*

JEREMIAH 22:30

Although his name means "The LORD will establish," Jehoiachin's character brought about the opposite result. God unseated Jehoiachin from the throne after three months. Jeremiah's scathing imagery captured God's disgust: "'As surely as I live,' declares the LORD, 'even if you, Jehoiachin son of Jehoiakim king of Judah, were a signet ring on my right hand, I would still pull you off'" (Jeremiah 22:24).

Jehoiachin became king when he was 18 years old. He spent his childhood in the court of his godly grandfather Josiah. But years of evil practices by his father Jehoiakim quickly undid the reforms of Josiah and returned Judah to idolatry. Jehoiachin perpetuated the evil behavior he learned from his father.

After three months of reign, Jehoiachin was taken prisoner by Nebuchadnezzar, king of Babylon. He spent the next 37 years under arrest. At age 55 he was released within the Babylonian court as a pitied prisoner of war. From then on he ate at the royal table.

Family traits can be difficult to change or get away from. But Jehoiachin had no excuses; he had the memory of Josiah and the message of God's judgment and mercy. Bad family traits that aren't replaced with good ones tend to be repeated generation after generation. Will your contribution be a benefit or a hindrance to those who follow you? ❖

### PRAYER

*Lord, help me establish good habits in my family . . .*

### READ

Jehoiachin's brief reign is recorded in 2 Kings 24:6–17; 25:27–30; 2 Chronicles 36:8–10 and Jeremiah 22:24–30.

## JEHOIADA
### A WISE MENTOR

*[Jehoiada] was buried with the kings in the City of David, because of the good he had done in Israel for God and his temple.*      2 CHRONICLES 24:16

Jehoiada the priest helped to save the life of Joash, the only survivor of an attempt to wipe out the male descendants of King David. He then became the child-king's mentor.

Six years later, Jehoiada organized the coup that removed Athaliah from the throne and replaced her with the rightful king. Joash took the throne at age seven and reigned forty years. Jehoiada acted as a chief counselor to the king during many of those years.

Jehoiada and Joash led a significant renewal of the nation. The temple of Baal was destroyed, and God's temple in Jerusalem was gradually renovated. Although Jehoiada was honored when he died, the memory of his deeds faded, and the king chose wrong paths. Jehoiada provided Joash with helpful counsel, but he couldn't compensate for the king's lack of internal stability. Joash was usually swayed by the latest counselor who had his ear.

Even the best advice must be received and followed if it is to be effective. The wisdom of parents, teachers and friends can't be forced on another person. Your responsibility is to present the truth and warn of the consequences of disobedience. Others must choose whether or not to follow.     ✤

**PRAYER**

*Lord, help me provide timely warnings to ...*

**READ**

Jehoiada's ministry is recorded in 2 Kings 11:4—12:21 and 2 Chronicles 22:10—24:22.

## JEHOIAKIM
### *ROYAL REBEL AGAINST GOD*

*Jehoiakim was twenty-five years old when he became king, and he reigned in Jerusalem eleven years. He did evil in the eyes of the LORD his God.*        2 CHRONICLES 36:5

Many good kings had children who refused to follow God. Perhaps these kings neglected the religious instruction of their offspring or delegated it to someone else. Maybe they were preoccupied with political and military affairs. Whatever the reason, faithfulness to God was clearly not hereditary!

Josiah followed God, but his son Jehoiakim was evil. Jehoiakim continued the lamentable tradition of royal rebelliousness against God. He killed the prophet Uriah (see Jeremiah 26:20–23). He was dishonest, greedy and unjust (see Jeremiah 22:1–19). While he ruled, Judah became a pawn in the power struggle between Egypt and Babylon. Jehoiakim cast his lot with Egypt against Babylon. This proved to be a crucial mistake. Nebuchadnezzar crushed Jehoiakim's rebellion and took him to Babylon. Eventually he was allowed to return to Jerusalem, where he died.

Parents who believe God's truths have no guarantee that their children will share those beliefs. Children require loving, intimate training about God and his Word. The Mosaic Law had included this mandate, that God's words be taught "to your children, talking about them when you sit at home and when you walk along the road, when you lie down and when you get up. Write them on the doorframes of your houses and on your gates, so that your days and the days of your children may be many in the land the LORD swore to give your ancestors, as many as the days that the heavens are above the earth" (Deuteronomy 11:19–21). Children must be taught about faith both in church and in their home. It is an important element of religious life that needs to be explained and exemplified by a child's parents.                                                                 ❖

PRAYER

*Lord, I want to practice what I preach . . .*

READ

Jehoiakim's reign is recorded in 2 Kings 23:34—24:6; 2 Chronicles 36:4–8 and Jeremiah 22:18–23.

## JEHORAM OF JUDAH
### *MISERABLE MONARCH*

*"You have also murdered your own brothers, members of your own family, men who were better than you."* 2 CHRONICLES 21:13

The reign of King Jehoram, son of Jehoshaphat, marked a low point in the history of Judah. His reign was filled with sin and cruelty. He married a woman who worshiped idols; he killed his brothers; he allowed and even promoted pagan worship. Jehoram's marriage to Athaliah was Judah's downfall, for Athaliah brought her mother Jezebel's wicked influence into Judah, causing the nation to forget God and turn to Baal worship (see 2 Chronicles 22:3). Yet he was not killed in battle or by treachery—he died of a lingering and painful disease (see 2 Chronicles 21:18–19).

The people of Judah willingly followed Jehoram's evil ways. But by the time he died, they were sick of him. Scripture points out that his tomb was placed away from the respected tombs of the kings. The people had chafed under the consequences of Jehoram's sin, but they blamed their suffering on him rather than accept their own responsibility.

Let the story of Jehoram encourage you to take a look at your own life. Are you tolerating sin by blaming its presence on someone else? Don't take the easy way out; remember that it's not too late own up to your wrongdoing and get right with God. ✣

**PRAYER**

*Lord, I want to be right with you . . .*

**READ**

The reign of Jehoram of Judah is recorded in 2 Kings 8:16–24 and 2 Chronicles 21:1–20.

## JEHOSHAPHAT
### *TURNING BACK TO GOD*

*They turned to attack him, but Jehoshaphat cried out, and the LORD helped him. God drew them away from him.*　　　　　　　　　　2 CHRONICLES 18:31

Jehoshaphat knew better than to make the mistakes he made. His troubles began when he joined forces with evil King Ahab. Ahab wined and dined King Jehoshaphat in hopes of securing Judah's help in an enemy attack. However, God warned Jehoshaphat through the prophet Micaiah that their plans would not succeed. Jehoshaphat's decision to ignore the message and proceed into battle anyway was thus a willful act of disobedience.

Almost at once, he found himself the target for soldiers who mistakenly identified him as Ahab. He could have accepted this deadly fate, because he richly deserved it. But instead, he mustered the nerve to cry out to God, who miraculously saved him.

Unfortunately, few believers remember Jehoshaphat's brazen request for God's mercy when they fall into sin. Instead of running to God for forgiveness and restoration, their guilt persuades them to run from him—a lingering instinct from the days in the garden. While we must accept the consequences of our mistakes, Jehoshaphat's predicament shows us that turning to God is always the best recourse. No matter how greatly you have sinned, God wants you to call on him for help.　　　　　❖

**PRAYER**

*Lord, I need you . . .*

**READ**

Jehoshaphat's story is told in 1 Kings 15:24; 22:2–50 and 2 Chronicles 17:1—21:1.

## JEHOSHAPHAT
### *FAITHFULNESS IN THE LITTLE THINGS*

*Later, Jehoshaphat king of Judah made an alliance with Ahaziah king of Israel, whose
ways were wicked.*                                                    2 CHRONICLES 20:35

When the challenges were obvious, Jehoshaphat turned to God for guidance and
made the right choices. To combat widespread idolatry, he sent out officials to
teach the law to the people. He also called for prayer and fasting when Judah was
threatened with war. His faithfulness resulted in a great victory.

Jehoshaphat, however, was not so reliant on God in his day-to-day affairs. He
allowed his son to marry Athaliah, the daughter of the wicked King Ahab of Israel,
who did her best to be as evil as Ahab. Later, he got involved in an unwise ship-
building venture with Ahab's son, Ahaziah—a venture that God shipwrecked.

We repeat Jehoshaphat's error when we fail to seek God's counsel in routine
decisions. Because we lack the patience or trust to consult with him, we find ourselves making foolish choices that hurt ourselves or others. Perhaps you are facing
no major crises today. Maybe it's just the same old routine. Have you paused long
enough to give your day to God anyway?                                        ♣

**PRAYER**

*Lord, here's my day...*

**READ**

Jehoshaphat's story is told in 1 Kings 15:24; 22:2–50 and 2 Chronicles 17:1—
21:1.

## JEHOSHEBA
### RESISTING EVIL IN SMALL WAYS

*Jehosheba, the daughter of King Jehoram and wife of the priest Jehoiada, was Ahaziah's sister, she hid the child from Athaliah so she could not kill him.* 2 CHRONICLES 22:11

Jehosheba made an impulsive decision that changed the course of a nation. Ruthless Queen Athaliah, Jehosheba's mother (or perhaps stepmother) was planning to murder every prince in the royal family. Jehosheba was painfully aware that her own brother Ahaziah, the recently deceased king, had been the only survivor when his brothers had all been murdered years before. History was about to repeat itself in a gruesome way.

Jehosheba decided to rescue at least one of the children. She kidnapped her nephew Joash and hid him away in the temple with her and her husband Jehoiada, a priest. For the next six years they became his parents in hiding. Providentially Jehosheba would preserve the ancestral line from which Christ would be born.

This crucial moment in Jehosheba's life demonstrates an important lesson: Even when evil has the upper hand, we are still called to do good where we can. We may not be able to change everything, but we ought to do whatever we can. It's impossible to know how great an effect a single act will have, but it could be huge. Let God help you do the best you can with the opportunities before you. ♣

**PRAYER**

*Lord, I want to do good ...*

**READ**

Jehosheba's courage is recorded in 2 Kings 11:1–3 and 2 Chronicles 22:10–12.

## JEHU
### *SETTLING FOR MEDIOCRITY*

*Jehu said, "Come with me and see my zeal for the LORD."*  2 Kings 10:16

Jehu had the basic qualities that could have made him a great success. By many accounts, he was a successful king. His family ruled the northern kingdom longer than any other. God used Jehu to topple Ahab's evil dynasty and to rid Judah of Baal worship. He came close to being God's kind of king, but he recklessly went beyond God's commands and failed to continue the obedient actions that began his reign. Within sight of victory, he settled for mediocrity.

God gives each person strengths and abilities that are most useful when used under his guidance. Outside of that control, they don't accomplish what they could and often become tools for evil. A natural talent in finances can become an avenue for greed. An outgoing and persuasive personality can be put to use promoting the wrong cause. One way to make sure this does not happen is to ask God to place you under his control. With his presence in your life, your natural strengths and abilities will be used to their greatest potential for the greatest good.  ❖

**PRAYER**

*When I'm tempted to settle, Lord, please help me ...*

**READ**

Jehu's story is told in 2 Kings 9–10.

## JEHU
### *A LACK OF HEARTFELT OBEDIENCE*

*Yet Jehu was not careful to keep the law of the LORD, the God of Israel, with all his heart.*

2 KINGS 10:31

Jehu was a man with big ideas but little spiritual resolve. His kingdom moved with excitement, but its destination was unclear. He fiercely eliminated Baal worship, only to tolerate the worship of golden calves. Despite all the good he accomplished, Jehu's reign was undermined by a crucial mistake: He did not follow God with all of his heart. He had become God's instrument for carrying out justice, but he had not become God's committed servant. He gave lip service to God while he worshiped the golden calves in his heart.

Likewise, we can be very active in our work for God and still not give him the heartfelt obedience he desires. To obey with all your heart means to give yourself fully to God—first in devotion to him and then to his service. So often our efforts to know and obey God's commands can best be described as halfhearted. How do you rate your heart's obedience? God is more than willing to give you the power to obey him with all your heart. All you have to do is ask. ❖

#### PRAYER

*Lord, I would rate my heart's obedience this way . . .*

#### READ

Read more about Jehu's reign in 1 Kings 19:16–18; 2 Kings 9–10.

## JEPHTHAH
### *THE WAY OF RECONCILIATION*

*Jephthah sent messengers to the Ammonite king with the question: "What do you have against me that you have attacked my country?"*          JUDGES 11:12

For some people, talking is not avoiding action; it is the beginning of action. They approach a conflict with the full intention of settling issues verbally, but they do not hesitate to use other means if words fail. Jephthah was this kind of person.

Jephthah's first approach to conflict was to talk it out. He tried this strategy of negotiation with the Ammonites. He clarified the issues so that everyone knew the cause of the conflict. He used firm but conciliatory language to state Israel's position. However, the king of Ammon ignored Jephthah's message and prepared his troops for battle. Although Jephthah was unable to reach a resolution through talking, he clearly thought it was worth a try.

How do you handle conflict? Do you lean toward reconciliation or quick retaliation? Even if you are inclined to talk it out first, choose your words carefully. In his message to the Ammonite king, Jephthah avoided using personal insults but refused to give in to threats. Remember his strategy the next time you encounter conflict. Make it your goal to talk peaceably through the problem if possible.   ❖

### PRAYER

*Help me, Lord, to reconcile with . . .*

### READ

Read more about Jephthah's style of conflict management in Judges 11:1 — 12:7.

## JEPHTHAH
### *PROMISES THAT SHOULDN'T BE MADE*

*And Jephthah made a vow to the LORD.*                    JUDGES 11:30

A promise is a promise. But some promises, like Jephthah's, should never be made. In Biblical times, a promise made to God carried as much force as a written contract between two parties. Jephthah, a brave warrior, made a weighty vow to God in return for his help in conquering the Ammonites. It is not clear why Jephthah felt compelled to make this promise; in any case, it was unnecessary.

We do not know what actually happened to Jephthah's daughter. She may have been burned as an offering or set apart as a virgin, thus denying Jephthah any hope of descendants, since she was his only child. What we do know is that his rash vow brought him unspeakable grief.

In the midst of personal turmoil, it is easy to make foolish promises to God. How many times have you found yourself beginning a prayer: "God, if you'll get me out of this one, I *promise* I'll ..."? These promises may sound especially spiritual when we make them, but they often produce guilt and frustration when it comes time to fulfill them. Jephthah reminds us of the cost of making spiritual "deals." Instead of pouring out rash promises to God for the future, commit to obey him today, and consider carefully whatever vows or promises you make to God.                                                                                    ❖

**PRAYER**

*Lord, I commit to ...*

**READ**

Jephthah's tragic story is told in Judges 11:1—12:7.

## JEREMIAH
### *THE PROPHET WHO ENDURED*

*"Do not be afraid of them, for I am with you and will rescue you," declares the LORD.*
JEREMIAH 1:8

Endurance is a rare quality. Many people lack the long-term commitment, care and willingness that are vital to sticking with a task against all odds. But Jeremiah was a prophet who endured.

Jeremiah had to depend on God's love as he developed endurance. His audiences were usually antagonistic or apathetic to his messages. He was sometimes ignored, sometimes hated. His life was often threatened. He saw both the excitement of a spiritual awakening and the sorrow of a national return to idolatry. With the exception of the good King Josiah, king after king ignored Jeremiah's warnings and led the people away from God. He saw fellow prophets murdered. He himself was severely persecuted. Finally, he watched Judah's defeat at the hands of the Babylonians.

Most people have felt like giving up at one time or another: in a relationship; during an overwhelming task at home, school or work; or during a persistent illness. But like Jeremiah, we are called not to despair but to endure. Instead of focusing your thoughts, prayers and energy on getting out of a problem, you can draw on God's resources to get through it. God's love enabled Jeremiah to bear the worst humiliation; it can see you through your problems too. Make endurance your theme throughout the trials of today. ❖

**PRAYER**

*Lord, help me to persevere . . .*

**READ**

Jeremiah's story is told in the book of Jeremiah.

## JEREMIAH
### *SHARING IN THE SUFFERING*

*Since my people are crushed, I am crushed; I mourn, and horror grips me.*

JEREMIAH 8:21

World tragedy is painful to observe. However, by the time it reaches us, through a glance at a headline or a flip through the channels, it has lost much of its sting. Not so for Jeremiah. He lived in the midst of Israel's tragedies and received from God himself a revelation about the dreadful future awaiting his people. He was so deeply sorrowful for the fallen condition of Israel that he was known as the weeping prophet.

Jeremiah's book is an emotional chronicle of a prophet who sees his nation beset by sin and cut off from God. Jeremiah was angered by the sinfulness of the people of Judah, but he had compassion for them too. He realized he was set apart from them by his work for God, but he still considered himself one of them. Anguish consumed the prophet as he anticipated the misery of his people who would be dragged off to captivity.

We watch that same world still dying in sin, still rejecting God. But how often is our heart broken for our lost friends and neighbors or our lost world? Only when we have Jeremiah's kind of concern will we be moved to help. We must begin by asking God to break our hearts for the world he loves. ❖

**PRAYER**

*Grant me your compassion, Lord . . .*

**READ**

Jeremiah's story is told in the book of Jeremiah.

# day182

## JEROBOAM
### *SIN'S CONSEQUENCES GUARANTEED*

*"Go, tell Jeroboam that this is what the LORD, the God of Israel, says: 'I raised yoı  p from among the people and appointed you ruler over my people Israel.'"*    1 KINGS 14:7

Even clear warnings can be hard to obey. God's warning to Jeroboam came through a prophet who declared that God would soon divide the kingdom of Israel to punish David's unfaithful descendants. Jeroboam would have the opportunity to rule ten of the twelve tribes. God made it clear that Jeroboam's family would suffer the same disaster that David's grandson Rehoboam had met if they refused to obey him.

Years later, Jeroboam assumed his reign over the tribes that had thrown off Rehoboam's rule. He forgot the prophet's words and led his kingdom away from the God who had allowed him to reign. The consequences of this action, while not immediate, were devastating. His family was eventually wiped out and the northern kingdom collapsed, never to be restored again.

Sin's consequences are guaranteed in God's Word. When we do something directly opposed to God's commands without any immediate consequences, we often fool ourselves into thinking we've gotten away with something. That is a dangerous assumption that can only do us harm. Jeroboam's life should make us recognize our frequent need to admit our disobedience and ask God to forgive us.

❖

### PRAYER

*Forgive me, Lord, for . . .*

### READ

Jeroboam's story is told in 1 Kings 11:26—14:20. He is also mentioned in 2 Chronicles 10–13.

## JEROBOAM II
### *SHARING THE WEALTH*

*He did evil in the eyes of the LORD and did not turn away from any of the sins of Jeroboam son of Nebat, which he had caused Israel to commit.* 2 KINGS 14:24

By worldly standards, Jeroboam II was a successful monarch. He consolidated the northern kingdom, as Jonah predicted (see 2 Kings 14:25). The son of Jeroboam, who reigned during the division of the kingdom of Israel, Jeroboam II cared little for God, yet under his skillful and aggressive diplomacy Israel enjoyed more national power and material prosperity than at any time since the days of Solomon.

The prophets Amos and Hosea, however, tell us what was really happening within the kingdom. Jeroboam and his government ignored the need for justice and compassion. As a result, the rich became richer and the poor became poorer. The people became self-centered, relying more on their power, security and money than on God.

Jeroboam's dubious legacy reminds us that prosperity brings obligations. Having once been poor and despised, Jeroboam and his people should have recognized the need to care for the needy and oppressed. Instead, they wallowed in luxury and turned their backs to the God who had restored them. ♣

### PRAYER

*Lord, please grant me wisdom to share ...*

### READ

The story of Jeroboam II's reign is told in 2 Kings 14:23–29. He also is referred to in the books of Hosea and Amos.

# day184

## JESSE
### *CHALLENGING OUR EXPECTATIONS*

*"I am sending you to Jesse of Bethlehem. I have chosen one of his sons to be king."*

1 SAMUEL 16:1

Jesse is most frequently mentioned in the Bible in connection with two of his descendants: King David and Jesus, the King of kings. Though never royalty himself, Jesse was chosen by God to father an eternal dynasty.

One day Samuel the judge showed up in Bethlehem with a flask of oil. He asked to see Jesse's sons. Jesse dutifully had them appear in their order of birth. But for some reason he failed to call his youngest, David. Samuel had to ask, "Are these all the sons you have?" (1 Samuel 16:11). Apparently Jesse's older sons *looked* good enough to pass for kings. But God told his judge, "The LORD does not look at the things people look at. People look at the outward appearance, but the LORD looks at the heart" (16:7). Jesse may have overlooked his youngest son, but God saw in the lad the makings of an outstanding leader.

Jesse's story reminds us that much of what God does in and through us comes from his choosing, not our expectations. It was logical, Jesse thought, that Samuel would choose one of his mature sons to be king. But God defied the conventional wisdom in choosing David. We should not always presume that God wants the same things we want. We can be confident that we will make good choices when we seek his guidance and study his Word.                                        ❧

> **PRAYER**

*Lord, I confess that my expectations concerning . . .*

> **READ**

Jesse's part in the grand story of God's plan is found in 1 Samuel 16:1–13; 17:12–58.

## JETHRO
### *WATCHING THE EVIDENCE*

*Jethro, Moses' father-in-law, brought a burnt offering and other sacrifices to God, and Aaron came with all the elders of Israel to eat a meal with Moses' father-in-law in the presence of God.* EXODUS 18:12

Seeing is believing, the old saying goes, but sometimes it is the only avenue to belief. Jethro's quiet observation of the faith of his son-in-law Moses was crucial to his own salvation.

Jethro was from Midian and belonged to a community that worshiped many gods. But God revealed himself to Jethro over the course of 40 years, during which time Moses worked as a shepherd for Jethro. Jethro was able to watch God at work, molding Moses into a leader. So when Jethro saw and heard from Moses what God had done for the Israelites, he needed no further evidence for the supremacy of Moses' God over all other gods.

Jethro's recognition is a critical reminder that unbelievers may watch our lives much more carefully than they listen to our words for evidence of God's power. The quality and genuineness of our relationship with unbelievers critically influences the effectiveness of our witness. More than 40 years passed before Jethro was ready to commit to God. Are you willing to be patient as you live out your witness in front of those you love? ❖

**PRAYER**

*Lord, I am finding it hard to be patient about . . .*

**READ**

Jethro's story is told in Exodus 2:15 — 3:2; 18:1 – 27.

## JETHRO
### *PRESCRIPTION FOR SPIRITUAL HEALTH*

*Moses listened to his father-in-law and did everything he said.*  EXODUS 18:24

Jethro had a good eye for seeing problems. During a visit to Moses' encampment in the wilderness, Jethro realized that the magnitude of his son-in-law's responsibilities was grinding him down. The people were constantly taking their disputes to Moses, who would graciously listen from sunrise to sundown and hand down the verdicts. Jethro observed how this task kept Moses from more important work and suggested that Moses delegate his arbitration to others. Jethro proposed guidelines for selecting his replacements and a list of job responsibilities for the new appointees. This formula, he believed, would relieve Moses' stress while caring for the needs of the people.

Sometimes life's pressures blind us to the more important duties we should be carrying out. At such times, we need to heed the advice of godly friends who can restore our perspective. Likewise, we need to be alert to our Christian brothers and sisters who may be so overwhelmed with church or career responsibilities that they may be neglecting time with God. Every believer can use a friend like Jethro to lessen the likelihood of spiritual burnout.          ❖

**PRAYER**

*Lord, I crave wise counsel in regard to . . .*

**READ**

Read the details of Jethro's visit to Moses in Exodus 18:1–27. Other details about his life are recorded in Exodus 2:15—3:2.

# day187

## JEZEBEL
### *A LIFE OF TREACHERY*

*There was never anyone like Ahab, who sold himself to do evil in the eyes of the LORD,*
*urged on by Jezebel his wife.*                                    1 KINGS 21:25

Jezebel ranks as perhaps the most evil woman in the Bible. The book of
Revelation makes her name synonymous with those who completely reject God
(see Revelation 2:20–21). Many pagan women married into Israel without
acknowledging the God their husbands worshiped. But no one was as determined
as Jezebel to make all Israel worship her gods. Her evil influence spurred the
idolatry that would eventually destroy the northern kingdom of Israel.

Jezebel's plan to wipe out the worship of God in Israel led to her own undoing.
Before she died, Jezebel suffered the loss of her husband in combat and her son at
the hand of Jehu, who took the throne by force. She died in the defiant and scorn-
ful way she had lived.

Jezebel's bones were all that remained of her evil life. Her power, money, prestige, royal finery, family and false gods failed to save her. In the end, her life of
treachery crashed down around her. Power, health and wealth may seduce you into
thinking life will continue indefinitely. But death strips everyone of all external
security. The time to set life's course is at the beginning. The end comes soon
enough.                                                                        ❖

**PRAYER**

*Lord, I admit I sometimes base my security on ...*

**READ**

Jezebel's story is told in 1 Kings 16:31 — 2 Kings 9:37.

## JOAB
### *FAILING TO MEET HIS POTENTIAL*

*"Now you yourself know what Joab son of Zeruiah did to me—what he did to the two commanders of Israel's armies, Abner son of Ner and Amasa son of Jether. He killed them, shedding their blood in peacetime as if in battle."*      I KINGS 2:5

Joab had the stuff of a great leader. He knew what he wanted. He was brilliant at planning and goal setting. He invariably implemented his plans without a hitch. He possessed boundless energy. He was confident and courageous. He was shrewd.

Yet, despite a few military successes, Joab never lived up to his potential. Why? Because even with his many talents and abilities, Joab lacked a moral compass. A true pragmatist, he concerned himself with what worked rather than with what was right. We find no evidence that Joab ever sought God's guidance or strove to live according to God's laws. Instead, the record reveals a man who generally reacted out of anger, resorted to treachery and did whatever it took to reach his goals.

Because Joab's life was ruled by vengeance, it is not surprising to discover that he died a violent death. The lesson from Joab's life is obvious—ignoring God's direction leads to pain and sorrow.

Are you seeking to do God's will today—in every area of your life? Or are you ignoring his standards in the ambitious pursuit of your own desires?     ❖

### PRAYER

*Lord, I submit my desires before you ...*

### READ

Joab's story is told in 2 Samuel 3:22–39 and 2 Samuel 20:1–16. He is also mentioned in 1 Chronicles 2:16; 11:4–39; 19:8–15; 20:1; 21:2–6; 26:28 and in the title of Psalm 60.

# day**189**

## JOANNA
### *CELEBRITY SERVANT*

*It was Mary Magdalene, Joanna, Mary the mother of James, and the others with them who told this to the apostles.*                                        LUKE 24:10

The Bible treats celebrities with wonderful indifference. It practices what it preaches: the humble are raised up while the proud are humbled. To people who are inclined to give fame and popularity entirely too much attention, Scripture provides a welcome antidote. The angels rejoice no more loudly when a celebrity repents than when an average person welcomes his or her Savior.

Joanna could have ranked as a celebrity among the early followers of Jesus. She had access to Herod's house. She might have been a person of some influence. Yet Joanna's important work took place far from the palace. She and several other women helped meet the needs of Jesus and his traveling band. She was also among those who heard and saw firsthand that Jesus had risen from the dead. Luke merely mentions her, but what an honor to be mentioned in the company of Jesus. Her persistent servanthood was rewarded with honor.

How could the basic intention of your life today best be summarized—a pursuit of service to God or service to yourself?                                        ❖

**PRAYER**

*Lord, my intention is to ...*

**READ**

Joanna appears in Luke 8:3; 24:1–10.

# day190

## JOASH
### *THE TRAGEDY OF BORROWED FAITH*

*Joash did what was right in the eyes of the LORD all the years of Jehoiada the priest.*
                                                                2 CHRONICLES 24:2

Imagine becoming the leader of a nation at the tender age of seven! That's exactly what happened to young Joash. He succeeded the wicked Queen Athaliah as the ruler of Judah in about 835 BC. Fortunately this boy king had a godly advisor, the priest Jehoiada. His influence can be seen in Joash's extensive plan to refurbish the temple. The new king made sure that sacrifices and burnt offerings were faithfully made to the God of Israel.

Then Jehoiada died. Almost immediately Joash abandoned his godly pursuits and plunged the nation into idolatry. When Zechariah, the son of Jehoiada, rebuked the king and the people for their waywardness, Joash ordered his execution. A short time later, his own officials assassinated Joash.

Joash epitomizes superficial spirituality. His decisions weren't based on his own deep-seated beliefs; rather, his was a borrowed faith. Like a chameleon, Joash changed to accommodate his surroundings. When Jehoiada was around, Joash behaved like a true believer. When his godly advisor was gone and he received bad advice, Joash joined the crowd of unbelievers.

What about you? Do you act like a follower of Christ all the time, no matter what? Or does your commitment change with the circumstances?                    ❖

### PRAYER

*Lord, my commitment level . . .*

### READ

Joash's story is told in 2 Kings 11:1 — 12:21 and 2 Chronicles 22:11 — 24:27.

# day191

## JOB
### *GOD IS IN CONTROL*

*The LORD said to Satan, "Very well, then, he is in your hands; but you must spare his life."*                                                                    JOB 2:6

The opening chapters of the book of Job reveal much about the person and work of Satan. He is depicted as a real being. He roams the earth. He has specific knowledge of those who love God. He tests the motives of God's servants and deceives them. He is given permission (within certain boundaries) to afflict the followers of God. He is ready, willing and eager to cause suffering and grief.

Since Job never mentions Satan, it is possible that he was unaware of the devilish source of his suffering. Christians today, however, have the completed Scriptures. We know Satan is real, and it is obvious that he would like nothing better than to wreck our lives. How are we to respond?

We can take comfort in the fact that God is in control. He defeated Satan at the cross and will soon crush him under our feet (see Romans 16:20). So put on the armor of God daily (see Ephesians 6:10–17) and be on the alert for the schemes of Satan. Also, realize that Satan uses sneak attacks much more often than full-frontal assaults!                                                                    ✤

**PRAYER**

*Heavenly Father, guard me against evil . . .*

**READ**

You can read more about Job and the difficulties he faced in the book that bears his name, as well as in Ezekiel 14:14, 20 and James 5:11.

## JOB
### *WHAT HARD TIMES CAN TEACH US*

*[Job] replied, "You are talking like a foolish woman. Shall we accept good from God, and not trouble?"*      JOB 2:10

Calamity can ambush us. Life is going well until a phone call or text message or knock at the door suddenly turns our world upside down.

That's what happened to Job. He was a family man, a successful businessman and a devoted follower of God. Then the roof caved in—figuratively and literally. In short order he lost his children, his wealth and his health. It's hard enough to understand why terrible things happen; it's even more difficult to comprehend why bad things happen to good people.

Both the Scriptures and our experience tell us that trials can stem from several sources. We may suffer because of our own sinful actions. Or our difficulties may be due to the wrong choices of others. Sometimes, like Job, we undergo inexplicable natural disasters.

Suffering is never pleasant—even when we understand its causes. But even in the darkest night of the soul we can reap positive benefits from our pain. Hard times remind us of our frailty and need for God. Hard times can build character if we respond with trust and obedience. Finally, hard times can teach us how to comfort others faced with similar problems. God will uphold and reward all his children who endure suffering patiently and faithfully. It will not be easy, but it can have surprising outcomes.      ✤

**PRAYER**

*Lord, I need your strength today, because . . .*

**READ**

In addition to the book that bears his name, Job is mentioned in Ezekiel 14:14, 20 and James 5:11.

## JOB
### *BEING THERE*

*"I have heard many things like these; you are miserable comforters, all of you!"*   JOB 16:2

When disaster fell on the house of Job, Eliphaz, Bildad and Zophar did what any friends would do. They dropped everything and came to sympathize with their devastated companion. For a solid week they said nothing. They simply made Job aware of their presence, weeping with him and suffering silently with him. But when Job began to question God and express the deep grief inside him, they forgot all about comforting and turned to correcting.

"Maybe you're in sin, Job," they speculated. "Your understanding of God is all wrong," they lectured. The more the accusations flew, the more heated the discussion became. Instead of sympathy, sarcasm flourished. In the place of tenderness grew hot tempers. Even when God speaks at the end of the book, Job never gets the answers he is looking for. The arguments of the comforters are neither confirmed nor rejected.

Here's what we can learn from the book of Job about helping those who hurt: Those who grieve need more than a Bible verse, a platitude, a Christian book or a sermon download. They need arms to hug them, ears to listen to them, shoulders to cry on and hands to help them. Talking is not as important as simply being available. Even small acts of support can be a great comfort to those who are suffering. ❧

**PRAYER**

*Lord, I am praying for . . .*

**READ**

Job's story is found in the book that bears his name. He is also mentioned in Ezekiel 14:14,20 and James 5:11.

# day194

## JOB'S WIFE
### *MISSING THE POINT*

*His wife said to him, "Are you still maintaining your integrity? Curse God and die!"*

JOB 2:9

Job's wife suffered almost as much as Job did. Except for her health, she too lost everything. Her attitude and response matched the one Satan had set out to evoke in Job—cursing God. How ironic that Satan achieved his goal in Job's sole surviving companion and not in Job himself.

Did Job's wife realize that she had surrendered to Satan's manipulative scheme? Did she feel her loss so greatly that she didn't care that she was wrong? Or did she respond to her calamity merely in a fit of emotion, which later passed, taking her bitterness with it? We don't know the answer to any of those questions. All we know is that she responded just as most people would have under the circumstances—she got angry at God and insisted that Job do the same. Most people would have responded that way, thereby missing the point, just as Job said.

Every time we suffer we also undergo a test of faith. Is God really in control? Is there any reason for what happens to us? Does any of this make any sense? If we let our emotions take over, as Job's wife did, then we will indeed curse God. We'll be just like her: bitter, angry and wrong. We have the power to choose how to react.

❧

### PRAYER

*Lord, sometimes I doubt that ...*

### READ

The story of Job's wife is told in Job 1:1—2:10.

# day195

## JOCHEBED
### *ENTRUSTING CHILDREN TO GOD'S CARE*

*She became pregnant and gave birth to a son. When she saw that he was a fine child, she hid him for three months.* EXODUS 2:2

During Jochebed's lifetime, conditions for the Israelites were harsh and hopeless. They were oppressed without mercy. They had even become slaves. Jochebed already had two young children when an edict was passed ordering all male Hebrew babies to be killed at birth. The people resisted, and babies continued to survive. Jochebed's third child turned out to be a handsome boy she determined to keep alive.

For three months, all went well. When the baby became impossible to hide, Jochebed chose in desperation to put his life in God's hands. So Moses was set afloat in the Nile's gentle waves. God performed the first of several miracles that would unfold over the years. Moses' rescuer turned out to be a princess. She in turn unwittingly placed the child back in his own mother's arms to raise for a time. God gave Jochebed's child back to her.

It is always difficult for a parent to let go of a child. If you are a parent, learn from Jochebed and realize that entrusting our children to God's care is the best security we have. Pray for their safety and spiritual well-being, and trust in God's promises. ❖

**PRAYER**

*Lord, I am praying for ...*

**READ**

Jochebed is mentioned in Exodus 2:1–10; 6:20; Numbers 26:59 and Hebrews 11:23.

## JOEL, SON OF SAMUEL
### *SHAPING OUR CHILDREN'S CHARACTER*

*His sons did not follow his ways. They turned aside after dishonest gain and accepted bribes and perverted justice.*
1 SAMUEL 8:3

As an old man, Samuel appointed his sons Joel and Abijah to be judges over Israel in his place. However, Samuel's boys turned out to be corrupt, much like Eli's sons (see 1 Samuel 2:12). We don't know where Joel and Abijah went wrong in their lives. Perhaps Samuel's mistake came when he appointed new judges instead of waiting for God to choose a successor in his office.

Was Samuel a bad parent? We may never know. We aren't even sure if he was unaware or simply ashamed of his sons' behavior. When the people demanded a king because of Samuel's age and the unreliable character of his sons, the prophet objected only to their wanting a king. Apparently, he couldn't argue with their other observations. Joel is not mentioned in 1 Samuel again.

Joel was certainly not the first child who was unable to handle the position and prestige his parents had possessed. We must be careful not to blame ourselves for the sins of our children or children we love. Yet we also must not excuse ourselves from the responsibility we have for in children in our lives.

Whether you have children or not, you are influential in the lives of young ones. If you have children, know that what you do and teach can profoundly affect them for a lifetime. ❖

**PRAYER**

*Heavenly Father, I would like my child(ren) to . . .*

**READ**

Joel and his brother are mentioned in 1 Samuel 8:1–22.

## JOHN THE APOSTLE
### *LOVE WITH NO STRINGS ATTACHED*

*This is love: not that we loved God, but that he loved us and sent his Son as an atoning sacrifice for our sins.*      1 JOHN 4:10

What motivated John to write five of the books of the New Testament? What sustained him through those turbulent first years of the church when persecution was rampant—when as many as eleven of his fellow apostles died violent deaths? What enabled him to cope with his own lonely exile on the isle of Patmos?

Perhaps the answer is found in an idea that John mentioned repeatedly in his writings. That recurring theme is love. The words *love, loves* and *loved* are used more than 50 times in John's Gospel, and there are at least that many references to love in John's epistles. John was so amazed by God's unconditional love and acceptance that he even began referring to himself as "the disciple whom Jesus loved" (John 13:23; 19:26; 21:7,20)!

It feels wonderful to be loved by another human, but when we catch a glimpse of the depths of the love of God, we are awestruck. His love comes with no conditions, no strings attached. And once embraced, it has transforming power, taking ordinary sinners like John and changing them into extraordinary servants of God.

Have you ever pondered God's infinite love for you? More than that, have you accepted the priceless gift of forgiveness and salvation that he offers?     ❖

**PRAYER**

*Of your love, O Lord, I . . .*

**READ**

More insights from the life of the apostle John can be found in the Gospels, Acts and Revelation.

## JOHN THE APOSTLE
### *TRANSFORMED BY GOD*

*James son of Zebedee and his brother John (to them he gave the name Boanerges, which means "sons of thunder").*                                     MARK 3:17

Because the apostle John wrote so much about love, it's easy to imagine him as a bookish, soft-spoken man with a squeaky-clean reputation. Not so fast. Let's go back and check the Biblical record:

- John was a professional fisherman without formal education (Mark 1:19–20).
- He and his brother James once wanted to call down fire from heaven on some unfriendly Samaritans (Luke 9:54).
- On another occasion John and James schemed (without success) to get special favors from Jesus (Mark 10:35–45).

Not the most glowing resume in the world. But then something revolutionary happened in John's life. The scared, inconsistent, self-centered, hot-tempered disciple of the Gospels reappears in the book of Acts as a bold, devoted, unselfish apostle of love. So extreme was the transformation that even the Jewish leaders noticed.

That's the kind of change that's possible when we make the commitment to follow Jesus. He's not that concerned with where we've been or even with what we are. Instead, he sees us for what we can be. When we give our lives to him, he can change us (for the better) in mind-boggling ways.                    ❧

> **PRAYER**

*Change me, O God ...*

> **READ**

Details about the life of the apostle John can be found in the Gospels, Acts and Revelation.

## JOHN THE BAPTIST
### *POINTING OTHERS TO JESUS*

*When [John] saw Jesus passing by, he said, "Look, the Lamb of God!"*     JOHN 1:36

The ministry of John the Baptist evokes a number of images: his strange diet of locusts and honey; his odd clothing; his take-no-prisoners preaching style; his gruesome death at the hands of Herodias. But perhaps the most striking aspect of John's life is the way that he constantly pointed others to Christ.

In the desert he had the perfect opportunity to make a name for himself and enjoy a bit of celebrity. Instead, he talked about Jesus. As more and more people came to hear him, he could have tried to gather and keep a following. Instead, he encouraged folks to follow Christ.

When John's disciples expressed concern that the crowds were thinning out because they were following Jesus, John might have sulked or dreamed up a gimmick to win back the allegiance of the masses. Instead, he said, "He must become greater; I must become less" (John 3:30). He understood that he was just a servant. Perhaps that is why Jesus said, "Among those born of women there has not risen anyone greater than John the Baptist" (Matthew 11:11).

You too can live your life the way John the Baptist did—with your mind focused on Christ. Resist the temptation to promote yourself, your church, your brand of theology, etc. Instead, make the commitment to "make Jesus greater" by pointing others to him.     ✤

**PRAYER**

*Give me the heart, Jesus, to seek your honor above my own desires ...*

**READ**

Read about John the Baptist in all four Gospels. He is also mentioned in Acts 1:5,22; 10:37; 11:16; 13:24–25; 18:25; 19:3–4.

# day200

## JOHN THE BAPTIST
### *HONEST DOUBTER*

*When John, who was in prison, heard about the deeds of the Messiah, he sent his disciples to ask him, "Are you the one who is to come, or should we expect someone else?"*

MATTHEW 11:2–3

Things were not turning out the way John the Baptist expected. He had done his best to tell people that Jesus was the long-awaited Messiah. He had faithfully preached his God-given message of repentance. He had even chastised Herod for adultery and called on him to repent!

The next thing John knew, he was in prison. Loneliness and self-pity eventually gave way to doubt. "If Jesus really were the Messiah," John likely reasoned, "God would never have allowed me to be locked up. I'm the messenger sent to prepare the way, so why am I here?"

And so John sent some of his disciples to Jesus to question him. "Are you the one who is to come?" they asked. Jesus didn't get offended. He simply reminded them of the evidence—his words and his works.

Even devoted people like John the Baptist have periodic episodes of honest doubt. They want to believe and as soon as they are reminded of the truth, their faith is restored. Like John, we all need a little reassurance on occasion. Don't be devastated if you have momentary lapses in your faith. Just remind yourself of the things you know are true, using the Bible to help you remember those truths. ✤

**PRAYER**

*Here are my doubts, Lord . . .*

**READ**

John the Baptist's story is found in all four Gospels. He is also mentioned in Acts 1:5,22; 10:37; 11:16; 13:24–25; 18:25; 19:3–4.

## JOHN MARK
### *OVERLOOKING OUR PAST*

*Barnabas wanted to take John, also called Mark, with them.*                    Acts 15:37

Put yourself in John Mark's place. You were selected to be an assistant on the first missionary journey of the Apostle Paul. You accompanied him and your cousin Barnabas (another leader of the church) as they preached the good news of Christ. But then you got scared. Or you felt homesick. Or the schedule was too demanding. Whatever the reason, you left the team and returned to Jerusalem.

Later, when it is time for the second missionary journey and Barnabas mentions your name, Paul is adamant. "John Mark? No way! He's not coming! Not after what he did last time!" Your self-esteem sinks to your knees.

But Barnabas, in spite of your track record, goes to bat for you. "Give the kid another chance, Paul. He'll be okay this time, I know it." Paul won't budge: "I can't afford to take that risk."

Barnabas is equally persistent. "Okay, Paul, if that's the way it's got to be then John Mark and I will strike out on our own." You can tell his words aren't just for show. He means them. Then Barnabas says to you, "Well, John Mark, I guess we'd better go pack our bags. We've got a big job ahead of us."

We all need someone who will overlook our past foul-ups and who will encourage us to become the people God made us to be. Do you have someone who believes in you? If not, ask God to put a Barnabas in your life.          ❖

**PRAYER**

*Lord, I need a Barnabas ...*

**READ**

John Mark's story is told in Acts 12:25 — 13:13; 15:36 – 40. He also is mentioned in Colossians 4:10 – 11; 2 Timothy 4:11; Philemon 24 and 1 Peter 5:13.

## JOHN MARK
### *COMING TO MATURITY*

*Only Luke is with me. Get Mark and bring him with you, because he is helpful to me in my ministry.* 2 TIMOTHY 4:11

We know Mark as the author of the earliest, liveliest and shortest of the four Gospels. He grew up during the turbulent first years of the church. In fact, he may be the young man among the followers of Jesus who fled in such terror that he shed his wrap and made his escape naked (see Mark 14:51–52). The inclusion of this unusual detail may indicate that the writer himself made that frantic flight.

Mark is first mentioned by name in the New Testament account of Peter's amazing, angel-aided escape from prison. They kept in touch and eventually spent time together in Rome (see 1 Peter 5:13).

Mark also accompanied Paul on his first missionary journey but returned home after a short time, earning Paul's displeasure. However, by the time Paul wrote to Timothy late in life, Mark had become a cherished companion. The instability of youth had apparently given way to dependability in adult life.

We too can benefit from the wisdom of mature believers. The floundering we do in our youthful years usually isn't as important as the faithfulness we display in our adult life. Take time today to remember the people who challenged and believed in you, especially during the early years of your faith. ✚

**PRAYER**

*Lord, I am grateful for ...*

**READ**

John Mark's story is told in Acts 12:25 — 13:13; 15:36–40. He also is mentioned in Colossians 4:10–11; 2 Timothy 4:11; Philemon 24 and 1 Peter 5:13.

## JONADAB
### *DEADLY ADVICE*

*Now Amnon had an adviser named Jonadab son of Shimeah, David's brother. Jonadab was a very shrewd man.*      2 SAMUEL 13:3

David's son Amnon had a close friend and a big problem. Amnon was sexually obsessed with his half-sister Tamar. Amnon's friend and cousin Jonadab eventually noticed something was wrong.

Amnon trusted Jonadab and told his friend about the problem. Jonadab proposed a "solution" that ignored the obvious moral questions, one virtually guaranteed to make Amnon's situation worse. Perhaps it didn't occur to Jonadab that Amnon would rape his half-sister if given a chance, but his scheme to get Amnon and Tamar together put both in danger. Jonadab's suggestion began a spiral of evil that climaxed with Amnon's murder at the hands of Absalom, Tamar's brother.

Careless advice can be dangerous if given without first considering the consequences. We may tell ourselves that we are not responsible for what others do, but we should never give advice flippantly. Before you suggest something, prayerfully consider what could happen if someone did just what you suggest.     ❖

**PRAYER**

*Grant me, Lord, the wisdom to advise …*

**READ**

Jonadab's friendship with Amnon is recorded in 2 Samuel 13:1–38.

## JONAH
### *GOD'S PATIENCE WITH HIS CHILDREN*

*Jonah ran away from the LORD and headed for Tarshish.*　　　　Jonah 1:3

Few Old Testament personalities are as transparent as the prophet Jonah. We can see right through him. And most of what we see we don't like. He reminds us too much of ourselves: fearful, selfish, spiteful and proud.

Jonah's call to service began disastrously. The Bible does not say why he chose to flee from his assignment to preach to the people of Nineveh, but we can guess that fear was the main motivation. Instead of staying put, Jonah imagined that if he put an even greater distance between him and Nineveh, God would give up and choose someone else. Clearly Jonah greatly underestimated God's determination that Jonah would fulfill his mission.

Encountering a violent storm on the boat to Tarshish, Jonah at last knew that fighting God's will was useless. Rather than risk the lives of the other travelers, he insisted that they throw him overboard, and was promptly swallowed by a great fish. But Jonah was not finished. God used this time of solitary confinement to encourage Jonah's repentance and recommitment. Three days later, Jonah was released, ready to begin the work he was called to do.

God's patience with us is amazing. Even though we run and rebel, he patiently corrects us and places us back on course. Even so, we should not test God's mercy. It is always better to do what he asks the first time. ❖

### PRAYER

*Lord God, when you call me to obey, I . . .*

### READ

Jonah's story is told in the Old Testament book of Jonah.

## JONAH
### *DESIRING MERCY*

*But to Jonah this seemed very wrong, and he became angry. He prayed to the LORD, "Isn't this what I said, LORD, when I was still at home?"*     JONAH 4:1–2

The outpouring of God's love on the parched, sinful land of Nineveh stunned Jonah. After all, he had gone through a lot to give the message of impending judgment to the imperial city of Nineveh. Now God had relented, showing mercy on the very ones he had earlier condemned. Jonah didn't want the Ninevites forgiven; he wanted them destroyed.

Unfortunately, we often share Jonah's you-get-what-you-deserve manner of thinking. We show our disgust, even in subtle ways, with others who defy or ignore God's commands. Some people can seem so far gone in our estimation that we would be shocked to learn they were destined for heaven. Maybe we would even feel disappointed with God's decision.

Jonah's understanding of God's love was distorted. Is it possible that our view is similarly narrow? We must not forget that God devoted himself to us even when we too were a lost and hopeless cause. If we are honest, it is not justice but mercy we desire most for ourselves. And yet, like Jonah, we often tend to hold others to a different standard. Begin now to confess to God any familiar reflections you see in the mirror of Jonah's life.     ❖

**PRAYER**

*Lord, I confess that . . .*

**READ**

Jonah's story is told in the book of Jonah.

## JONATHAN
### DEFYING THE ODDS

*Nothing can hinder the LORD from saving, whether by many or by few.* 1 SAMUEL 14:6

When Saul was chosen as king, God had guaranteed Israel rescue from the predatory Philistines. No doubt Jonathan was aware of this promise. So when Jonathan and his armor-bearer encountered a Philistine outpost at Mikmash, they decided to launch a two-man invasion.

After this dynamic duo had killed about 20 of the enemy soldiers, God shook the earth, causing the Philistines to panic even further. The ones who weren't killed by Jonathan or his sidekick or their own confused countrymen were killed by the other Israelites who joined the battle. The victory was decisive because Jonathan decided to believe God and show his faith.

Logic tells us that Jonathan was foolish to attempt such a feat in the face of overwhelming odds. At least he should have notified his father of his plans! But faith by its very nature includes taking risks. Occasionally faith requires us to do illogical things on a grand scale.

In what area of your life today do you need to rely on your faith and believe in God to do the impossible? Do you have a relationship that needs mending? A friend who needs to know Christ? A habit that needs to be broken? Realize this: the same God we serve is the same God who proved faithful to Jonathan. ♣

### PRAYER

*Lord, I need you to do the impossible . . .*

### READ

The life of Jonathan is depicted in 1 Samuel 13–31. He is also mentioned in 2 Samuel 1 and 9.

## JONATHAN
### *THE COVENANT OF FRIENDSHIP*

*Jonathan made a covenant with David because he loved him as himself.* 1 SAMUEL 18:3

The deep friendship between Jonathan and David is surprising for a number of reasons. For starters, God selected David—instead of Jonathan, son of Saul and prince of Israel—to become the second king of Israel. Second, Jonathan's father, Saul, was intensely jealous of David and tried repeatedly to kill him. Third, David was a multitalented individual who was much more popular with the masses than either Saul or Jonathan. Finally, David had at one time lived among the hated Philistines and seemed to have joined up with them against Israel.

Jonathan and David should have been at least wary of each other, if not outright enemies. Yet they were able to overcome these potential obstacles and forge a model friendship. Perhaps the outstanding quality of their relationship was loyalty. That loyalty was grounded in a profound devotion to God. This higher commitment is what enabled their friendship not just to survive, but to thrive amid confusion and conflict.

Are you a fair-weather friend? Do you walk away from relationships when difficulties arise? Or do you defend a friend under attack? Can you rejoice when friends succeed, or are you secretly jealous and bitter? If your human relationships are weak, examine the depth of your loyalty to God. You may be surprised at what you find. ❖

**PRAYER**

*As far as my loyalty to you is concerned, Lord...*

**READ**

The life of Jonathan is depicted in 1 Samuel 13–31. He is also mentioned in 2 Samuel 1 and 9.

## JORAM, KING OF ISRAEL
### *PRESUMING ON GOD'S PATIENCE*

*[Joram] did evil in the eyes of the LORD, but not as his father and mother had done. He got rid of the sacred stone of Baal that his father had made.*     2 KINGS 3:2

Those who recorded the history of Israel noted that while things under Ahab and Jezebel's son Joram didn't get any worse, they didn't improve much either. Joram clearly knew what God required of him as king, but he chose not to obey.

Joram clashed often with Elisha the prophet during his reign. Once, the combined forces of Joram and two other kings became stranded in the desert without water. Joram immediately wondered about God's action in creating their predicament. King Jehoshaphat, however, called for the counsel of a "prophet of the LORD" (3:11). Elisha informed Joram and the king of Edom that his own presence and God's help were meant for Jehoshaphat. The other kings were merely absorbing the overflow of blessings.

God also used Elisha to preserve the king and his army from the Arameans. But Joram missed the point. When famine and the armies of Ben-Hadad surrounded Samaria, the king decided Elisha should be blamed. The city and Elisha were rescued, but Joram was soon killed by Jehu.

Joram knew about God and had many opportunities to submit to the Lord. He resisted to the end. How often we too presume on God's patience! Choose to live this day conscious of God's presence.     ❖

### PRAYER

*Today, O God, I choose to . . .*

### READ

Joram's reign is recorded in 2 Kings 3:1—9:26.

## JOSEPH
### HOLDING YOUR TONGUE

*They hated him all the more because of his dream and what he had said.*    GENESIS 37:8

Joseph couldn't help the dreams he kept having. They were visions from God about the future. But Joseph was perhaps a little too eager to share these dreams with his brothers, who were already jealous of the great affection their father Jacob had for him.

In one dream, the brothers were binding sheaves of grain, when suddenly Joseph's sheaf stood up and the others hurried to bow down to it. In the second vision, Joseph observed the sun, moon and eleven stars bowing down to him. These were obvious glimpses into the future—divine peeks at what lay ahead for Jacob's family down in Egypt.

Common sense would seem to say, "I'd better keep such dreams to myself. The situation with my siblings is volatile enough." But Joseph, obviously immature, blabbed it all. The results were what we might expect.

While self-assurance and confidence are admirable qualities, we need to be careful that we don't become cocky or boastful. Nobody likes a braggart. Remember the wisdom of Proverbs 27:2: "Let someone else praise you, and not your own mouth; an outsider, and not your own lips." Resist the urge to make yourself look better than others. The Scriptures say that those who exalt themselves will be humbled (see Matthew 23:12; Luke 14:11).    ❖

**PRAYER**

*Lord, please weed out any tendency to boast . . .*

**READ**

Joseph's story is found in Genesis 37–50. He is also mentioned in Hebrews 11:22.

## JOSEPH
### *NO EXCUSES FOR SIN*

*"No one is greater in this house than I am. My master has withheld nothing from me except you, because you are his wife. How then could I do such a wicked thing and sin against God?"*                                                    GENESIS 39:9

Mistreated by his brothers, torn away from his family, sold into slavery, transported to a foreign country, made to be a household servant—no question about it, Joseph knew all about raw deals.

The average Joe, no doubt, would have become bitter in Joseph's situation—angry at the ones directly responsible and angry at God for sitting back and letting it all happen. With that resentment at full boil, how do you think most people would have responded when offered the opportunity for some secret sexual pleasure? The rationalization would no doubt sound like this: "I'm miles from home. No one will ever know. I deserve some happiness. Besides, I didn't initiate this thing."

But look closely at Joseph's response. He recognized that sin is still sin—no matter what the circumstances. So he fled from Potiphar's wife like a scalded dog! Joseph was a man of impeccable integrity. The opportunity for indulgence merely highlighted his uprightness.

What about you? Do you rationalize and compromise when situations become unpleasant? What is revealed about your character when life deals you a losing hand?                                                                                      ♣

### PRAYER

*Lord, when I'm tempted to rationalize . . .*

### READ

Joseph's story is found in Genesis 37–50. He is also mentioned in Hebrews 11:22.

## JOSEPH
### *THE SOVEREIGN HAND OF GOD*

*"You intended to harm me, but God intended it for good to accomplish what is now being done, the saving of many lives."* GENESIS 50:20

When Joseph finally revealed himself to his brothers, they were terrified and rightly so. After all, years ago they had very nearly killed him before they decided to sell him into slavery. Somehow, however, much to their amazement, Joseph had become the second most powerful man in Egypt. The brothers recognized that their lives were in Joseph's hand. They cowered before him, trembling and waiting for him to pronounce judgment.

Instead they heard their long-lost brother speak words of consolation. Joseph told them not to be angry with themselves, for God had sent him to Egypt so he could preserve his family from the famine that had engulfed the land. Joseph encouraged his brothers to make the reunion complete by bringing their father Jacob to Egypt.

Rather than being vengeful, Joseph was thrilled. "Isn't it amazing?" he seemed to be saying, "God orchestrated this whole episode!" By standing back and looking at the big picture, Joseph saw the sovereign hand of God. He realized that God can master terrible situations to benefit his children.

What a marvelous, comforting truth! God is in control of your life today. Trusting in that fact can be the difference between joy and despair.                    ♣

**PRAYER**

*Lord, I take joy in the fact that you . . .*

**READ**

Joseph's story is found in Genesis 37 – 50. He is also mentioned in Hebrews 11:22.

## JOSEPH, MARY'S HUSBAND
### *RESPONDING TO ADVERSITY*

*Because Joseph her husband was faithful to the law, and yet did not want to expose her to public disgrace, he had in mind to divorce her quietly.*　　MATTHEW 1:19

Mary informed Joseph of the staggering news that she was pregnant. Her claims of angelic visits and her explanation that the baby inside her was the child of God may have soothed his mind a little bit, but still ... the news must have hit him like a punch in the gut. What would people think? What would Joseph tell his family and friends? And the most disturbing thought—was Mary telling the truth?

Joseph might have reacted in any number of ways. He could have publicly shamed Mary. He could have demanded that she be stoned as an adulteress. He could have disappeared in the night.

Instead Joseph tried to find a solution that would please God and spare Mary any sort of public ridicule. Isn't that interesting? In the midst of a severe personal crisis, Joseph's primary thoughts were, first, "What does God want me to do?" and second, "How can I best show mercy and kindness to Mary?" Ultimately God sent an angel to Joseph with the instructions to go ahead and take her as his wife.

Think back to the last crisis in your own life. How did you react? If a writer summarized your response in a sentence or two (like Matthew summarized Joseph's response above), how would that assessment read?

Ask God to help you become the kind of person who responds righteously to life's tough situations.　　❖

**PRAYER**

*Lord, I want to respond rightly ...*

**READ**

Joseph's story can be found in Matthew 1:16—2:23 and Luke 1:26—2:52.

## JOSEPH, MARY'S HUSBAND
### *URGENT OBEDIENCE*

*When Joseph woke up, he did what the angel of the Lord had commanded him and took Mary home as his wife.*    MATTHEW 1:24

Joseph had made up his mind. His fiancée was pregnant, and he was not the father. There was only one thing to do. He would end his relationship with Mary quietly and get on with his life. Then he had a dream in which an angel of the Lord explained Mary's pregnancy and the importance of the child. Joseph listened and obeyed.

After the child was born, an angel told Joseph to leave Israel immediately and go to Egypt to avoid violence at the hands of King Herod. Joseph listened and obeyed.

Imagine for a moment if Joseph had ignored the clear revelation of God. Suppose Joseph had awakened from one of the dreams and tried to explain it away: "How can I be sure that dream was really from God? It certainly seemed urgent, but maybe I should just wait for more evidence." Can you imagine the blessings Joseph would have missed or the dangers he would have encountered?

For us, obedience might not seem so urgent. We're not faced with world-changing events or life-and-death choices very often. But the principle is still true: God wants to guide us and bless us. However, we can't know the full extent of his blessing unless we follow his lead.

What clear command of God do you need to obey today?    ❖

**PRAYER**

*Heavenly Father, I sense that you are calling me to . . .*

**READ**

Joseph's story can be found in Matthew 1:16 — 2:23 and Luke 1:26 — 2:52.

## JOSEPH OF ARIMATHEA
### *ACTING IN SPITE OF FEAR*

*Joseph of Arimathea, a prominent member of the Council, who was himself waiting for the kingdom of God, went boldly to Pilate and asked for Jesus' body.*  MARK 15:43

A crisis reveals true commitment. When the pressure is life-threatening, those who don't have a clear reason for their faith give up. Jesus' disciples demonstrated these all-too-human traits. They fled and hid; some, like Peter, denied knowing Christ. But in the chaos a few disciples remained true. One of them was Joseph of Arimathea.

John's Gospel points out that Joseph was an undercover disciple until this point because he was afraid (see John 19:38). But Mark describes his request of Jesus' body as "bold." It was bold because it challenged the appearance that all leading Jews were opposed to Jesus and because it placed Joseph's career at risk. Joseph stepped out of the shadows at a crucial moment in history.

We may be tempted to look down on Joseph's timid discipleship, but such an attitude is not fair to Joseph. All the disciples were afraid! Joseph did not stand out because he was afraid; he stood out because he acted in spite of his fear. He had every reason to keep his faith under wraps, but he chose to risk everything to make public his faith in Jesus.

The big struggle for us is not to admit our fears. Those are usually pretty apparent. The challenge is to follow Jesus anyway. What fears keep you from being an effective disciple? Turn them over to God today.  ❖

### PRAYER

*Lord, I offer you my fear . . .*

### READ

For accounts of Joseph's bravery, see Matthew 27:57–61; Mark 15:42–47; Luke 23:50–56 and John 19:38–42.

## JOSHUA
### *TRAINING A LEADER*

*Moses did as the LORD commanded him. He took Joshua and had him stand before Eleazar the priest and the whole assembly. Then he laid his hands on him and commissioned him, as the LORD instructed through Moses.* NUMBERS 27:22–23

Regardless of what some people claim, leaders are made, not born. Gifted individuals must have training, hands-on experience and good role models if they are ever going to realize their leadership potential. Joshua had it all.

He led the attack on the Amalekites. He accompanied Moses (at least halfway up the mountain) when God issued the law on Mount Sinai. He was at the tent of meeting where God spoke to Moses face-to-face. He was one of the 12 men sent to spy on the land of Canaan. All in all, Joshua's was an impressive resume.

But perhaps the most valuable aspect of Joshua's leadership preparation was the privilege he had of observing Moses in action. As Moses's personal aide, Joshua got to watch him deal with jealous, rebellious and stubborn people. He saw how Moses handled national crises and smaller administrative nightmares. Most important, Joshua got an insider's look at Moses' intimate relationship with God.

In fact, the Bible frequently features this kind of leadership mentoring program: Elisha had Elijah; the disciples had Jesus; Timothy had Paul. Do you have an older, wiser role model to whom you can look? Ask God to provide you with a Moses. Then ask God to help you become a Joshua. ❖

### PRAYER

*Lord, make me a Joshua . . .*

### READ

In addition to the book that bears his name, details about the life of Joshua can be found throughout Exodus, Numbers and Deuteronomy.

## JOSHUA
### *BEING STRONG AND COURAGEOUS*

*"Have I not commanded you? Be strong and courageous. Do not be afraid; do not be discouraged, for the LORD your God will be with you wherever you go."*    JOSHUA 1:9

It's easy to understand Joshua's fear. One, he was following in the footsteps of the legendary Moses. Two, his "army" was as awe-inspiring as a ragtag band of schoolchildren. Three, the land before them was filled with fierce tribes of people who were not exactly going to lie down and play dead.

God recognized these concerns in Joshua. How else do we explain the repeated attempts by the Lord to comfort Israel's new leader? Four times in the very first chapter of the book of Joshua we hear the words, "Be strong and courageous." But these weren't just empty exhortations. God gave Joshua solid reasons why he didn't need to fear. "I will give you every place where you set your foot, as I promised Moses," God promised (Joshua 1:3). "I will never leave you nor forsake you," God declared ( Joshua 1:5). "Keep this Book of the Law always on your lips; meditate on it day and night, so that you may be careful to do everything written in it," God reminded (Joshua 1:8).

In short, Joshua faced the same decision we all face every single day of our lives: "Am I going to trust what God has said, and am I going to obey what God has said?" That was, and is, the bottom-line issue for the people of God.

Are you feeling anxious today? The solution lies in doing what Joshua did: Remember the promises of God and respond in faith.    ♣

**PRAYER**

*Lord, I am anxious about . . .*

**READ**

In addition to the book that bears his name, details about the life of Joshua can be found throughout Exodus, Numbers and Deuteronomy.

# day217

## JOSHUA
### FORGETTING TO ASK GOD

*The Israelites sampled their provisions but did not inquire of the LORD.* JOSHUA 9:14

Before the Israelites entered the promised land, God warned his people not to get chummy with their new neighbors. Inspired (but perhaps a little fearful), the Israelites conquered Jericho and, with some difficulty, Ai. Then they encountered the Gibeonites.

The people of Gibeon were aware of the fate of Jericho and Ai. It was obvious to them that the Israelites (and their God) were invincible in battle. So the Gibeonites concocted an elaborate trick. They pretended to be people from a faraway nation. They came humbly, asking for a peace treaty, offering to become slaves.

The ploy worked. Rather than checking out the Gibeonites' story carefully, Joshua and his people dispensed with the need to seek wisdom and guidance from God. Days after signing an agreement with this supposedly distant enemy, the Israelites discovered the Gibeonites practically lived next door!

In a similar way we need discernment as we attempt to sort out the various deals and offers that come our way daily. How often we make harmful—if not devastating—decisions, all because we forget to ask God what he thinks. Today, rather than making your own plans and then asking God to bless them, ask God to show you his will and then act accordingly. ❖

### PRAYER

*Please show me your will, O God ...*

### READ

In addition to the book that bears his name, details about the life of Joshua can be found throughout Exodus, Numbers and Deuteronomy.

## JOSIAH
### *TEARING DOWN THE IDOLS*

*While he was still young, [Josiah] began to seek the God of his father David. In his twelfth year he began to purge Judah and Jerusalem of high places, Asherah poles and idols.*

2 CHRONICLES 34:3

Josiah had been on the throne of Judah for 12 years when he began a crusade to eradicate idolatry from the land. The Scriptures tell us of the determination of the young king. He was intense. He was zealous. He was thorough. To put it bluntly, Josiah was a one-man wrecking crew! Josiah understood the ageless truth that God will have no rivals. He realized that as long as the nation of Judah flirted with false gods, they would never know the blessings of the one true God.

Christians in modern cultures often think of idolatry as a quaint ancient curiosity or a superstitious practice found only among primitive peoples. Wrong! Idolatry thrives today in the most sophisticated societies on earth.

An idol can be anything or anyone that comes to take the place of God in our life. If we give more of our devotion and commitment and energy to a human relationship, a job, a possession, a skill or an activity, rather than to God, we are living just as idolatrously as the pagans of old. All of our earthly loyalties and loves need to be oriented and ordered toward our highest love: God.

Ask the Spirit of God to show you anything in your life that has come between you and your heavenly Father. Then ask God for the courage to do whatever it takes to remove the obstacle. ❖

### PRAYER

*Remove the obstacles between us, Lord . . .*

### READ

Josiah's story is found in 2 Kings 21:24—23:30 and 2 Chronicles 33:25—35:26. He is also mentioned in Jeremiah 1–3.

## JOSIAH
### *A BLUEPRINT FOR ACTION*

*When the king heard the words of the Law, he tore his robes.*      2 CHRONICLES 34:19

As a young man of 26, Josiah, king of Judah, instituted a campaign to repair and refurbish the temple. During the renovation process, Hilkiah the high priest discovered a scroll in the temple. What books of the law this long-lost document contained is not known. What is recorded is Josiah's response upon hearing God's law.

King Josiah tore his clothes! In the ancient Near East, this was (and still is) a way of expressing deep grief or remorse. Why was Josiah so upset? Because as he heard the holy standards of God's law, he immediately realized that the nation of Judah had neglected God's commands.

It's important to note that Josiah didn't just feel bad and let it go at that. He immediately began making decisions, issuing directives and taking actions so as to comply with what God expected of his people. His response was both immediate and radical.

Is that how we react when we hear God's Word preached or when we read the Scriptures for ourselves? Do we instantly seek to apply the truth to our lives? Or do we procrastinate and rationalize with thoughts like, "That's true, and one of these days, I'm going to stop/start doing that?" Determine today that with God's help you will obey instantly and completely.                                   ❖

**PRAYER**

*Make me completely yours, Lord . . .*

**READ**

Josiah's story is found in 2 Kings 21:24—23:30 and 2 Chronicles 33:25—35:26. He is also mentioned in Jeremiah 1–3.

## JOTHAM
### *LEAVING THE JOB UNFINISHED*

*The high places, however, were not removed; the people continued to offer sacrifices and burn incense there.*                                        2 KINGS 15:35

Although Jotham's official reign lasted 16 years, he actually governed longer. When his father Uzziah was forced into quarantine because of leprosy, Jotham performed the day-to-day functions of the crown.

Much good can be said of Jotham's time as king of Judah, but he failed in an important area: He didn't destroy the high places of idol worship, even though leaving them clearly violated the first commandment (see Exodus 20:3). Apparently, Jotham preferred to build. He added to the architecture surrounding the lovely temple. He constructed cities, forts and towers around Jerusalem. But his failure to remove the pagan worship places undermined the good he did. The consequences were fully realized in the life of his son Ahaz, who became one of Judah's most wicked rulers.

Like Jotham, we may live basically good lives and yet miss doing what is most important. A lifetime of doing good is not enough if we make the crucial mistake of not following God with all our hearts. God sometimes requires that certain habits or influences be removed from our lives. Our lives only have room for one God. A true follower of God puts him first in all areas of life.                    ❖

### PRAYER

*Lord, my number one priority is . . .*

### READ

The brief accounts of Jotham's reign are found in 2 Kings 15:1–7; 32–38 and 2 Chronicles 27:1–9. See also Isaiah 1–5 for a picture of Judah in Jotham's day.

# day221

## JUDAH
### THE DIFFERENCE GOD HAS MADE

*"How can I go back to my father if the boy is not with me? No! Do not let me see the misery that would come on my father."*  GENESIS 44:34

When we first get a good introduction to Judah in Scripture, he is successfully urging his brothers to sell Joseph into slavery. All agree that it seems like a good plan. Joseph is the favorite son with the colorful jacket and the big head. "Might as well make a little money off this cocky troublemaker!" the brothers agree.

Yet toward the end of Genesis, we notice that Judah's callousness is gone. When it appears that young Benjamin (the new favorite son of Jacob) will be arrested for theft, Judah makes an appeal for the release of his baby brother. Judah pleads to his yet unrecognized brother Joseph, "Take me instead."

Judah's transformation is a marvelous example of how God can change a life. The younger Judah was opportunistic, selfish, dishonest and indifferent to the feelings of others. The older Judah was thoughtful, unselfish, responsible and compassionate.

In what areas have you seen God change you? What would your close friends or family members say is the biggest difference Christ has made in your life? Spend a few minutes thanking God for the way he has worked in your life. Then ask him to show you new ways in which you need to change.  ❖

### PRAYER

*Lord, please change . . .*

### READ

Details about Judah's life can be found in Genesis 29:35 — 50:26.

## JUDAS
### *THE WRONG AGENDA*

*The evening meal was in progress, and the devil had already prompted Judas, the son of Simon Iscariot, to betray Jesus.*                                                              JOHN 13:2

Judas, like so many others Jews, may have been looking for a military Messiah, a conquering king who would free Judea from Roman oppression. Judas had watched the way Jesus enthralled the masses with his words. Certainly Jesus had the power—hadn't he performed great miracles?

But Jesus wasn't interested in political or military liberation. He spoke instead of being a servant and turning the other cheek and being changed from within and taking up one's cross. What kind of talk was that for someone with so much potential? And so, the argument goes, Judas tried to force Jesus' hand. He hoped that Jesus' arrest would wake this reluctant Messiah to his "true" calling: the overthrow of Roman rule. We all know, however, that Jesus did not deviate from his divine mission.

Perhaps the lesson for us in all of this is that we must be careful not to try to dictate to God. Rather than trying to manipulate him into implementing our agenda, we need to submit ourselves to his plan. When we think we know what is best, when we are most determined to get our own way, when we fail to consult God about what he wants—then we are most likely to make choices that will lead to sorrow and remorse.

Whose agenda are you pursuing today?                                                    ❖

**PRAYER**

*Lord, not my way, but yours ...*

**READ**

The story of Judas Iscariot is told in the Gospels and in Acts 1:16–26.

# day223

## JUDAS
### PHONY COMMITMENT

*Going at once to Jesus, Judas said, "Greetings, Rabbi!" and kissed him.*

MATTHEW 26:49

Scholars and laypeople have long speculated about Judas. Why did Jesus pick him to be a disciple? Why did he betray Jesus? What are we to think about the sorrow he felt after committing his treacherous act?

Most of these questions are beyond our ability to answer. But these facts are beyond dispute: (1) Judas was one of the twelve disciples; (2) Judas lived and traveled with Jesus for about three years; (3) Judas heard Jesus teach; (4) Judas witnessed the miraculous works of Christ.

To onlookers, Judas appeared to be a committed follower of Christ. After all, he was the treasurer of the group. Judas had to have been a true believer, right? Wrong! Jesus warned that one of his disciples was "a devil" (John 6:70) and hinted that this follower was "doomed to destruction" (John 17:12).

The sad story of Judas should remind us of a sober truth: It is possible to be deeply involved in Christian activities, to learn the lingo of the church, to look and act like a follower of Christ and still be lost in your sins.

What about you? Your religious activity aside, have you ever come to Jesus on his terms and bowed before him as Savior and Lord? This decision is what separates those who know about Christ from those who truly know him. ♣

### PRAYER

*Lord, this is what's true about my activities . . .*

### READ

The story about Judas Iscariot is told in the Gospels and in Acts 1:16–26.

## JUDE
### CONTENDER FOR THE FAITH

*Jude, a servant of Jesus Christ and a brother of James.* JUDE 1

We know very little about Jesus' brother Jude. Like his other siblings, Jude found it hard to believe his older half-brother was God's Son. His doubt was understandable. The members of Jesus' family weren't always sure he was God's Son, but they *were* sure *they* weren't divine. Even though the authority and power of Jesus was plainly evident, they were not willing to call themselves followers.

Jude at first likely rejected the claims of his half-brother but later became convinced that Jesus is Lord. The brief letter he eventually wrote reflected his personal odyssey to the truth. He urged Christians to "contend for the faith" (Jude 3). Jude, who now treasured that faith above all else, was anxious to prevent false teachers and immorality from snuffing out the life of the church. Undoubtedly he recalled the folly of his youthful skepticism and was determined to bolster the faith of young believers who may have been troubled by their own doubts.

It is often the person who has wrestled long and hard with the claims of Christianity who emerges with a strong faith and transformed life. Jude was slow in acknowledging the claims of Jesus, but his letter leaves no doubt that he developed into a loving, mature Christian eager to serve God with his whole life. If you are struggling with the tough questions of the faith, take encouragement from Jude's life. ❖

### PRAYER

*Lord, I struggle with ...*

### READ

For more on Jude, see Matthew 13:54–58; Mark 3:31–35; 6:1–6 and the epistle of Jude.

# day225

## JULIUS
### INFLUENCING THE AUTHORITIES

*When it was decided that we would sail for Italy, Paul and some other prisoners were handed over to a centurion named Julius, who belonged to the Imperial Regiment.*

ACTS 27:1

Once he became a messenger for Christ, Paul spent a great deal of time in prison. While under arrest, an unusual relationship developed between Paul and a centurion named Julius, who had received orders to escort several prisoners to Rome. Julius and Paul may have known each other during the two years the apostle was detained in Caesarea. Julius showed kindness and trust toward Paul from the start, even allowing him to visit friends along their route.

When their ship ran into bad weather, Paul warned Julius of danger and loss. Yet Julius felt pressure to accomplish his mission, and others convinced him to journey on to a better port. Paul's warning proved true and the ship sank. Only the passengers survived.

During the shipwreck, the soldiers planned to kill the prisoners rather than run the risk of allowing them to escape. Julius overruled the plan. He wanted to protect Paul. From then on, Luke's account indicates that Julius allowed Paul a voice in the decision-making. We can easily imagine that Julius met Christ through Paul.

No relationship is accidental. Every person we meet gives us an opportunity to be faithful to Christ in our words and actions.                                    ❖

**PRAYER**

*Lord, help me be aware of my sphere of influence ...*

**READ**

Paul and Julius's adventure is recorded in Acts 27:1—28:16.

## JUSTUS
### AN OPEN HEART, AN OPEN HOME

*Paul left the synagogue and went next door to the house of Titius Justus, a worshiper of God.* ACTS 18:7

The apostle Paul frequently got mixed reviews when he visited a new city. His method was quite consistent. He began in a familiar place—the synagogue. Paul announced his message about Christ as the fulfillment of all that the Jews truly believed. Some responded, some resisted, while others objected. In Corinth, Paul met stiff opposition from local Jewish leaders and decided to try a different strategy of evangelism. He took up the offer of a man named Titius Justus, who lived next door to the synagogue.

For the next year and a half, Paul taught and ministered from Justus's home. We could say that Justus had both his heart and his hearth in the right place. The strategic location of his house allowed Paul's message to reach Jews even while he was gaining a hearing among the Greeks. Within a short time, Crispus, the leader of the synagogue, became a believer in Jesus. So did many others.

Justus's hospitality was motivated by his relationship with God. His open home was an act of worship! He shows us that even those of us with little can give what we can. When we make the best we have available to God, the results are often wonderful! What opportunities are you aware of for worshiping God through acts of hospitality? ❖

**PRAYER**

*Lord, I offer my ...*

**READ**

Justus's role in the spread of the gospel is recorded in Acts 18:1–17.

## KETURAH
### *SMOOTHING OVER A ROUGH SITUATION*

*Abraham had taken another wife, whose name was Keturah.*     Genesis 25:1

Keturah became Abraham's second wife after Sarah died. What a complicated family system she faced! Her husband was perhaps thrice her age. Although she gave birth to six sons, Abraham's entire estate was inherited by Isaac, the only son Sarah had borne him. The memory of the "other woman," Hagar, and her son, Ishmael, no doubt lingered. We read that concubines lived in the household as well. These women had children. Keturah was a late arrival in the household.

We don't know how Keturah handled the problems she faced, but her life bears witness to God's compassion for family messes. God honored Keturah with significant offspring. Among her descendants were the Midianites. Keturah was the ancestor of Moses' wife Zipporah and his wise father-in-law Jethro.

God's Biblical guidelines are intended to steer us around potential problems, including family difficulties. Like Keturah, we may not enjoy ideal family circumstances. Parents divorce. Children rebel. Siblings quarrel. But if you obey God and show love even to those who are unloving, you may be surprised at the results. God is always working for our good. He is eager to restore broken relationships. Invite him today to begin the healing process.     ❖

**PRAYER**

*Lord, please heal . . .*

**READ**

Keturah's place in Abraham's life is recorded in Genesis 25:1–8.

## KISH
### *PASSING ON FAMILY VALUES*

*There was a Benjamite, a man of standing, whose name was Kish son of Abiel, the son of Zeror, the son of Bekorath, the son of Aphiah of Benjamin.*                    1 SAMUEL 9:1

In ancient Israel a person could be identified in three ways: by family lineage, tribal ancestry and social status. The Bible introduces Kish in all three ways, but he is chiefly remembered as the father of Saul, the first king of Israel.

Kish lived in a time of change. The people of Israel had failed to conquer Canaan. They were led by judges who responded to crises but who could not restore spiritual health to Israel. Instead, the nation clamored for a king.

One day Kish sent Saul to find several donkeys that had wandered off. Saul never found the donkeys but did meet Samuel the judge during his search. Though the events appeared to be coincidental, God had arranged a divine appointment between Samuel and Saul. Kish's son returned home as the newly appointed king of Israel.

When Kish sent Saul after the donkeys, he was preparing his son for the responsibilities he would inherit one day. He trained Saul to be his heir without knowing his son would be king. Like Kish, we seldom know what paths our children will follow. We can't even be sure they will absorb the best we can offer them. But a stable family provides the best way to transmit important values. How do you help your children develop skills they will need every day? Ask God to help you develop the wisdom and discernment you need to be the best parent you can be.          ❖

**PRAYER**

*Lord, I need your discernment . . .*

**READ**

Kish is mentioned briefly in 1 Samuel 9:1–3; 14:51 and Acts 13:21.

## KORAH
### *CULTIVATING BITTERNESS*

*Korah son of Izhar, the son of Kohath, the son of Levi, and certain Reubenites — Dathan and Abiram, sons of Eliab, and On son of Peleth — became insolent and rose up against Moses.*
         NUMBERS 16:1 – 2

Korah was a whiner, a complainer, a grumbler. Rather than concentrating on all his blessings (and they were many), he focused on what he didn't have. His discontentment turned into jealousy and then resentment. Overcome with bitterness, he challenged Moses, God's appointed leader. His rebellion resulted in his death and that of many other Israelites.

Imagine how differently things might have turned out. Suppose Korah had spent his time, energy and emotion thanking God for delivering him and his family from Egyptian bondage. Imagine if Korah had regularly expressed appreciation to God for the privilege of being a Levite and for the opportunity to work in and around the tabernacle. Consider the difference if Korah had prayed daily for Moses and Aaron, the leaders of Israel. There's no doubt that if Korah had cultivated contentment, his witness would have brought glory to God.

How can we guard against grumbling? Practice the art of appreciation. Thank God often for the many blessings he has given you. Focus on what God has called you to do. Serve faithfully, and leave issues like prestige, prominence and position in God's hands.

If you're trying to grab the spotlight, or if you're mad that someone else is enjoying it instead, beware!      ✤

**PRAYER**

*Lord, help me focus on you . . .*

**READ**

The sad story of Korah is found in Numbers 16:1 – 40. He is also mentioned in Numbers 26:9 – 10 and Jude 11.

## LABAN
### *RIDING A COATTAIL OF BLESSINGS*

*Laban said to him, "If I have found favor in your eyes, please stay. I have learned by divination that the LORD has blessed me because of you."*        GENESIS 30:27

What does Scripture tell us about Laban? He was the brother of Rebekah, the brother-in-law of Isaac and the uncle of Jacob. He had two daughters: Leah and Rachel. Laban was a wealthy shepherd with a history of deception in his dealings with others. (That may explain how he became wealthy!)

Nowhere in Genesis do we find any evidence that Laban ever had much interest in the God of Abraham, Isaac and Jacob. In fact, he seemed much more devoted to his pagan idols. And yet, Laban was no dummy. He recognized the unmistakable overflow of benefits that surrounded Jacob.

It is easy to fall into a routine where we ride the spiritual coattails of others. We discover that we can taste a little bit of the goodness of God even from a distance, even without a life of commitment. Yet, if we're selfish and worldly like Laban, we don't really belong. We're just along for the ride. We're on the outside looking in. We're close to God ... but not really.

Don't settle for that kind of long-distance, secondhand relationship with God. Tell God today that you want to know him intimately. Then wait to see what happens.                                                                              ❧

**PRAYER**

*Father God, I want to know you ...*

**READ**

Laban's life story is found in Genesis 27:43 — 31:55.

## LAMECH
### *THE RAPID GROWTH OF SIN*

*"If Cain is avenged seven times, then Lamech seventy-seven times."*     GENESIS 4:24

Lamech earns just a few brief verses in Scripture, but those words say much about the rapid advance of sin in the days after Adam and Eve. A descendant of Cain, Lamech was the father of the first musician and the first metalworker. But Lamech's contribution to the spiritual condition of humankind was a pitiful one.

First, we note that Lamech was the first polygamist, taking two wives, Adah and Zillah. This attempt to "improve" on God's design for marriage would bear sorrow and frustration for many who followed in his footsteps—Jacob, David and Solomon are obvious examples.

Second, Lamech had a cavalier regard for the value of human life. He tells his wives that he killed a young man (actually, "child" in the Hebrew) for striking him. Instead of showing remorse, he boasts of his deed and throws down a challenge: If anyone dare settle the score for this murder, Lamech would be avenged "seventy-seven times"! Unlike Cain, who took God's protection gladly, Lamech seems to laugh off the need for any divine discipline or refuge.

Sin is like a weed. It can grow rapidly even in adverse conditions. Are you ignoring the sprouts that are shooting up in your life? Ask God to help you pull up the weeds of selfishness and rebellion before the problem gets out of control.   ✢

**PRAYER**

*Lord, please pull these "weeds" . . .*

**READ**

Lamech's story appears in Genesis 4:18–24.

## LAZARUS
### *OBEYING THE CALL*

*When he had said this, Jesus called in a loud voice, "Lazarus, come out!"*　　John 11:43

A scene like the one in Bethany that John describes is repeated around the world each day. A grieving family gathers at a graveside. Friends are silent, agonizing over what to say. Their downcast eyes and shifting feet provide more distraction than comfort. On this day, drawn by grief and duty, people came from Jerusalem and the surrounding area to pay their last respects to a citizen of Bethany.

Jesus' friend Lazarus was dead. His brief sickness overpowered the medicine available. Jesus had been sent for but failed to arrive in time. Death, on the other hand, failed to wait. The body was quickly wrapped and buried in a tomb. Four days later, Jesus arrived.

Lazarus was spoken about and spoken to but we don't have a record of a single word he said. We do know that he listened to Jesus. Even when death separated them, Lazarus responded to Jesus' voice. We know because he came hobbling out of the tomb, still wrapped in the burial cloths. Jesus raised him from the dead!

When all is said and done, what will really matter will be what God accomplished through us. We will not be able to take much credit. We have Christ's invitation to participate in his work, but we must not forget that he can do much more than we are able to do. Our obedience to Jesus' call will make the difference. Do you listen to Christ faithfully by reading his Word?　　❖

**PRAYER**

*Lord, I am listening ...*

**READ**

Lazarus's role as an "active spectator" is recorded in John 11:1—12:11.

## LEAH
### *PRISONER OF INSECURITY*

*Then Leah said, "God has presented me with a precious gift. This time my husband will treat me with honor, because I have borne him six sons."*     GENESIS 30:20

Leah lived in a world where women were considered property. Daughters were tokens used by fathers to finish deals. Leah's father Laban gave her to Jacob, who did not love her as much as he loved her younger sister Rachel. But God loved her completely.

Leah desperately wanted her husband to cherish her. The names she chose for her sons expressed her longing to be noticed. She also competed fiercely with Rachel. The sisters began to measure their worth by the number of children they could bear. Leah won the fertility contest, but the victory most likely did not capture Jacob's affection.

When we fail to live at peace with the important people in our lives, we create problems that may last for years. Although God loved Leah, we are not told that she acknowledged that fact. Her refusal to appreciate God's love and his blessings also made her unable to love others in a healthy way. When we struggle to love others, we need to remember the simple fact that God loves us. Only God's love can free us from desperate love.     ✣

### PRAYER

*Lord, I struggle to love ...*

### READ

Leah's story appears in Genesis 29–35.

## LOT
### *HIGH PLAINS DRIFTER*

*Abram lived in the land of Canaan, while Lot lived among the cities of the plain and pitched his tents near Sodom.*                    GENESIS 13:12

Perhaps you have heard this old saying: "There are three kinds of people in life — those who make things happen, those who watch what happens and those who say, 'What happened?'"

Lot seems to have been the third type of person. As you read about him in Scripture, you get the impression of a guy who floated through life, taking the path of least resistance. He never seemed to wrestle with difficult questions such as, "What are the long-term consequences of this choice?" or "I wonder what God wants me to do?" Instead he lived for the moment. He never anchored himself to the truth of God; consequently, he was swept along by a corrupt culture to places he probably never wanted to go. Lot and his family suffered death, incest and disgrace because he allowed the world to shape his life and determine his direction.

Are you drifting? Do you have firm convictions about how God expects you to live? Have you anchored yourself to the truth of God? Do you have some definite goals in view? If you don't take specific steps to place yourself under God's direction, you may turn out like Lot, one of those poor souls who gets into one mess after another. Don't let your life be a tragic example of what might have been. ♣

**PRAYER**

*Lord, I crave your direction . . .*

**READ**

The story of Lot is found in Genesis 11 – 14; 19.

# day235

## LOT'S WIFE
### DON'T LOOK BACK

*Lot's wife looked back, and she became a pillar of salt.*          GENESIS 19:26

Lot's wife was one look away from reaching a safe haven with her family. Gulping the sulfurous air, she frantically followed her husband through the smoke. Perhaps she was startled to a sudden halt by the fiery orange bursts that ruptured the dim morning sky. The thunderous crack of fire striking her neighbors' homes and the rooftops of familiar buildings might have instinctively made her whip around to see what was happening. Instantly, her eyes took in the dreadful scene and her mortal frame disintegrated—her disobedience memorialized in grains of salt.

Why did Lot's wife so foolishly look back? Likely for the reason most familiar to us: She was thoroughly human. Like her, we often receive clear instruction from God yet still feel frightened and uncertain about where God is taking us.

When we are following God in a new direction, the awareness of our former dreams and goals going up in flames behind us may cause us to distrust his leading. Are you looking back longingly at what you are leaving behind while trying to move forward into a deeper relationship with God? Jesus' clear warning to us is to "Remember Lot's wife!" (Luke 17:32). The only way out of this dilemma is to trust him in spite of your fears.                                                                    ❖

### PRAYER

*Lord, I am tempted to look back on ...*

### READ

The full story of Lot's wife and her family's escape from Sodom is found in Genesis 18:16 — 19:29.

## LUCIUS
### *OBSCURE OBEDIENCE*

*Now in the church at Antioch there were prophets and teachers.*       Acts 13:1

Lucius may well have been one of the unnamed Christians from Cyrene who traveled to Antioch to plant a church there (see Acts 11:19–21)—the first of its kind among non-Jews. Later, Lucius became a leader in the Antioch church along with Paul and Barnabas. He was one of those who recognized God's call for missionaries to advance the gospel. His church's prayerful response led to Paul and Barnabas's departure to evangelize the peoples of Europe and Asia.

For every well-known person within the church, many must be content to live out their lives in obscure obedience. The direction of the church may come from strong leaders, but the strength of the church comes from strong followers. We may want to be praised like Paul, but we will probably receive little more mention than Lucius.

Jesus never promised earthly recognition for his faithful disciples. He actually predicted the opposite. In any case, the chance for fame makes a very poor reason for obedience. The lives of Lucius and many other Biblical figures provide us with healthy models of simple obedience. They lived their answer to the question, "How faithful to God are you when no one else is watching?" How will you answer that question today?                                                                   ✤

**PRAYER**

*When no one is watching, Jesus, I . . .*

**READ**

Lucius is mentioned in passing in Acts 13:1.

## LUKE
### *THE DOCTOR HAS GOOD NEWS*

*I myself have carefully investigated everything from the beginning.*      LUKE 1:3

Luke was a medical doctor who experienced spiritual healing in his own life when he heard the gospel of Jesus Christ, probably from the lips of the apostle Paul. He later traveled with Paul and became a leader in the early church.

Doctor Luke's greatest achievements are the two New Testament books he authored—Luke and Acts—under the inspiration of the Holy Spirit. Both books are marked by excellent style and are supported by comprehensive personal research. Clearly Luke approached his writing of church history with the same care he approached his practice of medicine!

Unfortunately, many modern-day believers fail to serve God with excellence. They give their best time and efforts to other endeavors. Consider the man who willingly spends hours preparing a report for his supervisor and then throws his Bible study lesson together in 30 minutes. Think of the woman who wouldn't dream of missing her weekly tennis lesson but who is often "just too tired" to get to church many Sundays. How do these people rank their priorities?

If we are going to serve God—whether through writing as Luke did, leading a small group or volunteering to keep the church building clean—we need to serve with excellence.     ✤

**PRAYER**

*Lord, I want to serve you with excellence...*

**READ**

Luke refers to himself in Luke 1:3, Acts 1:1; 16–28. He also is mentioned in Colossians 4:14; 2 Timothy 4:11 and Philemon 24.

## LYDIA
### HOUSEHOLD OF HOSPITALITY

*When she and the members of her household were baptized, she invited us to her home. "If you consider me a believer in the Lord," she said, "come and stay at my house."*

ACTS 16:15

Lydia's day may have begun like any other Sabbath as she made her way outside of Philippi to meet with other women to pray. As women and Gentiles, this group was not allowed to do much, but their gatherings by the river to pray to the God of the Old Testament must have been a significant break from their pagan surroundings. On this day, she met Paul, Silas, Timothy, and Luke, and through them she met Jesus Christ. She had been seeking God and on that day she found him.

Lydia's response to the gospel was personal, profound and practical. She opened her life to Jesus and then led her entire household in committing themselves to him. Also, she insisted on having the missionaries make her house their base of operations.

We do not know what God has planned for each of our days. There is profound guidance in the old saying, "Wherever you are, be all there." To the extent that Lydia understood God, she obeyed. She displayed a willing heart. When God showed her more, she immediately responded. Does your plan and schedule for today reflect your desire to respond to God wherever you may be? ❧

**PRAYER**

*Meet me, Lord, today...*

**READ**

Lydia's story is told in Acts 16:11–40.

## THE MAN BORN BLIND
### *A REASON FOR REJOICING*

*"One thing I do know. I was blind but now I see!"*      John 9:25

Was the man born blind listening when the disciples asked Jesus, "Who sinned, this man or his parents, that he was born blind?" (John 9:2). Did the man understand Jesus' answer? Was there something in that voice that gave him hope? What did he think when he heard Jesus spit? How did it feel to have mud rubbed on his eyes? Did he hesitate for even a moment at Jesus' prescription? Who helped him stumble his way to the Pool of Siloam? The Bible reduces it all to a sentence: "The man went and washed, and came home seeing" (John 9:7).

The miracle of this man's new sight caused the Pharisees to throw a fit about Jesus. "He can't do that. He broke the Sabbath. He must be a sinner. This guy is crazy!"

The Pharisees had their reasons for complaining, and today we have our own. Many of us complain at every injustice, every ache, every pain—even after it's over—as if God owes us better. Or we think life isn't fair: why *them* and not *me*?

But the man born blind held no grudges. He just rejoiced. Why can't we all do that?      ❖

**PRAYER**

*Lord, I rejoice in you . . .*

**READ**

The blind man's story is told in John 9.

## MANASSEH
### CHANGING THE HARDEST HEART

*When [Manasseh] prayed to him, the LORD was moved by his entreaty and listened to his plea; so he brought him back to Jerusalem and to his kingdom.*     2 CHRONICLES 33:13

Despite being the son of godly King Hezekiah, Manasseh lived a most ungodly life. He was a confirmed idolater, and as king, he introduced to Judah sorcery, witchcraft and the consulting of mediums. He put carved images of other gods in the temple of the Lord. He built an altar to Molek, sacrificed his own son there, and encouraged others to sacrifice to the pagan idols. According to tradition, it was King Manasseh who ordered that the prophet Isaiah be sawn in two!

After repeated warnings, God judged the evil king. He raised up the Assyrians, who took Manasseh into captivity in Babylon. There a surprising thing happened. Manasseh cried out humbly to God for help! Apparently his pleas were sincere, for God restored him. Upon returning to Jerusalem, Manasseh began purging every vestige of idolatry from the land and developed a regular habit of offering sacrifices to the one true God.

The story of Manasseh's transformation should encourage us. God's grace is greater than any sin we commit. His forgiveness reaches to the lowest depths. He can change even the hardest heart.                                                    ♣

**PRAYER**

*Lord, change me . . .*

**READ**

King Manasseh's story is found in 2 Kings 20:21—21:18 and 2 Chronicles 32:33—33:20. He is also mentioned in Jeremiah 15:4.

## MANOAH
### *AWESTRUCK BY GOD'S GOODNESS*

*As the flame blazed up from the altar toward heaven, the angel of the LORD ascended in the flame. Seeing this, Manoah and his wife fell with their faces to the ground.*

JUDGES 13:20

Dark and painful episodes marked the Old Testament time of the judges. The people occupied the land of Israel, but they had not conquered it completely. Instead of trusting the God who had been so faithful to them, the Israelites traveled in a confused circle of sin, judgment, repentance and rescue. God sent judges to clean up the mess: women like Deborah and men like Gideon. And the birth of Samson, one of the most famous judges, was announced to his parents.

Like many fathers, Manoah was nervous about the prospects of fatherhood. Anxious to do what was right, Manoah asked God to send the messenger with further counsel. The angel repeated instructions he had already given Manoah's wife.

Apparently Manoah thought it might be a good idea to stay in touch with this mysterious being. He offered the angel a meal and tried to learn his name. The angel insisted instead that an offering to the Lord would be more appropriate, and then the angel ascended in the flame of their offering fire. Manoah and his wife realized they had received a divine messenger. Hearing from God scared Manoah even more than having a child!

Manoah's experience teaches us that God's help may come in many forms, but we should never forget its true source. Nor should we forget to be grateful!     ❖

PRAYER

*Lord, teach me your ways . . .*

READ

Manoah and his wife are introduced in Judges 13.

## MARTHA
### *CAUGHT UP IN THE URGENT*

*[Martha] came to him and asked, "Lord, don't you care that my sister has left me to do the work by myself? Tell her to help me!"*                    Luke 10:40

Martha was a bit of a perfectionist. You know the type. They may agonize over details and bustle about trying to make sure everything is just so. They are fanatical about order. They compulsively plan and prepare. They don't like letting things slip through the cracks. People like Martha can find it hard to relax—even on vacation. Their sense of worth is often tied to how much they accomplish (and how well they do it).

When Jesus came to visit, Martha's stress levels shot through the roof. She wanted everything to be flawless. But her priorities were clearly out of whack. The Lord of the universe was in her living room, and she was back in the kitchen frantically concerned about rolling out a good meal!

Jesus gently reminded Martha of this important truth: It is more important to spend time with God than to do things for him. God wants us more than he wants our busy activity.

Perhaps you suffer from "Martha syndrome." You may get so caught up in your service that you forget to spend time with the Savior. Make it your goal this week to take at least a few minutes each day to just sit quietly in the presence of God. As you let God speak to you from his Word, you will see more clearly the things in life that matter most.                                                                  ❖

**PRAYER**

*Jesus, I lay my "to-do" list at your feet . . .*

**READ**

Details about the life of Martha can be found in Luke 10:38–42 and John 11:17–45.

## MARY MAGDALENE
### *OVERFLOWING GRATITUDE*

*Some women who had been cured of evil spirits and diseases: Mary (called Magdalene) from whom seven demons had come out.*      LUKE 8:2

Many churches teach new Christians to share their spiritual story by using this simple formula: (1) describe your life before you put your faith in Christ; (2) describe how you met Jesus; and (3) describe the changes in your life since trusting him.

Given those guidelines, here's how we could reconstruct Mary Magdalene's testimony: Before she met Christ, Mary was possessed by seven evil spirits and, given the descriptions of demonic activity in the New Testament, we can only assume hers was a life of misery and madness.

At some point early in his ministry—we don't know precisely when or where—Jesus encountered Mary and freed her from the demons that had tormented her for so long. She was forever changed.

After this life-altering event, Mary Magdalene became a devoted follower of Jesus. She supported his ministry financially. She stayed with him at his crucifixion (when all the male disciples except John had run away). She was there at the tomb on the morning of his resurrection.

We find no trace of "I guess I ought to serve Jesus" or "I probably should give some money to the Lord" in the life of Mary. Instead we see the overflowing gratitude of one who grasped the blessings of her salvation. If your Christian life has become a dull routine of obligations, ask God to help you recapture the joy of your salvation.        ♣

**PRAYER**

*Thank you, Lord . . .*

**READ**

More about Mary Magdalene can be found in Matthew 27–28; Mark 15–16; Luke 8 and John 19–20.

## MARY, MOTHER OF JESUS
### *A FAITHFUL RESPONSE*

*"I am the Lord's servant," Mary answered. "May your word to me be fulfilled."*

LUKE 1:38

The gist of Gabriel's announcement was this: Mary, even though you're a virgin, you're going to have a baby.

How does a young-bride-to-be explain that fact to her fiancé, to parents and soon-to-be in-laws, to friends and neighbors? No matter what Mary said, she had to know that people would talk. Her pregnancy was scandalous. The religious community would condemn. The story would spread like wildfire. Gossips would have a field day.

How unfair! Both Joseph and Mary were devoted followers of God. They knew and God knew that they had been morally pure. But the world that loves to whisper didn't know and probably didn't care. How ironic! To God, Mary was chosen; to the world, Mary was cheap. She might have protested. Instead, she humbly submitted to the plan and purpose of God.

Mary's response to the surprising will of God is a great example for us. When we are confronted by situations that seem crazy or unfair, do we balk and complain? Or do we say, "God, I trust that you are in control, that you are good, and that you know what is best. If this is your plan for my life, then I accept it willingly"? Ask God today to help you develop confidence in his faithfulness in every situation. ❖

**PRAYER**

*Lord, I am your servant...*

**READ**

Mary is mentioned throughout all four Gospels. She is also found in Acts 1:14.

## MARY, MOTHER OF JESUS
### REFLECTING ON GOD'S KINDNESS

*Mary treasured up all these things and pondered them in her heart.*     LUKE 2:19

Mary and Joseph had endured a whirlwind week: the arduous trip from Nazareth to Bethlehem for the census of Caesar Augustus; no vacancy for rooms anywhere; the birth of Jesus in a dirty stable; and then the visitation by the shepherds, wild-eyed with excitement, who told of seeing an angelic army in the heavens and jabbered nonstop about the baby, calling him "Messiah" and "Lord." Mary, the Scriptures say, soaked it all in. In her mind, she gathered these images and experiences so that she could later recall them and contemplate their profound implications.

Luke's portrait of Mary is that of a pensive woman. Unlike many who are busy and distracted, Mary valued moments of quietness so that she could meditate on the works of God. It is probably this quality—this desire to fully appreciate God's character and actions—that makes the difference between ordinary and extraordinary Christians.

The command of Psalm 46:10 is this: "Be still, and know that I am God." Unfortunately, many modern-day believers have a superficial knowledge of God because they are never still long enough to hear his still, small voice. What about you? How long has it been since you spent time quietly reflecting on God's workings in your life?                                                                            ❖

### PRAYER

*Father God, I am amazed that you . . .*

### READ

Mary is mentioned throughout all four Gospels. She is also found in Acts 1:14.

# day246

## MARY, SISTER OF LAZARUS
### *LAVISH GIFTS*

*Mary took about a pint of pure nard, an expensive perfume; she poured it on Jesus ̣ ̣t and wiped his feet with her hair.*                                                JOHN 12:3

During the final week of his life, Jesus attended a dinner given in his honor. Right in the middle of the meal, Mary, the sister of Lazarus and Martha, broke open a bottle of nard and poured it over Jesus' head and feet. Nard was rare, costly and reserved only for the most special occasions (like the ritual anointing of kings). This small vial of perfume, the Gospel writers tell us, was worth more money than the average laborer could make in a year!

As the aroma filled the air, several partygoers began grumbling. "What a waste!" they cried. "This money could have been put to better use!" Jesus shocked the naysayers when he praised Mary's extravagant behavior and commended the love that prompted it.

Most of us can learn a lot from Mary's example. Our Lord, because of who he is and what he has done, deserves our best. He is worthy of our most lavish gifts. We cannot thank him, love him, serve him or honor him too much.

Give God your best efforts and your most precious hours today. Use whatever you can for his glory. Such devotion not only pleases God but also tells the world how great he is.                                                                                   ❖

**PRAYER**

*Lord Jesus, I offer you . . .*

**READ**

Mary's story is found in Matthew 26:6–13; Mark 14:3–9; Luke 10:38–42 and John 11:17–45; 12:1–11.

## MATTHEW
### *SEEING JESUS AS HE REALLY IS*

*While Jesus was having dinner at Matthew's house, many tax collectors and sinners came and ate with him and his disciples.*      MATTHEW 9:10

Christians are capable of cooking up some elaborate evangelism programs. God can (and does) use such methods to draw people to himself. But perhaps we've overlooked a more natural strategy for reaching out to the spiritually needy—creating nonthreatening situations in which our non-Christians friends and neighbors can see what Christ is really like.

That's what Matthew the tax collector did. After he decided to follow Jesus, he threw a party. He invited all his tax collector buddies and made sure Jesus and his disciples showed up. Instead of bringing his friends into a religious setting where they would be unwelcome, Matthew brought the Good News into their world. Though these tax collectors and "sinners" were considered outcasts by the religion of the Pharisees, they were attracted to and intrigued by Jesus!

Before you worry about reaching total strangers with the gospel, think about your non-Christian friends, neighbors and colleagues at work. God has put these individuals in your life (and you in theirs) for a reason. Take some time to think about how you can best cultivate those relationships.      ❧

**PRAYER**

*Lord, please grant me the courage to bring others to you . . .*

**READ**

Besides appearing throughout the Gospels, Matthew is also mentioned in Acts 1:13.

## MATTHEW
### *ATTENTION TO DETAIL*

*These are the names of the twelve apostles ... Matthew the tax collector.*
MATTHEW 10:2−3

When Matthew listed the names of the twelve apostles in his Gospel, he also mentioned his former occupation—tax collector. This meant that Matthew had formerly gathered revenues from his own Jewish countrymen and turned them over to the hated Roman government. Since a standard practice of tax collectors was to overcharge people and pocket the excess, we can safely assume that Matthew was rich—and despised. Branded a traitor and treated like a leper, Matthew was an unlikely disciple.

Then Jesus came along. Jesus not only changed Matthew's life but he also chose Matthew to be one of his most trusted followers. It may seem odd for God to use a man with a shady past to advance his kingdom, but consider the situation. Matthew obviously had a knack for keeping records. In his career as a tax collector, he had to be a keen observer, careful and detail-oriented. What better individual to write an accurate history of the life of Christ?

The story of Matthew is an encouraging one. It reminds us that God is in control of the affairs of our lives. He has given each one of us an individual personality, special abilities and unique experiences.

What about you? Have you surrendered your life—your past, present and future to God? ❖

### PRAYER

*Lord, use me ...*

### READ

Besides appearing throughout the Gospels, Matthew is also mentioned in Acts 1:13.

# day249

## MATTHIAS
### *LABORING OUT OF THE PUBLIC EYE*

*They cast lots, and the lot fell to Matthias; so he was added to the eleven apostles.*

ACTS 1:26

After Judas killed himself and before the coming of the Holy Spirit at Pentecost, the followers of Jesus huddled in Jerusalem. Gathered in an upper room, they waited and prayed. At some point during these 50 days, Peter addressed the group. He reviewed the sad defection of Judas and asked the disciples to choose a replacement. Peter cited both the job qualifications and description. The individual had to have been present during the entire course of Jesus' public ministry; they would also be responsible to help proclaim and oversee the apostles' teaching about Jesus for the church.

Two names were proposed—Barsabbas and Matthias. God revealed through the casting of lots that Matthias was the man for the job. Matthias is not mentioned again in the New Testament. Various legends and traditions say that he either preached the gospel in Judea and was stoned by the Jews, or that he was martyred in Ethiopia or Colchis.

From this scant description of Matthias we can glean these truths: (1) He had been a long-term, faithful follower of Christ. (2) Being chosen to serve does not guarantee a position of prominence. (3) Whoever we are and whatever we accomplish is all due to the grace of God.

Are you being faithful today in following Christ? Are you willing to serve in obscurity, doing things that others may never know about? Do you feel resentful when others get more attention or more praise? Remember the life of Matthias, chosen by God to serve out of the public eye.                                                    ❖

**PRAYER**

*Lord, I humbly offer to release my will to your service ...*

**READ**

The sketchy story of Matthias is found in Acts 1:12–26.

## MELCHIZEDEK
### KING OF RIGHTEOUSNESS

*Melchizedek king of Salem ... was priest of God Most High, and he blessed Abram.*
GENESIS 14:18–19

Lot and his family had been taken prisoner in a war between several kings who lived in the regions surrounding Sodom. Abram (later known as Abraham) with the help of 318 men, had rescued his imperiled nephew. In the aftermath of this victory, we are introduced to the mysterious character named Melchizedek. Coming out to congratulate Abram, this king-priest offered physical nourishment and spiritual encouragement. Then he disappeared, never to be heard from again. What are we to make of this unusual Bible personality?

The name Melchizedek means "king of righteousness" or "king of peace." He was a priest, not of a local deity (as was common among the Canaanite peoples) but of the one true God. Melchizedek blessed the Lord and also Abram.

Many scholars have speculated about the identity of Melchizedek. Some regard him as a king who was a "type" of Christ, meaning aspects of his life prefigure or illustrate some later truth from the earthly life of Jesus. He is sometimes understood to be representative of a remnant of true religion that had survived from the earliest days of human life. Other commentators argue that Melchizedek was actually a pre-incarnate appearance of Christ. The most important thing about Melchizedek, however, is not so much *who* he was, but *what* he did. He sought to know and worship the one true God. Furthermore, he honored the followers of the Lord.                                                                ✤

**PRAYER**

*Father, I worship you ...*

**READ**

The few details we have about the life of Melchizedek are found in Genesis 14:17–20; Psalm 110:4 and Hebrews 5–7.

## MEPHIBOSHETH
### *MARVELING AT GRACE*

*Mephibosheth bowed down and said, "What is your servant, that you should notice a dead dog like me?"*      2 SAMUEL 9:8

Mephibosheth was the son of David's best friend Jonathan. At the age of five, Mephibosheth had been crippled in an accident — this tragedy right on the heels of the death of his father and grandfather Saul.

Because of a covenant he had made with Jonathan, David located Mephibosheth and treated him with extreme generosity and kindness. David restored Mephibosheth's family property to him and invited him to be a regular guest at his table.

As you read the story of Mephibosheth, you may be struck by his grateful attitude. He never quite seemed to understand the reason for David's graciousness. Yet he never took the king's generosity for granted. He just enjoyed and marveled at the goodness that was constantly poured out on him.

Is this your response as you consider all that God has done for you? Stop what you are doing and take a few minutes to review the blessings that God has lavished on you. Let his grace bowl you over. Then express your gratitude through prayer, song and a life that is devoted to him.      ❖

**PRAYER**

*O God of heaven, I praise your name . . .*

**READ**

The story of Mephibosheth is told in 2 Samuel 4; 9; 16; 19 and 21.

## MEPHIBOSHETH
### A RELIABLE MASTER

*Mephibosheth said to the king, "Let him take everything, now that my lord the king has returned home safely."*                    2 SAMUEL 19:30

David faced an unusual test of his mercy and wisdom after he was forced by Absalom, his own son, to flee Jerusalem. Mephibosheth stayed behind. Mephibosheth's servant Ziba betrayed his master by reporting to David that Mephibosheth hoped to gain the throne himself as a result of Absalom's revolt against the king. Circumstances seemed to verify Ziba's account, but David allowed Mephibosheth to defend himself. He claimed to have been left behind by Ziba.

After Ziba's accusation, David had turned all of Mephibosheth's lands over to Ziba. Following Mephibosheth's plausible defense, David ordered the two to divide the estate. But the crippled son of Jonathan quietly gave up his claim to any property. He considered his life and the lands to have been David's unexpected gifts to him, and he did not take them for granted. He was simply grateful to see David back on the throne and his own relationship with the king renewed.

There may well be times in which we identify with Mephibosheth: alone, hurt, betrayed, unworthy. But God will keep his word to us. We can trust him. Mephibosheth had a dependable king; we have an absolutely reliable and sovereign one. How do you recognize God's rule in your life?                    ❖

PRAYER

*Lord, reign in me . . .*

READ

The story of Mephibosheth is told in 2 Samuel 4; 9; 16; 19 and 21.

## METHUSELAH
### *LIVING LIFE TO THE FULLEST*

*Altogether, Methuselah lived a total of 969 years, and then he died.*   GENESIS 5:27

If you asked most people whether or not living a long life is a desirable goal, they would probably say yes. If you asked them why, they might tell you that they could travel to exotic places, experience the wonders of future technology, read book after book and live life to the fullest. But how many have truly pondered what living life to its fullest means?

Methuselah's sole claim to Biblical fame is his amazing lifespan—an incredible 969 years. But we know little else about him. He is never mentioned in Scripture as a man of faith. We don't know if he even had a relationship with God, as did his father Enoch. His long life certainly would have given him countless opportunities to draw close to God, but he may have ignored those chances just the same.

The length of our lives is not as important as who we live them for. A short life given in service to Christ brings more joy to God than a long life lived in selfishness and empty pursuits. Thank God today for the precious gift of life he's given you and resolve with his help to dedicate it to obeying him and serving others. ❖

**PRAYER**

*For the gift of life, I offer you my thanks, Lord . . .*

**READ**

Methuselah is mentioned in Genesis 5:21–27 and in the genealogies of 1 Chronicles 1:3 and Luke 3:37.

## MICAH
### *STRONG FAITH FOR TOUGH TIMES*

*As for me, I am filled with power, with the Spirit of the LORD, and with justice and might, to declare to Jacob his transgression, to Israel his sin.*      Micah 3:8

Micah was a prophet during the reigns of Jotham, Ahaz and Hezekiah. A contemporary of Isaiah, Micah faced the daunting task of preaching to a people who were drifting further and further from God. Because his culture was so corrupt, Micah needed special insight to fulfill his mission. What qualities stand out from his life?

*He was filled with the Spirit* (see Micah 3:8). This gave Micah the power and boldness to speak truth—even unpopular, convicting truth—to the most powerful leaders of the nation.

*He knew the difference between empty religion and true devotion* (see Micah 6:8). Micah recognized that actions mean little; God wants to change his people from the inside out. This fundamental truth permeated his life's message.

*He trusted God in hard times* (see Micah 7:7). Despite the sad decline of his culture, Micah prayed and waited for God to work. This hope sustained him even in his darkest hours.

*He understood the character of God* (see Micah 7:18–20). Micah knew that God, in his justice, must punish sin; however, he also knew that the Creator longs for a relationship with his beloved creatures.

We need to develop these same qualities if we are to live for Christ in a corrupt culture. Pick out the one or two attributes from the life of Micah that are most meaningful to you and share them with a fellow believer today.     ❖

**PRAYER**

*Fill me with your Spirit, Lord ...*

**READ**

What little bit we know about Micah is found in the prophetic book that bears his name.

## MICAIAH
### *FACING UNPLEASANT FACTS*

*Micaiah said, "As surely as the LORD lives, I can tell him only what the LORD tells me."*
1 KINGS 22:14

Have you ever met someone who seems to prefer to avoid the truth? It is almost as though these people have consented to a conspiracy of deception. The rules of this arrangement are simple: "Forget the truth—tell me what I want to hear! And in return, I'll lie to you as well."

We see this perverted principle in the story of Micaiah, a prophet of Samaria. Unimpressed by King Ahab's yes-men, King Jehoshaphat of Judah wanted to hear from a true prophet of God before committing his armies to battle. When Micaiah's name came up, the evil Ahab made this classic statement, "I hate him because he never prophesies anything good about me" (1 Kings 22:8).

Nevertheless, Micaiah was summoned. When first questioned by Ahab, Micaiah indulged in a bit of sarcasm and then announced his determination to speak the truth. When Micaiah announced a depressing (yet true) picture of the immediate future, he received a sharp slap in the face and was sentenced to prison by the angry Ahab.

What about you? Are you like the prophet Micaiah, always adhering to the truth, even when it's unpleasant? Have you ever twisted the truth out of a desire to be liked or to avoid confrontation? We do not honor God when we lie. In fact, when we distort the truth we act as children of the father of lies, Satan himself! While others may find our fiction flattering, God finds it offensive. He is a God of truth. ❖

**PRAYER**

*Lord, root out any dishonesty in me ...*

**READ**

The story of Micaiah is found in 1 Kings 22:1–28 and 2 Chronicles 18:1–27.

## MICHAL
### *CONSUMED BY JEALOUSY*

*As the ark of the LORD was entering the City of David, Michal daughter of Saul watched from a window. And when she saw King David leaping and dancing before the LORD, she despised him in her heart.*                                        2 SAMUEL 6:16

Michal had seen firsthand how jealousy had turned her father, King Saul, into a bitter, suspicious, paranoid man. His inordinate fear of potential rivals ruined most of his relationships, robbed him of joy in life and eventually rendered him insane.

Michal unwisely followed in her father's footsteps. Her immature love for David was possessive and selfish. She craved his affection and became envious of the devotion and passion he reserved for God. Eventually she voiced her feelings, chiding David for his extravagant display of emotion in worshiping before the returning ark of God. David explained to his jealous wife that he didn't care how silly his celebrating looked—his highest allegiance was to God. To one right with God, such a statement would be cause for joy. But to a soul consumed by jealousy and bitterness, David's words cut like a knife.

How do you rank on the jealousy scale? Do you demand that your spouse or best friends or children put you first? How do you feel when those you love most love God most? As believers we should be careful that we don't look to other people to fill the deep needs of our souls. That approach to relationships can lead to jealousy and disappointment. Let God meet the deep emotional needs of your heart. Embrace his will for your life. Then you will be able to rejoice when those closest to you put him first.                                        ✣

**PRAYER**

*Heavenly Father, not my will, but yours be done ...*

**READ**

The story of Michal is found in 1 Samuel 14:49; 18:20–30; 19:11–18; 25:44 and 2 Samuel 3:13–16. She is also mentioned in 1 Chronicles 15:29.

## MIRIAM
### *WANTING BACK IN THE SPOTLIGHT*

*Miriam and Aaron began to talk against Moses because of his Cushite wife, for he had married a Cushite.*                    NUMBERS 12:1

Miriam stood by as Moses was raised in the luxury of Pharaoh's palace. She watched as God used her kid brother to lead the Israelites out of Egyptian bondage. She remained at the foot of Mount Sinai with the people of Israel, while Moses got to go up on the mountain and enjoy a face-to-face discussion with God. Moses was often in the spotlight, while Miriam's role was less visible and more subordinate.

Miriam, of course, did serve God. She had watched out for her baby brother while he was a helpless infant (see Exodus 2:1–10). After the Israelites crossed the Red Sea, she led the Israelite women in dancing and instrumental accompaniment while she sang the song of victory. But she also let herself be overcome by feelings of resentment toward her little brother, Moses. She and Aaron attacked Moses' choice of a wife. Then they got around to their real complaint. "Has the LORD spoken only through Moses?" they asked. "Hasn't he also spoken through us?" (Numbers 12:2). It was a clear case of rebellion against Moses's leadership, and God quickly ended it by inflicting Miriam with leprosy.

We serve in the place where God has put us, with the abilities he has given us. Instead of worrying about others, our efforts would be better spent looking after our own faithfulness. When we thank God regularly for the gifts he has given, we find that we don't have the time to be envious of others—not even our siblings! ❖

PRAYER

*Lord, forgive me for the times when I have envied . . .*

READ

The story of Miriam is found in Exodus 2; 15 and Numbers 12; 20.

## MORDECAI
### *WORKING FOR THE GOOD OF HIS PEOPLE*

*Mordecai ... worked for the good of his people and spoke up for the welfare of all the Jews.*
ESTHER 10:3

The book of Esther reads like a great suspense novel. A foolish king. A beautiful young woman and her devoted relative. A power-hungry government official. A devious decree that causes thousands of lives to hang in the balance. An impossible plan. A plot twist. The demise of the bad guy. But don't get so caught up in the thrills and chills that you miss the lesson from the life of Mordecai.

Simply put, Mordecai was a positive influence everywhere he went. Even though Esther was only his cousin, Mordecai essentially adopted her and reared her as his own daughter. Later he was instrumental in helping his God-fearing Jewish "daughter" to become the new queen of Persia. He also helped thwart an assassination plot he overheard being planned at the city gate. Then when the wicked Haman was exposed and executed, Mordecai became prime minister in his place. The Scriptures record that Mordecai spent the balance of his life working for the good of his people.

Do you approach life with the same determination Mordecai displayed? Is it your goal to make a positive difference in the lives of the people God has placed in your life? Do you use your position, your power, your possessions and your "pull" to help others? You can make a huge difference today with a simple phone call, note of encouragement or letter of protest. How will you exert your influence today? ❖

**PRAYER**

*Lord, show me where I can make a difference today ...*

**READ**

The story of Mordecai can be read in the book of Esther.

# day259

## MOSES
### *RUNNING AHEAD OF GOD*

*Moses thought that his own people would realize that God was using him to rescue them, but they did not.*                                                ACTS 7:25

Even though Moses had been reared as an Egyptian in Pharaoh's household, he was unable to forget his heritage or turn a deaf ear to the plight of his enslaved countrymen. Somewhere along the line he sensed that he might be the one chosen by God to bring freedom to his people.

So when he witnessed a slave being mistreated, Moses came to the man's aid, killing the tormentor. The next day Moses tried to mediate a dispute between two Hebrews. From a human perspective Moses' actions were gutsy, risky and praiseworthy. From a divine perspective Moses' behavior was all wrong. God had a better way and a better time planned for bringing about the deliverance of his people. Moses still had some lessons to learn — lessons in humility and patience — before he would be ready for the great task of leading the children of Israel out of Egyptian bondage and into the promised land.

It is admirable to want to serve God. It is not, however, admirable to run ahead of God. We must wait until he clearly leads. Before you begin any new venture for God, seek the counsel of older, wiser Christians. Spend a great deal of time in prayer. Make sure your motives are pure and that God has obviously directed you. Then serve with all your heart!                                                ❖

### PRAYER

*Show me your paths, Lord ...*

### READ

The story of Moses is recorded in the books of Exodus, Leviticus, Numbers and Deuteronomy. Moses is also mentioned in Matthew 17:3–4 and Hebrews 11:23–29.

## MOSES
### *LIVING WITH AN ETERNAL PERSPECTIVE*

*He chose to be mistreated along with the people of God rather than to enjoy the fleeting pleasures of sin.*                                        HEBREWS 11:25

There came a time in Moses' life when he had to make a big decision: would he enjoy the good life as an adopted Egyptian, or would he cast his lot with his poor, enslaved Jewish brethren? The contrast between the two options could not have been starker—a life of sensual ease versus a life of hardship, uncertainty and pain.

Moses chose what most people would consider the less attractive option. He somehow caught sight of the vast reality of God. He looked beyond the temporary glitter of Egypt to the eternal truths that had been revealed to his Jewish ancestors.

In slightly different ways we each must make the same decision: Will we remember the life-changing truth that one day we each must stand before God and give an accounting for the way we have spent our time on earth? Will we side with a corrupt culture that makes choices on the basis of feelings, hormones, majority rule and statistics or will we embrace the eternal truths of Scripture and let them be our only rule for life and practice?

Look back over the last month of your life. Evaluate your attitudes, motives and actions. Have you been living with heaven in view? If not, ask God to help you develop an eternal perspective.                                        ❖

### PRAYER

*Lord, look over my days and my ways . . .*

### READ

The story of Moses is recorded in the books of Exodus, Leviticus, Numbers and Deuteronomy. Moses is also mentioned in Matthew 17:3–4 and Hebrews 11:23–29.

## MOSES
### *NO EXCUSE WILL SUFFICE*

*Moses said to the LORD, "Pardon your servant, Lord. I have never been eloquent, neither in the past nor since you have spoken to your servant. I am slow of speech and tongue."*
                                                                    EXODUS 4:10

The more Moses listened to the voice emanating from the burning bush, the more fearful he became. God was in the bush, telling Moses he had been selected to lead the Israelites out of Egyptian bondage.

"There must be some mistake," Moses thought. He had a long list of excuses for why he couldn't be God's man. He was 80 years old, having spent the previous 40 years tending sheep in the desert. He wasn't theologically trained and therefore wouldn't be able to adequately explain why God had sent him. To top things off, Moses was not an eloquent speaker.

One by one, God shot down Moses's excuses. Then he provided the surprised and scared Moses with the ultimate audiovisual lesson. Before his very eyes, God transformed an ordinary shepherd's staff into an extraordinary tool for deliverance. It was as if God was saying, "Moses, I can do the same thing with your life. But first you have to quit making excuses. And then you have to trust me."

God says essentially the same thing to you. He has an exciting purpose for your life. He has amazing plans he wants you to accomplish. But if you focus on your weaknesses and cling to your doubt, you'll never know anything beyond mediocrity. Let him work in you and through you, and the world may very well marvel at the results.                                                                    ✦

### PRAYER

*Work in me, Lord . . .*

### READ

The story of Moses is recorded in the books of Exodus, Leviticus, Numbers and Deuteronomy. Moses is also mentioned in Matthew 17:3–4 and Hebrews 11:23–29.

## MOSES
### A MOMENT TO REGRET

*The LORD said to Moses and Aaron, "Because you did not trust in me enough to honor me as holy in the sight of the Israelites, you will not bring this community into the land I give them."*
NUMBERS 20:12

The nation of Israel has had many grim moments in its history, but for sheer misery few eras can match the period of wandering recorded in the book of Numbers.

Instead of enjoying a new life of blessing in the promised land, the 12 tribes had been sentenced to stumble around in the desert because of their unwillingness to trust God. If the people of Israel weren't complaining about the lack of water, they were moaning about the food. In between they were grumbling against the leadership of Moses and attending about 20 funerals per day!

We can hardly blame Moses for getting fed up with this bunch of bellyachers. But he let anger and pride consume him. Instead of speaking to the rock from which God intended to provide water for his people, Moses struck it. And he whacked it not once, but twice!

God's judgment was immediate. For failing to obey, Moses and Aaron would not be permitted to enter Canaan. Should we regard this decree as harsh and extreme? No. We should see it as a sobering reminder of the holiness of God and the ugliness of sin.

There is no question that Moses was forgiven for his impulsive act. However, that one incident changed the course of his life. As Moses found out, it is possible to do something in an instant you will regret for the rest of your life.      ♣

### PRAYER

*Forgive me, Lord, for ...*

### READ

The story of Moses is recorded in the books of Exodus, Leviticus, Numbers and Deuteronomy. Moses is also mentioned in Matthew 17:3–4 and Hebrews 11:23–29.

## NAAMAN
### *THE BARRIER OF PRIDE*

*"There were many in Israel with leprosy in the time of Elisha the prophet, yet not one of them was cleansed—only Naaman the Syrian."*                    LUKE 4:27

Naaman was a brilliant leader with a severe handicap. His successes on the battlefield did not erase the shame and isolation of his leprosy. The depth of his desperation can be measured by his readiness to accept the suggestion of a young Israelite slave (see the devotion at December 24) who served his wife. Naaman went to the king for permission to visit Elisha the prophet.

Perhaps he thought Elisha would be impressed to have such a celebrity for a patient. Elisha curtly dismissed the general with his prescription: "Go, wash yourself seven times in the Jordan, and your flesh will be restored and you will be cleansed" (2 Kings 5:10). Clearly, Naaman resented the treatment he received. Fortunately, he had some clearheaded and devoted servants. After following Elisha's directions, Naaman's wounds and scars were healed.

As he did with Naaman, God will meet our needs, but not on our terms. God is not impressed with our pride or intimidated by our demands. When we approach God with the intention of earning his acceptance and love we are pursuing a hopeless plan. God's prescription is painfully simple: repentance, followed by wholehearted acceptance of his free gift of salvation. Is your pride standing in the way of a restored relationship with God? If so, confess your sin and get right with him today.                                                                                    ❖

**PRAYER**

*Lord, I confess that I . . .*

**READ**

Naaman's encounter with God is recorded in 2 Kings 5:1–27.

## NABAL
### *SINGLE-MINDED SELFISHNESS*

*Nabal answered David's servants, "Who is this David?... Why should I take my bread and water, and the meat I have slaughtered for my shearers, and give it to men coming from who knows where?"*                                                   1 SAMUEL 25:10–11

Nabal lived during David's rise to power. In fact, Nabal benefited from David because his men offered a region of security for Nabal's herds to graze. But when David sent men to Nabal's house with a courteous request for supplies, they were rudely turned away. Nabal's own men were shocked at Nabal's harshness. They hurried to warn Nabal's wife Abigail, who clearly possessed the level head in the family.

Meanwhile, David set out with 400 angry men to confront Nabal. Abigail met him, armed with gifts and apologies. David accepted Abigail's excuse and spared Nabal's household. While his wife was pleading for his life, Nabal was home hosting a party. When he was sober the next morning, Abigail explained his close call with David. Nabal's shock and fear were such that he died within days.

A person who refuses to be distracted by the needs of others can focus all their energies on their own goals. But if we allow anyone or anything to become the center of our lives other than the God who made us and loves us, our world will be as fragile and fearful as Nabal's. The lesson is clear: everything we have comes from God. How can we be selfish when God has given to us so freely?          ❧

### PRAYER

*Take what stands between you and me, Lord...*

### READ

Nabal's folly is recorded in 1 Samuel 25:1–39.

## NABOTH
### *BRINGING INJUSTICE TO LIGHT*

*Naboth replied, "The LORD forbid that I should give you the inheritance of my ancestors."*

1 KINGS 21:3

Evil King Ahab owned many vineyards, but he wanted one that was located next to the palace in Jezreel. So when Naboth, the owner of the vineyard, respectfully refused his offer to trade for an even better property, Ahab became angry and sullen.

King Ahab's wife, Jezebel, then schemed to take by force what Naboth would not willingly give up. The vineyard owner was publicly accused of having cursed God and the king—a crime punishable by immediate stoning. Jezebel arranged a ruthless betrayal, coercing Naboth's neighbors to speak against him, and the sentence was carried out. Naboth appeared to be just another simple person ground under the wheels of greed and power.

Yet God made public the injustice. Elijah was dispatched to meet Ahab just as the king arrived to gloat over his new acquisition. Through the prophet, God leveled a crushing indictment on Ahab and his family for their murder of Naboth and their theft of his property.

Naboth's tragedy can comfort us when we are treated unjustly and convict us when we mistreat others. Even when injustice appears victorious, we know a God who guarantees ultimate justice. We dare not treat lightly God's holiness.    ❖

**PRAYER**

*Holy God, you see all forms of injustice . . .*

**READ**

Naboth's story is found in 1 Kings 21.

## NADAB AND ABIHU
### *DOING WHAT WE KNOW*

*Aaron's sons Nadab and Abihu took their censers, put fire in them and added incense; and they offered unauthorized fire before the LORD, contrary to his command.*

LEVITICUS 10:1

Nadab and Abihu had quite a spiritual pedigree. They were the sons of the high priest Aaron and therefore in line to take his place. They were nephews of Moses, the great leader who spoke face-to-face with God. They were part of God's covenant people Israel, recipients of a miraculous redemption from Egypt. They had seen God's power and holiness demonstrated in the plagues on Egypt and in the giving of the Law on Mount Sinai. They had been consecrated for ministry in a solemn ceremony in front of the tabernacle and all the people. They had a firsthand knowledge of the Jewish sacrificial system and the ugliness of sin that necessitated it.

And despite such exposure to the truth about God, Nadab and Abihu disobeyed him in a very public way. Their sin cost them their lives. It is believed that the sons of Aaron brought unconsecrated coals from elsewhere to burn on the altar of God. Whatever the particulars, their behavior was brazen enough to warrant immediate, deadly discipline from God.

The deaths of Nadab and Abihu remind us of this truth. It is not enough to *know* what to do; we must also do what we *know*! Are you ignoring certain commands of God? Is your obedience selective? If so, what changes do you need to make to avoid negative consequences?                                             ♣

**PRAYER**

*Lord, cleanse me of anything unworthy . . .*

**READ**

The story of Nadab and Abihu is found in Leviticus 8–10.

# day267

## NAHUM
### *MESSENGER OF DOOM*

*The LORD is good, a refuge in times of trouble.*                    NAHUM 1:7

Nahum was a prophet from Elkosh (a village of Galilee) who was sent by God to prophesy to the people of Nineveh. This was not the first time the Assyrians—a people with an unrivaled reputation for evil and cruelty—were confronted with God's truth. A century earlier, Yahweh had sent another prophet (the reluctant Jonah) to Nineveh with a message of judgment. When Jonah delivered his prophecy, the Assyrians renounced their wicked ways and turned to God. The Lord mercifully spared this idolatrous nation.

Over time, however, the Assyrians reverted to their godless lifestyle, and so God summoned Nahum. This time, there would be no mercy. The nation known for its pride and power would be completely destroyed.

Ironically, Nahum's name means "consolation" or "full of comfort." But the prophet's message to the Assyrians was anything but soothing! They could only listen to his stern words and wait for the wrath of God to fall. However, for the godly remnant in Israel, Nahum's sermon was full of comforting reminders of God's power and justice.

The next time you see injustice or evil, remember that God will one day right every wrong and punish those who defy him. Remember too that those who cling to him will forever be kept safe.                                              ❖

### PRAYER

*Lord, you are a just God ...*

### READ

All that we know about Nahum can be found in the book that bears his name.

## NATHAN
### CONFRONTING SIN

*The LORD sent Nathan to David. When he came to him, he said, "There were two men in a certain town, one rich and the other poor."*　　　　2 SAMUEL 12:1

It's appropriate that the name Nathan means "God has given," for in Nathan, God had given King David a very great gift. Nathan was a prophet, an advisor and a chronicler of Israel's history. He was the man who brought David the good news of God's blessing. He was also the man who brought David the bad news of God's discipline for committing adultery with Bathsheba and sending Uriah to his death in battle.

The twelfth chapter of 2 Samuel recounts how Nathan confronted David about his sin. Nathan told David a moving parable about a wicked rich man (with plenty of sheep) who took the only lamb of a poor man to serve to his guest. When Nathan finished his story, David was livid. "As surely as the LORD lives, the man who did this must die!" he snapped (2 Samuel 12:5).

Nathan had the courage to look the king in the eye and say, "You are the man!" (2 Samuel 12:7). Then Nathan outlined for David the consequences of his sin. God used this bold prophet to bring David to his senses and to repentance.

Do you have someone in your life who holds you accountable, who asks you the tough questions, who loves you enough to tell you the truth—even when it hurts? If you do, thank God for the wonderful gift he has given you. If not, ask the Lord to bring such a person into your life. We all need a Nathan!　　　❖

### PRAYER

*Lord, thank you for the Nathans in my life . . .*

### READ

The story of Nathan is found in 2 Samuel 7:1–17; 12:1–12; 1 Kings 1:1–27. He is also mentioned in 1 Chronicles 17:1–15 and 2 Chronicles 9:29; 29:25–26.

## NATHANAEL
### *WORKING IN UNEXPECTED WAYS*

*When Jesus saw Nathanael approaching, he said of him, "Here truly is an Israelite in whom there is no deceit."*　　　　　　　　JOHN 1:47

Nathanael was a devout Jew from Cana in Galilee. Like so many other Hebrews who knew and obeyed the Scriptures, Nathanael was waiting for the arrival of the Messiah who would bring salvation to Israel. One day, Nathanael was approached by Philip, a friend from Bethsaida. Philip was clearly excited as he told Nathanael that the Messiah was in their midst. He was a Nazarene named Jesus.

Nathanael was surprised and skeptical. Nazareth was the site of a Roman army garrison. How could the Messiah come from such a tainted town? Why not Jerusalem or some other Jewish city with better credentials?

Philip convinced Nathanael to come see for himself. Fortunately Nathanael went and met Jesus for himself. A short conversation with Jesus was all Nathanael needed to become convinced that Jesus was, in fact, the long-awaited Messiah. Nathanael became one of Jesus' most devoted disciples.

Honest people don't form hard and fast opinions based merely on their presuppositions, their prejudices or their past experiences. They know that things are not always what they appear to be and that God often works in unexpected ways. Be hungry for the truth but willing to let God change your ideas about what he is like.　　　　　　　　❖

**PRAYER**

*Lord, I hunger for your truth . . .*

**READ**

The story of Nathanael (also known as Bartholomew) is found in Matthew 10:3; Mark 3:18; Luke 6:14; John 1:43–51; 21:2 and Acts 1:13.

## NEBUCHADNEZZAR
### HUMBLED BY GOD

*Now I, Nebuchadnezzar, praise and exalt and glorify the King of heaven, because every-thing he does is right and all his ways are just. And those who walk in pride he is able to humble.*
DANIEL 4:37

Nebuchadnezzar was the Babylonian king who subdued and expelled the people of Judah. As the ruler of a vast empire and the most powerful army on earth, Nebuchadnezzar was an arrogant man.

Nebuchadnezzar's pride reached its zenith when he fancied himself to be a god. He had a 90-foot-tall statue of himself created and ordered all of Babylon to worship it. When the Hebrew exiles Shadrach, Meshach and Abednego refused to bow to this idol, Nebuchadnezzar had them thrown into a fiery furnace. Even when they came out of the blaze unharmed, Nebuchadnezzar realized only dimly that his greatness was a sham. Still, his pride remained.

Since he wouldn't humble himself, God humbled him. He caused Nebuchad-nezzar to go insane for seven years, during which time he literally grazed like a cow on the palace lawn! At the end of that time, Nebuchadnezzar looked up to God and acknowledged his kingship over the universe. Then, and only then, was his health restored. ❖

PRAYER

*Father God, my pride is . . .*

READ

The story of Nebuchadnezzar is found in 2 Kings 24–25; 2 Chronicles 36; Jeremiah 21–52 and Daniel 1–4.

## NEHEMIAH
### *A LIFE OF PRAYER*

*"LORD, the God of heaven ... let your ear be attentive and your eyes open to hear the prayer your servant is praying before you day and night for your servants."*
NEHEMIAH 1:5−6

Around 445 BC Nehemiah led a group of Jewish exiles from Persia back to Jerusalem for the purpose of rebuilding the city's broken-down walls. Despite strong opposition from without and extreme discouragement from within, the Jews accomplished this monumental task in only 52 days! What was Nehemiah's secret? How was he able to get such a disorganized, disillusioned bunch of people to accomplish such a remarkable feat?

Some cite his leadership and organizational skills. Others laud his ability to motivate. Perhaps the real key is found in Nehemiah's prayer life. The story of Nehemiah reveals a man who was intimate with God and highly dependent on his Creator.

When discouraged, he prayed (see Nehemiah 1:4−11). Even during his busy schedule, he carried on a running conversation with God (see Nehemiah 2:4). When under attack, he prayed (see Nehemiah 4:4−5,9). When weak and power-less, he prayed (see Nehemiah 6:9). When happy, he spent time thanking and praising God (see Nehemiah 12:27−47).

What about you? Is prayer a regular part of your daily life? Do you rely on God during hard times? Do you regularly thank and praise him for his blessings? Spend some time today thinking about Nehemiah and let his example motivate you to a life of power ... through prayer.     ✤

### PRAYER

*Motivate me, Lord, to do your will ...*

### READ

Nehemiah's story is found in the book that bears his name.

# day272

## NEHEMIAH
### *TAKING THE WISEST COURSE OF ACTION*

*We prayed to our God and posted a guard day and night to meet this threat.*

NEHEMIAH 4:9

From the start, Nehemiah's effort to rebuild the walls of Jerusalem was met with opposition. His enemies were Sanballat the Horonite, Tobiah the Ammonite and Geshem the Arab. These men tried everything to slow down or stop the work. They mocked Nehemiah and his builders. They accused the Jews of treason. They even threatened physical violence.

Nehemiah met each verbal attack with patience and prayer. When he heard rumors of an impending military attack, Nehemiah not only prayed but also prepared for action by posting guards and arming his workers. Often workers finished their tasks with one hand while holding a weapon in the other.

Nehemiah's response is a great example for us. Prayer should be the first thing we turn to when facing trouble; however, it should not be the only thing. We must also use common sense. We must do whatever we can do, trusting God all the while. God calls us both to prayer and work!

Are you facing a difficult situation in your life? By all means, pray! Then study the situation and consider what steps you can take to alleviate the problem. The Christian life is a joint venture. God works in us, but at the same time, we are expected to work out our own salvation (see Philippians 2:12–13). Grasping this truth is crucial if we are to find success in walking with God. ❖

**PRAYER**

*Lord, I need you today ...*

**READ**

Nehemiah's story is found in the book that bears his name.

## NICODEMUS
### *GROWING IN BOLDNESS*

*[Joseph of Arimathea] was accompanied by Nicodemus, the man who earlier had visited Jesus at night. Nicodemus brought a mixture of myrrh and aloes, about seventy-five pounds.*      JOHN 19:39

When we first meet Nicodemus in the Gospel of John, he is coming to Jesus under cover of night (see John 3). He is a Pharisee, one of Israel's prominent and respected religious leaders. He knows the Scriptures inside and out yet seems to be searching for something more. Nicodemus discovers that eternal life comes only when people put their faith in Jesus.

Exactly when Nicodemus became a follower of Christ, we do not know. But we can see definite signs of growth in his life. In John 7, as the Pharisees are having a heated discussion about what to do with Jesus, Nicodemus sticks his neck out: "Does our law condemn a man without first hearing him to find out what he has been doing?" (John 7:51). It's not exactly a ringing endorsement, but Nicodemus catches heat for even attempting to be fair.

Later, when the religious leaders have succeeded in getting rid of Jesus, Nicodemus and Joseph of Arimathea boldly ask for Jesus' body so they can give it a proper burial. We have no record of either man suffering any consequences for their actions, but very likely Nicodemus was scorned and perhaps even shunned by the other Pharisees.

Nicodemus's spiritual pilgrimage was marked by slow but steady growth. He gradually became bolder in revealing his love and devotion for Christ. Can others see similar growth in your life? What one action can you take today to identify publicly with Christ?      ✤

**PRAYER**

*Lord, help me to lead others, using my experiences with you ...*

**READ**

The Bible mentions Nicodemus in John 3:1–21; 7:50–51; 19:39.

# day274

## NOAH
### *A RIGHTEOUS REPUTATION*

*Noah was a righteous man, blameless among the people of his time, and he walked faithfully with God.*                                     GENESIS 6:9

Against the backdrop of a culture darkened by evil, Noah lived a sparkling, exemplary life. He was the only follower of God left in his generation, so God chose his family to survive the great flood. In a sense, Noah became the second father of the human race.

In completing the giant boat that would bring him and his family through God's watery judgment, Noah demonstrated patience, faithfulness and obedience. (The task took more than 100 years!) In 2 Peter 2:5, Noah is called "a preacher of righteousness," implying that he warned his friends and neighbors of the wrath to come.

Noah wasn't perfect. He demonstrated a lack of self-control late in life when he got drunk on wine from his own vineyard. But when Scripture summarizes his life, Noah is called—in sharp contrast to the others of his day—a righteous man who walked with God.

If someone today were to sum up your life in a sentence or two, what would they say about you? What is your reputation? If you are serious about wanting to live in a way that pleases God, you might wish to ask these questions of a trusted friend. The answers might surprise you or even hurt your feelings, but they will give you some clear ideas on what areas of your life need to change.          ❖

**PRAYER**

*Lord, help me live for you ...*

**READ**

The story of Noah is found in Genesis 5:29—10:32.

278

## NOAH
### *DOING WHAT GOD COMMANDS*

*Noah did everything just as God commanded him.*      GENESIS 6:22

Put yourself in Noah's sandals for a few moments. You see the world around you becoming more and more evil. God then announces to you his intention to judge the earth. You think, "It's about time something was done about all this ungodliness!" Then God tells you to begin building an ark—a ship large enough to house your entire family and representatives of each species of the animal kingdom!

As you reflect on these strange commands, you ponder the implications: "Build a giant boat miles from any water ... what will the neighbors think? How do I explain this to my family? What do I, a man of the soil, know about boat building?"

Noah's response to his newfound responsibilities was immediate. Genesis, not once but twice, says that Noah "did everything just as God commanded him." No rationalizing, no complaining, no stalling. Noah went right to work.

God has promised that we will never again need to practice the craft of ark building. However, he still asks us to do certain things that our society will scorn. What does your lifestyle say to your non-Christian neighbors and friends? Are you living an obedient, Noah-like life? Pick one area of your life today in which you have been resisting God and take some steps toward obedience. You'll definitely have a better conscience, and your actions just might provide you an opportunity to share your faith with others.      ✤

PRAYER

*Lord, I offer you my resistance to ...*

READ

The story of Noah is found in Genesis 5:29—10:32.

## NYMPHA
### AN OASIS OF MINISTRY

*Give my greetings to the brothers and sisters at Laodicea, and to Nympha and the church in her house.* COLOSSIANS 4:15

Nympha was a Christian whose home was used as a gathering place for believers. While this person's gender remains a mystery at least in some translations (some use the masculine form—Nymphas), her generosity does not. Nympha allowed a congregation of believers to meet and worship in her home. This was a normal practice, since separate church buildings did not become common until the third century.

Hosting a church was a major commitment. It meant clear, public identification with a new, questionable and radical religious faith. It meant accommodating large numbers of people weekly, with many men and women coming and going all the time. It meant little privacy and no doubt a lot of extra cooking and cleaning.

Nympha deserves to be commended for such a hospitable attitude. It just goes to show that we all don't have to be preachers or teachers or evangelists to play a significant role in the building of Christ's church.

Do you make your home available for the work of the kingdom? Is it a place where other believers can come and find warmth, love and encouragement? ❖

**PRAYER**

*Lord, my home is yours to use ...*

**READ**

The one reference we have to the life of Nympha is found in Colossians 4:15.

## OBADIAH
### *THE PROUD BROUGHT LOW*

*"Though you soar like the eagle and make your nest among the stars, from there I will bring you down," declares the LORD.*     OBADIAH 4

Obadiah was a Judean prophet and a contemporary of Ezekiel and Jeremiah. He was sent to the nation of Edom with a message of judgment. Specifically, the Edomites were doomed to destruction for mistreating Judah, their northern neighbor.

What made Edom's actions even more reprehensible was the fact that the Edomites and Israelites weren't just neighbors, they were related! The fathers of Edom and Judah were Esau and Jacob, respectively. The countries should have been on friendly terms. Edom, however, constantly took advantage of Judah. Beginning with their journey to the promised land, the Edomites constantly opposed the Israelites (see Numbers 20:14–21). When other nations attacked Judah, Edom either sided with the enemy or ignored pleas for help. Worse still, the Edomites would at times loot the Judean countryside.

God sent Obadiah to deliver a short but stern message concerning Edom's pride and the promise that God would destroy this nation and lift up Israel. In 185 BC it happened. Judas Maccabeus overran the Edomites. By the first century AD, Edom had vanished from the map!

God humbles proud and wicked people. Hostility to him — or his people — will never go unpunished! If you are being mistreated because of your faith, remember that God sees your situation and will have the last word.     ♣

**PRAYER**

*Lord, I come before you as humbly as I know how . . .*

**READ**

Obadiah's words are found in the Old Testament book that bears his name.

## ONESIMUS
### *RUNNING BACK TO THE PROBLEM*

*[Tychicus] is coming with Onesimus, our faithful and dear brother, who is one of you. They will tell you everything that is happening here.* COLOSSIANS 4:9

God must have a special love for runaways. From Adam and Eve's attempt to elude God, to Jacob's escape from his brother, to Moses' retreat to the desert, to that inner circle of disciples who fled when Jesus was captured, the Bible abounds with runaways. Perhaps the best-known runaway, however, is a slave named Onesimus.

We are not told why Onesimus ran away from Philemon's house. Eventually, he and Paul were united in Rome. There Onesimus became a follower of Jesus. His spiritual depth prompted Paul to call him a "faithful and dear brother" (Colossians 4:9).

Eventually, Paul and Onesimus decided it was time for Onesimus to return home. Paul wrote to his friend Philemon (see the devotion at October 16), assuring him that Onesimus would now serve him wholeheartedly. At the same time Paul challenged Philemon to look upon his former servant as a brother.

As God transforms your life, you may also need to confront your past. Do you need to forgive others or be forgiven? Do you need to resolve a painful situation? Don't keep running—rely on your relationship with Christ to face what you used to run away from. ✤

### PRAYER

*Here I am, God, just as I am ...*

### READ

Onesimus is mentioned in Colossians 4:9 and is the subject of Paul's letter to Philemon.

## ONESIPHORUS
### *A SOURCE OF REFRESHMENT*

*May the Lord show mercy to the household of Onesiphorus, because he often refreshed me and was not ashamed of my chains.*                                          2 TIMOTHY 1:16

In 2 Timothy, the last letter that Paul ever wrote, he listed some of the people who meant the most to him. One obscure name that sticks out is the name Onesiphorus. Who was he? Listen to the way Paul described his friend:

1. Onesiphorus was a constant source of refreshment. Perhaps he brought food. Certainly he provided emotional and spiritual support—so much so that Paul was strengthened by his visits.

2. Onesiphorus was not ashamed of Paul's troubles. Paul had many fair-weather friends—people who had turned on him or deserted him. Onesiphorus, on the other hand, was a foul-weather friend. Rather than avoiding Paul, he sought him out. He took the risk of visiting Paul in prison (a gutsy move that might have caused trouble for Onesiphorus and his family!).

3. Onesiphorus helped Paul minister in Ephesus. Obviously he was a kind, generous and willing servant.

What kind of friend are you? Do you refresh others? When you leave a friend's company, is your companion likely to be replenished or drained? In four verses, Onesiphorus shows us what a true friend is like. Ask God to give you a friend like that—and to make you one!                                                                    ❖

### PRAYER

*Lord, grant me the gift of friendship ...*

### READ

The story of Onesiphorus is found in 2 Timothy 1:16–18; 4:19.

## ONESIPHORUS
### *GOING OUT OF THE WAY TO HELP*

*Greet Priscilla and Aquila and the household of Onesiphorus.*     2 TIMOTHY 4:19

Paul and Timothy shared a strong and effective relationship. Thousands heard the gospel because of their collaboration. As they traveled, preached and planted local churches, Paul and Timothy also built a team of diligent fellow workers. Among them was Onesiphorus, who had been a vital link between the imprisoned Paul and the outside world.

Onesiphorus arrived in Rome at a crucial time for Paul. Many of his associates had left him. But Onesiphorus tracked him down, overlooked his humiliating circumstances and offered him real encouragement, ministering in the same way he had in Ephesus. Paul expressed to Timothy his profound gratitude for this servant. Apparently Onesiphorus kept alert to any opportunity where he might be of service.

Discipleship involves our willingness to respond when people ask for help. Onesiphorus carried this attitude further. He went out of his way to help. His willingness to help those in need is a quality all Christians should desire.

Do your opportunities for service come because others ask or because you actively seek them out? Ask God to make you more aware of the needs of those around you each day.     ❖

**PRAYER**

*Lord, open my eyes to those who are hurting ...*

**READ**

Onesiphorus was recognized by Paul in 2 Timothy 1:16 – 18; 4:19.

## PARMENAS
### *A MATTER OF SERVING*

*"Brothers and sisters, choose seven men from among you who are known to be full of the Spirit and wisdom. We will turn this responsibility over to them."*       Acts 6:3

As the early church grew, so did its administrative work. One particular ministry that was requiring more and more oversight from the apostles was the care of widows in the church. The twelve disciples realized that in devoting too much of their energy to the physical needs of their church, they were neglecting its spiritual needs. So they conferred and decided to delegate the feed-the-widows ministry to seven other qualified men.

The men selected had to meet exacting standards. It was stipulated that they be godly, wise men. Among those chosen was Parmenas, a man we know very little about. His name means "constant" or "abiding," and various church traditions say that he was either martyred at Philippi during the reign of Trajan or that he become the bishop of Soli.

Assume for a moment that your church leaders decided to pick seven individuals to serve on a special ministry team. If the requirements for service were the same as those mentioned above—being wise and filled with the Spirit—do you think you would be nominated? Would it even come up in the discussion?

Leadership in the church is not a matter of getting a position and then serving; it is about serving, period. If you are letting God work in you and through you, others will eventually notice. Even if they don't, God will. And that's what ultimately matters. ❖

**PRAYER**

*Lord, work in me . . .*

**READ**

Parmenas is mentioned in Acts 6:5.

## PAUL
### *THE SOURCE OF SPIRITUAL FERVOR*

*Never be lacking in zeal, but keep your spiritual fervor, serving the Lord.*

ROMANS 12:11

Paul was full of zeal. He was a passionate man who threw himself into everything he did. Before he met Christ on the road to Damascus, Paul (then known as Saul) zealously persecuted Christians. Then, after his conversion, Paul developed a burning desire to know Christ more intimately (see Ephesians 3). Throughout the book of Acts, we see Paul's intense commitment to take the gospel to the world. In Paul's letters we witness Paul's fervent effort to see believers grow up into "all the fullness of God" (Ephesians 3:19).

What enabled Paul to maintain such spiritual fervor? He had been captured by the love of Christ. Jesus was real to Paul. He was not just a theological idea or a religious concept. Christ saved Paul and gave him a mission. Paul's life was consumed with the love of Jesus.

Remember how you felt the first time you fell in love? Remember how you wanted nothing else but to be with your significant other? Remember how you were willing to do anything—anything at all!—for their sake? That's a good, although imperfect, picture of the kind of passion with which we are to serve Christ. If you have "forsaken the love you had at first" (Revelation 2:4), ask the Lord to help you regain a deep passion for him. ♣

### PRAYER

*Rekindle the fire within me, Lord God...*

### READ

Paul's life story is told in Acts 7:58—28:31. Other details about him are found throughout the New Testament epistles.

# day283

## PAUL
### *THE DIFFERENCE PRAISE MAKES*

*Greet Tryphena and Tryphosa, those women who work hard in the Lord.*

ROMANS 16:12

Few things in life motivate us more than words of sincere praise. To be affirmed publicly is a tremendous reward. To be recognized for one's faithful service—especially by a respected leader—is a richly satisfying payoff.

The apostle Paul understood the importance of a well-timed word of encouragement. In every letter he wrote, he looked for godly attitudes and actions to commend. Here are just a few examples:

- "Greet Apelles, whose fidelity to Christ has stood the test" (Romans 16:10).
- "I was glad when Stephanas, Fortunatus and Achaicus arrived, because they have supplied what was lacking from you. For they refreshed my spirit and yours also. Such men deserve recognition" (1 Corinthians 16:17–18).
- "Tychicus, the dear brother and faithful servant in the Lord" (Ephesians 6:21).
- "Welcome [Epaphroditus] in the Lord with great joy, and honor people like him, because he almost died for the work of Christ. He risked his life to make up for the help you yourselves could not give me" (Philippians 2:29–30).
- "Epaphras ... is always wrestling in prayer for you, that you may stand firm in all the will of God, mature and fully assured" (Colossians 4:12).

Do you notice and applaud the efforts of others? Do you make a big deal out of their praiseworthy accomplishments? Make it your goal today to affirm those you interact with. Then watch what a difference a few words of praise can make! ❖

### PRAYER

*Lord, show me someone who needs affirmation today ...*

### READ

Paul's life story is told in Acts 7:58—28:31. Other details about him are found throughout the New Testament epistles.

## PAUL
### *THE THORN IN THE FLESH*

*Therefore, in order to keep me from becoming conceited, I was given a thorn in my flesh, a messenger of Satan, to torment me.*      2 CORINTHIANS 12:7

Christians throughout the centuries have speculated as to the nature of Paul's "thorn in [the] flesh." Was it—as various commentators suggest—a disease of the eyes, malaria, epilepsy, a stomach disorder like dysentery, or was it something else? We can't say for sure. We do know, however, that it caused him great discomfort. It was painful enough that he repeatedly asked God to take it away.

Yet Paul's prayers went unanswered. In time, Paul was able to recognize the hidden blessing of his debilitating condition. It kept him humble, forced him to depend on God, shaped his character and turned him into a valuable role model for other Christians.

Do you suffer from unpleasant things that you wish God would remove? Perhaps you are struggling with a financial reversal, a lingering illness, a physical handicap, an unwarranted attack on your character, a relational breakdown beyond your control, a parenting dilemma or a job crisis. Know that God understands your suffering. Depend on him to turn your thorn in the flesh into an opportunity to trust him more deeply and to see his power more clearly in your life.      ❖

**PRAYER**

*Lord, I depend on you . . .*

**READ**

Paul's life story is told in Acts 7:58—28:31. Other details about him are found throughout the New Testament epistles.

# day285

## PENINNAH
### *PROTECTING OURSELVES FROM THE HURT*

*Because the LORD had closed Hannah's womb, her rival kept provoking her in order to irritate her.*                                                        I SAMUEL 1:6

Elkanah's household was a cauldron of simmering emotions. Like many of his contemporaries, he had two wives. Hannah, the real love of his life, had no children; Peninnah, his other wife, had many. Hannah was despondent over her infertility, while Peninnah was bitter because Elkanah loved Hannah more. Peninnah taunted Hannah for her inability to conceive. At long last, God heard Hannah's prayers and gave her a son named Samuel, who would grow up to become a great judge and prophet.

Most people can relate to Peninnah's feelings. We've all felt pain or rejection in a relationship dear to us. To protect ourselves from any future hurt, we devise strategies to keep others from causing us pain. Sometimes, like Peninnah, we keep people at a safe distance by lashing out at them. Unfortunately, the result of such behavior is often isolation and loneliness.

Have you been deeply hurt by others in your family? Do you have feelings of jealousy, anger or bitterness toward someone else? Are you tempted to get back at that person? It may sound trite, but know that Christ wants to meet you in your pain, show you his compassion and give you the courage to reach out in love to others — even to those who have hurt you most. Will you let the Lord show you how to forge better relationships in your family?                                    ❖

PRAYER

*Lord, guide me in my family relationships . . .*

READ

Peninnah's story is found in 1 Samuel 1.

## PETER
### *OBEYING WHEN IT DOESN'T MAKE SENSE*

*Simon answered, "Master, we've worked hard all night and haven't caught anything. But because you say so, I will let down the nets."*              LUKE 5:5

Peter (also called Simon), Andrew, James and John—colleagues in a commercial fishing business—were tired and frustrated. They had spent the entire night lowering and raising their nets into the Sea of Galilee with nothing to show for their strenuous labors—not so much as a minnow.

As they cleaned and mended their nets on the shore, a crowd began to gather to hear Jesus, an itinerant evangelist. The fishermen had heard him before and his words intrigued them. As the audience grew and inched closer, Jesus retreated to one of the boats. After concluding his message, Jesus asked Peter to go fishing again! Peter might have thought, "What do you know about fishing, Jesus? You're just a preacher!" or "We're exhausted. Maybe another time." But Peter pushed his reluctance aside and headed out.

The results were astonishing—a greater catch of fish than Peter had ever seen in his life! What did it mean? Peter's head was spinning. But in that moment, he and his friends suddenly realized what they had to do. They left everything there on the beach and followed Jesus.

The same Jesus who suddenly and abruptly brought purpose, hope and help to Peter wants to do the same thing for you. Are you willing to "let down [your] nets," to do something odd or inconvenient to know Jesus better?              ♣

**PRAYER**

*Lord, help me trust, even when what I hear doesn't make sense ...*

**READ**

Peter's life story is found in the Gospels and the book of Acts.

## PETER
### *STANDING AGAINST THE EVIL ONE*

*Jesus answered, "I tell you, Peter, before the rooster crows today, you will deny three times that you know me."*      LUKE 22:34

After the Last Supper, Jesus told Peter that he would deny being one of Jesus' followers. Peter was both shocked and offended: "Lord, I am ready to go with you to prison and to death" (Luke 22:33). No doubt, Peter meant these words. His intentions were honorable. And yet he was weak. Peter was completely unprepared for the trials that lay ahead. The faithful prayers of Christ were Peter's only hope.

Sadly, but not surprisingly, the events turned out just as Jesus said they would. Peter was unable to stand up and speak the truth even to a servant girl. With the words still on his tongue, Peter heard the plaintive cry of a rooster. Looking across the courtyard into the sad but loving eyes of Jesus, Peter ran away and wept bitterly.

This episode from the life of Peter reminds us of several important truths: (1) Satan wants to wreck our lives and our relationship with Jesus (1 Peter 5:8); (2) In our own strength, we cannot stand against his attacks (Ephesians 6:10–18). (3) When we repent, admitting our weakness and failure, we can once again "strengthen [our] brothers" (Luke 22:32).

Ask God to protect you from the temptations of the evil one and trust him for the strength to respond as you should in trying situations. If you have failed, turn to God for cleansing and another chance.      ❖

**PRAYER**

*Lord, I am weak . . .*

**READ**

Peter's life story is found in the Gospels and the book of Acts.

# day288

## PETER
### FEEDING HIS SHEEP

*The third time he said to him, "Simon son of John, do you love me?" Peter was hurt be-*
*cause Jesus asked him the third time ... Jesus said, "Feed my sheep."*   JOHN 21:17

Much has been made of the question Jesus asked Peter three times: "Do you love me?" Pastors and teachers talk about how this question intentionally parallels Peter's three denials of Christ. Others stress the different Greek words translated as "love" in this passage. But we must also recognize the emphasis Jesus placed on ministering to others.

"Feed my sheep," Jesus said each time Peter affirmed his love for Christ. If Peter really loved Jesus, he would care for those who belong to Jesus. Notice that not once did Jesus ask Peter if he loved Jesus' sheep. The bottom-line motivation for ministry was and is love for Jesus and a willingness to act. There is another message here as well. "Even if you have failed," Jesus seems to be saying, "I can still use you in the lives of others."

What about your life? Do you love Jesus? Are you proving your love for him by serving others? Is your motivation in ministry to show love for Christ? Anything less will not endure.

Are past failures haunting you and keeping you from seeking Christ? Look at the lesson of Peter and realize that God can and still wants you to be a fruitful servant for him.                                                                        ❖

**PRAYER**

*Lord, in my barren times, help me to still bear fruit ...*

**READ**

Peter's life story is found in the Gospels and the book of Acts.

## PHILEMON
### *GROWING IN CHRIST*

*Confident of your obedience, I write to you, knowing that you will do even more than I ask.*     PHILEMON 21

Philemon was a wealthy citizen of Colossae. The church in that city gathered in his home. It was to this man that Paul wrote concerning a slave named Onesimus who had run away (see devotion at October 5). Onesimus was now a believer but still a slave. Onesimus may have feared for his life, for a master had the legal right to kill a runaway slave. Paul wanted to assure both his friends that their relationship in Jesus meant that reconciliation and restitution were possible.

Because Paul was an elder and an apostle, he could have used his authority to force Philemon to deal kindly with his runaway slave. Paul appealed instead to Philemon's Christian commitment. He wanted Philemon's heartfelt obedience. To make his case more convincing, Paul gently reminded Philemon of his personal obligation to him. He was confident that Philemon would see Onesimus's return as a reminder of God's mercy in his own life.

Can others count on the consistency of your character? As you have grown in the Christian faith, have others trusted you with greater responsibilities and expectations? Do you forgive others completely? If not, determine today to address the issues that are hindering the growth of spiritual fruit in your life.     ✤

**PRAYER**

*Lord, my life is an open book before you ...*

**READ**

Our knowledge of Philemon comes from Paul's letter to him.

## PHILETUS
### *SINCERELY WRONG*

*Their teaching will spread like gangrene. Among them are Hymenaeus and Philetus.*

2 TIMOTHY 2:17

Philetus may have known many of the believers in Ephesus. He seems to have been well versed in Scripture and able to debate theology and doctrine. He had strong convictions and sincerely argued his beliefs. But being sincere is not enough. It is possible to be sincere and wrong at the same time.

Philetus and his cohort Hymenaeus were upsetting believers with a "new" theology that denied the Scriptural teaching of a bodily resurrection. Paul warns that Philetus and Hymenaeus "say that the resurrection has already taken place, and they destroy the faith of some." (2 Timothy 2:18). The idea was that Christians already experience the resurrection spiritually, but could not hope in a physical resurrection. Such a view struck at the very heart of Christianity, since the faith rests squarely on the evidence of the empty tomb! Because such beliefs and teachings were (and are) so dangerous, Paul sought to warn others to steer clear of Philetus.

Within the Christian faith, there is plenty of room for contrasting viewpoints. For example, godly people interpret the Bible's teaching on the end times differently. But when it comes to the essentials—the reliability and authority of the Scriptures, the deity of Christ and salvation by grace alone, to name just three— there can be no disagreement. Anyone who denies or trifles with the key articles of the faith is headed for trouble.

Creeds and doctrine may seem boring, but they are vital to all Christians. Ask your pastor to recommend a good, comprehensible theology book for laypeople. This will help you to understand why a good grasp of doctrine is important to every Christian's faith.                                                                ♣

**PRAYER**

*Lord, here's what I believe about you ...*

**READ**

Philetus is mentioned in 2 Timothy 2:14–19.

## PHILIP
### *CHANCE ENCOUNTER?*

*The Spirit told Philip, "Go to that chariot and stay near it." Then Philip ran up to the chariot and heard the man reading Isaiah the prophet.*     ACTS 8:29–30

Philip, the deacon and evangelist, saw God work in a powerful way. Driven from Jerusalem because of persecution, Philip had journeyed to Samaria and began preaching about Christ. God confirmed Philip's message with miraculous signs — exorcisms and healings — and the Samaritans began putting their faith in Christ and finding joy.

Suddenly, right in the midst of this intense time of revival, God summoned Philip to the desert. From a human perspective, this might have seemed illogical: Why leave a place where many people were finding God for a place where few people even live? But Philip obeyed.

There on the road from Jerusalem to Gaza, Philip *just happened* to encounter an Ethiopian government official. *Coincidentally* this man was reading a scroll of Isaiah. *By chance* the man invited Philip to his chariot to explain to him the meaning of the Scriptures, after which the man embraced the truth about Jesus. After baptizing the man, "the Spirit of the Lord suddenly took Philip away" (Acts 8:39). The Ethiopian returned home, where, according to tradition, the gospel began to spread throughout Africa.

God still works through chance encounters. The next time you meet a stranger, get delayed in traffic or end up in a place you did not intend to visit, pay careful attention to the Spirit of God. You may be on the verge of a divine appointment with eternal ramifications!    ❖

**PRAYER**

*Please lead me this week, Lord ...*

**READ**

Philip's story is found in Acts 6:1 – 7; 8:5 – 40; 21:8 – 10.

## PHINEHAS
### A NECESSARY ZEAL

*"[Phinehas] and his descendants will have a covenant of a lasting priesthood, because he was zealous for the honor of his God and made atonement for the Israelites."*

NUMBERS 25:13

Phinehas grew up during the 40 years of Jewish wandering in the wilderness. He was born into a priestly family. Aaron was his grandfather and Eleazar was his father. He was convinced that it was time to obey God and enter the promised land. He hoped the lessons from the wilderness had been learned.

How dismayed Phinehas and other godly people must have been when the Israelites left the wastelands and almost immediately plunged into worship of pagan gods and sexual sin. God demanded that the ringleaders be put to death, along with those who indulged in blatant immorality.

As if to aggravate the crisis, an Israelite flouted God's directive by taking a Midianite woman into his tent for sex in the sight of Moses and the nation. Phinehas resolutely carried out God's punishment, killing them both with a spear. God confirmed the justice of his action by stopping a plague that had taken thousands of lives.

Someone with zeal like that of Phinehas takes obedience to God with utmost seriousness. Such a person recognizes that sin is death and that obedience is life. In what areas of your life have you developed zeal for God's causes? How could you bolster your passion for him in other ways? ✤

### PRAYER

*Lord, increase my zeal for you ...*

### READ

Phinehas appears in the following Old Testament passages: Exodus 6:25; Numbers 25:1–13; 31:6; Joshua 22:13–20,30–33; 24:33; Judges 20:26–28 and 1 Chronicles 6:4,50; 9:20.

## PHOEBE
### *A PROVEN DISCIPLE*

*[Phoebe] has been the benefactor of many people, including me.*          ROMANS 16:2

Paul provided us with his most mature summary of the Christian faith when he wrote his letter to the Roman church while in Corinth. It remains one of the most widely studied books of the New Testament. Yet for several weeks the single, handwritten copy of this letter probably traveled under the personal care of a woman who was a courier for Paul. Her name was Phoebe.

Though she was not mentioned anywhere else in the New Testament, Paul warmly praised her to the church in Rome. She was a deacon of the church in the Corinthian suburb of Cenchreae. She was a proven disciple, providing financial support for Paul and other believers. He encouraged the Roman Christians to extend whatever assistance Phoebe might need. Paul was confident Phoebe would find like-minded believers during her visit to Rome.

Paul's introduction of Phoebe reveals his confidence in her character. What traits do people mention when they introduce you? To what degree are you a dependable person? Have you practiced the kind of trustworthiness that makes others desire to introduce you to their friends? Who's counting on you today?  ❖

**PRAYER**

*Lord, make me truly faithful . . .*

**READ**

Phoebe was introduced to us by Paul in Romans 16:1–2.

## PILATE
### *THE PRICE OF INDECISION*

*When Pilate saw that he was getting nowhere, but that instead an uproar was starting, he took water and washed his hands in front of the crowd. "I am innocent of this man's blood," he said. "It is your responsibility!"*                    MATTHEW 27:24

Pilate was in political hot water. As governor of Judea, he was already in disfavor with the emperor (being assigned to govern the Jews was considered a demotion). Now the Jews were stirring up trouble again—some sort of religious matter involving a supposed miracle-worker. Pilate did not want to get involved, but he had no choice.

Pilate's conscience (what was left of it, anyway) told him that this Jesus had done nothing to deserve death. Even his wife was having strange dreams about this man and begged her husband to leave him alone. But the masses were calling for Jesus' hide, making the choice clear: justice or expediency? Pilate decided to pacify his critics. He may not have hammered the nails into Christ's hands and feet, but his cave-in to popular pressure served that very purpose. No matter how many times Pilate washed his hands, he could not wash away his guilt.

When faced with tough situations, we often wrestle with similar temptations: to abstain from voting, to refuse to get involved, to make excuses, to remain silent. We do nothing and then convince ourselves that our passivity absolves us of guilt. But in doing nothing, we are doing something.

Ask God for the courage to do what is right, regardless of the consequences. ✤

### PRAYER

*Heavenly Father, give me courage to ...*

### READ

Pilate's story is found in each of the Gospels. He also is mentioned in Acts 3:13; 4:27; 13:28 and 1 Timothy 6:13.

# day295

## PILATE
### SEARCHING FOR THE TRUTH

*"What is truth?" retorted Pilate.*                                        JOHN 18:38

Standing before Pilate, Jesus probably looked like anything but a king. He was most likely bound and may have been beaten and bloodied. "The reason I was born and came into the world is to testify to the truth. Everyone on the side of truth listens to me," Jesus stated (John 18:37).

Pilate studied this curious teacher from Galilee and uttered his famous question: "What is truth?" We don't know for sure if he was being sarcastic or if his query came from a heart hungry for real answers.

Whatever his motivation or attitude, Pilate didn't wait for an answer. This may tell us something about his perspective. Not only did he not wait for an answer, but neither did he pay enough attention to Jesus. Too bad Pilate didn't ask a few more questions. Perhaps then he might have recognized that the one on trial before him did not just know the truth but was, in fact, the truth (see John 14:6)! Then Pilate might have recognized that the better question would have been, "Who is Truth?"

Is your life fully committed to the truth? Are you seeking to know Christ? Are you listening to him? Are you convinced he is who he claimed to be? Ask God to keep you from falsehood and to help you recognize, embrace and live by the truth.                                                                ❖

### PRAYER

*I am committed to your truth, Lord ...*

### READ

Pilate's story is found in each of the Gospels. He also is mentioned in Acts 3:13; 4:27; 13:28 and 1 Timothy 6:13.

## POTIPHAR
### *RECOGNIZING THE TRUE SOURCE OF OUR BLESSINGS*

*From the time he put him in charge of his household and of all that he owned, the LORD blessed the household of the Egyptian because of Joseph. The blessing of the LORD was on everything Potiphar had, both in the house and in the field.* GENESIS 39:5

Potiphar was the captain of Pharaoh's royal guard. One day he purchased Joseph from some Ishmaelite slave traders and "left everything he had in Joseph's care" (Genesis 39:6). This was the best decision Potiphar ever made. Joseph was not only talented but God was also with him. Joseph was a man of integrity. Because of Joseph, Potiphar began to prosper greatly.

What lesson can we learn from the life of Potiphar? Potiphar was the first, but not the last to benefit from Joseph's insight. Later Pharaoh would put Joseph in a similar position of responsibility, but this time over the entire nation rather than a single household. And like his work for Potiphar, Joseph helped Egypt to flourish, even in the midst of harsh famine.

Had Potiphar and Pharaoh been more observant, they would have seen that Joseph was not merely an administrative whiz, he was also a young man of integrity. Joseph knew that the source of his talents was God. Whatever ways he was able to bless others was only because of the blessings and abilities that God had given to him. Joseph recognized that God is the true source of blessing, no matter where we find them. ❖

### PRAYER

*Lord, make me a person of character . . .*

### READ

The story of Potiphar is found in Genesis 37:36; 39.

## POTIPHAR'S WIFE
### *SATISFYING SELFISH DESIRES*

*And though she spoke to Joseph day after day, he refused to go to bed with her or even be with her.*      GENESIS 39:10

Potiphar's wife knew what she wanted and knew his name too! He was Joseph, the handsome young Hebrew servant her Egyptian husband had purchased from a caravan of Ishmaelite slave traders. She tried to seduce Joseph day after day after day. He repeatedly spurned her tempting offers, until finally she literally grabbed him. Joseph did what any godly person would do—he fled like a scared rabbit. But Potiphar's wife—feeling scorned and embarrassed—cried, "Rape!"

Never mind that Joseph had done nothing wrong. Never mind that he had done everything right. All Potiphar's wife recognized was that she didn't get what she wanted. Denied the thrill of chasing and capturing her prey, of feeling a few moments of illicit pleasure, Potiphar's wife became angry and hurt. Consumed with selfish feelings, she wanted Joseph to pay. He would spend several years in jail because of her lie.

The behavior displayed by Potiphar's wife not only dishonors God but also leads to sin and disappointment. Instead of using others to meet your needs and wants, ask God to help you encourage and serve them. Joseph is a perfect example of one who lived out such a commitment. His life wasn't easy, but he was blessed at every turn.      ❖

**PRAYER**

*Lord, I lay my agenda at your cross . . .*

**READ**

The story of Potiphar's wife is found in Genesis 39.

## QUARTUS
### *THE VALUE OF ENCOURAGEMENT*

*Erastus, who is the city's director of public works, and our brother Quartus send you their greetings.* ROMANS 16:23

Quartus would be an ideal character for a historical novel. We know a handful of details about his life (there's the history), and we can imagine the rest (there's the novel).

Here's what we know for sure: (1) Quartus's name means "a fourth." (2) He was a Christian. (3) He lived in Corinth (where Paul wrote the book of Romans). We also have ancient church traditions that say that Quartus was one of the 72 disciples mentioned in Luke 10:1,17 and later became the bishop of Berytus (Beirut).

Beyond this smattering of information, we know nothing about Quartus, except this: When he heard that Paul was writing a letter to the Christians in Rome, Quartus said, "Tell them I said hello."

What did this greeting mean to the Roman Christians? Here are a few possible reactions:

- "Our brother Quartus? You mean Quartus has become a Christian? That's fantastic! Praise God!"
- "Quartus sends his greetings? That means he's still alive. It means God healed him! How wonderful!"
- "So old Quartus is still serving the Lord. Great!"

We'll never know for sure how Quartus's greeting affected these Christians. But in all likelihood, his message was encouraging. Think of someone in your own life today who could use encouragement. Drop that person a note or give them a call. A few words can make a big impact. ❧

**PRAYER**

*Lord, use me to encourage someone today . . .*

**READ**

Quartus is mentioned in Romans 16:23.

## RACHEL
### *BEAUTY SECRETS*

*Leah had weak eyes, but Rachel had a lovely figure and was beautiful.*    GENESIS 29:17

Rachel was, in today's language, a head turner. She quickly caught the eye of Jacob, who found her so desirable that he agreed to work seven years for her father, Laban, in order to marry her.

And yet, if we look beyond Rachel's figure and face to her underlying character, we see some very unattractive qualities. First, she is portrayed as jealous and demanding. When she learned she was unable to bear children, her complaining and accusing sent Jacob into a rage.

Second, she is pictured as desperate and conniving. Rather than trusting God to provide her with children in his timing, she tried to "help God out" by sending her servant girls to bed with Jacob. She stole religious artifacts from her father and then lied about her involvement in the theft. All in all, the Scriptures do not paint a pretty picture of this pretty woman!

The lessons learned from Rachel's life are especially relevant to people who live in a culture obsessed by youth and glamour. Keep in mind that outer loveliness quickly fades. Inner beauty is far more critical to God, and he makes that character available to anyone who is filled with the Spirit of God. The longer and closer we walk with God the more attractive we become.    ❖

**PRAYER**

*Mold my character, Lord . . .*

**READ**

The complete story of Rachel is found in Genesis 29:1 — 35:20.

# day300

## RACHEL
### *THE TRAP OF ENVY*

*When Rachel saw that she was not bearing Jacob any children, she became jealous of her sister. So she said to Jacob, "Give me children, or I'll die!"*  GENESIS 30:1

Why did godly men like Abraham, Jacob, King David and Solomon have multiple wives? It may have been that God allowed this practice to assure the continuation of family lines or to provide for women who might have otherwise remained single in a warlike culture where men were frequently killed in battle. Whatever the reason, polygamy created great tension and bitterness in families.

Rachel and Leah, Jacob's wives, are a good case in point. Jacob favored Rachel, who was barren, while Leah, whom he loved less, was extremely fertile. Rachel became jealous of her sister and fearful of losing her husband's love. This, in turn, caused her to become obsessed with motherhood. "Give me children, or I'll die!" she panicked.

When we struggle (with infertility, financial reversal, family troubles or any setback), we are prone to notice others who are doing well. We often become envious. In time we may turn bitter, falling into the trap of thinking that life itself hinges on our problems being fixed or solved.

While it won't necessarily make our circumstances go away, a better response in the midst of difficulty is to look to God. His presence is far more valuable than anything else. Remember the words of the psalmist: "Whom have I in heaven but you? And earth has nothing I desire besides you" (Psalm 73:25). ❖

### PRAYER

*Lord, whom have I in heaven but you ...*

### READ

The complete story of Rachel is found in Genesis 29:1—35:20.

## RAHAB
### *GOD CAN CHANGE ANYONE*

*By faith the prostitute Rahab, because she welcomed the spies, was not killed with those who were disobedient.*          HEBREWS 11:31

From a human perspective, it's difficult to understand why the Bible should speak favorably of Rahab. She was a prostitute and a Canaanite, a member of a heathen people who indulged in idolatry. She was a liar who deceived her own leaders and helped "the enemy" escape. She was a traitor who helped orchestrate the overthrow of Jericho.

Yet look at Rahab from a divine perspective. She had developed a healthy fear of the God of Israel. She was willing to become a part of God's covenant nation. The writer of Hebrews explicitly tells us that Rahab's welcoming of the Jewish spies was a visible demonstration of faith.

In her post-Jericho life, Rahab married Salmon and ultimately became the ancestress of King David! Imagine that—a Canaanite prostitute becoming part of the ancestral line of Israel's kings, including the nation's greatest King, Jesus. Rahab epitomizes the kind of transformation that is possible when a person puts their faith in God.

The issue for us today is not what we are doing for God, but what he is willing to do for us. Our efforts at right living cannot make us right with God. Have you recognized God as the true king of your life? Have you trusted in his power alone to save you and change you? If God can transform a heathen prostitute, he can certainly change you!     ❖

**PRAYER**

*Lord, you are my King . . .*

**READ**

The complete story of Rahab is found in Joshua 2; 6.

## REBEKAH
### *FAMILY FAVORITES*

*Isaac, who had a taste for wild game, loved Esau, but Rebekah loved Jacob.*

GENESIS 25:28

The sons of Isaac and Rebekah were very different people. Esau is described as a skillful hunter, a man of the open country. He comes across as rough and tough, impulsive and spiteful. Jacob, on the other hand, is depicted as a quiet man, staying among the tents. We see him preparing stews and cooking up schemes to take advantage of others.

Perhaps these differences explain (at least in part) the parental favoritism that developed in Isaac's household. Isaac had a special bond with Esau, while Rebekah clearly favored Jacob. These preferences caused strife between Isaac and Rebekah and may have encouraged the poor choices and flawed personalities of each brother. Jacob became a trickster while Esau became a rebel.

It is normal to feel drawn to certain individuals. We cannot help those feelings, nor should we feel guilty for having them. What is wrong is to accentuate the special feelings we may have for one family member. When we play favorites and give special treatment or extra attention to a mother, father, child or sibling, we invite friction into our homes and cause emotional hurt in those we slight.

If family relations have turned sour, ask for an honest assessment from a Christian friend about how you are relating to each person in your family. Then ask God to supply the love that will heal the hurt.                    ❧

**PRAYER**

*Lord, love others through me ...*

**READ**

The story of Rebekah is found in Genesis 24–27. She is also mentioned in Romans 9:10.

## REBEKAH
### *DECEPTION'S PRICE TAG*

*[Jacob's] mother said to him, "My son, let the curse fall on me. Just do what I say; go and get them for me."*         GENESIS 27:13

Rebekah remembered what the Lord had said: "the older [son] will serve the younger" (Genesis 25:23). As the firstborn son, Esau was entitled to special privileges. He would be the recipient of Isaac's special blessings.

Perhaps that is how Rebekah reasoned. Maybe that is how her scheme of deception came about. Rebekah eventually got Isaac to bless Jacob instead. She planned and orchestrated the whole scam and it worked. Isaac gave the blessing he had reserved for his eldest son to his younger son.

Rebekah got what she wanted, but she also got some additional unpleasant surprises: a rift between Esau and Jacob that took years to heal; a bitter Esau who threatened violence and was a source of frustration to his parents; and a demanding daughter-in-law named Rachel

Rebekah was exposed to a truth we still wrestle with today: Sin doesn't pay; it only costs! An immoral or unethical action may offer a desirable payoff, but down the road we will begin receiving notices of payment due!

Pragmatism is not the same as obedience. Don't do things on the basis of what will work. Make your decisions based on what is right in the eyes of God.    ✤

**PRAYER**

*I depend on you, God, to help me make wise decisions . . .*

**READ**

The story of Rebekah is found in Genesis 24–27. She is also mentioned in Romans 9:10.

## REHOBOAM
### *NOT-SO-WONDERFUL COUNSELORS*

*Rehoboam rejected the advice the elders gave him and consulted the young men who had grown up with him and were serving him.*                     I KINGS 12:8

Perhaps you have heard the old saying, "Never follow a legend." That was Rehoboam's dilemma. His father was Solomon—the king renowned for his wisdom, wealth and fame. Solomon's immense talent and vision made Israel the envy of the civilized world.

One small problem: To finance this state-of-the-art kingdom, Solomon increased taxes to the point that the average citizen was near financial ruin. The people of Israel hoped that his son Rehoboam would relieve their misery.

Rehoboam listened to his subjects and then sought the advice of the elders who had served his father Solomon. Their counsel was to lower the tax rate. Rehoboam dismissed them and asked his friends for their advice. They replied, "Tell them, 'My little finger is thicker than my father's waist. My father laid on you a heavy yoke; I will make it even heavier. My father scourged you with whips; I will scourge you with scorpions" (1 Kings 12:10–11). Unfortunately, Rehoboam followed the advice of his foolish friends. The result was an immediate split in the kingdom.

Clearly, it is not enough to merely seek out advice. We must consider the source of the counsel and weigh their guidance against the truth of the Scriptures.

Do you have an older, wiser Christian in your life who provides you with godly counsel? If so, talk with that person this week. If not, ask God to put a wise counselor (or two) in your life soon.                                           ✤

PRAYER

*Lord, I need wise counsel today ...*

READ

The story of Rehoboam is told in 1 Kings 11:43 — 14:31 and 2 Chronicles 9:31 — 13:7.

## REUBEN
### *TURBULENT CHARACTER*

*"Turbulent as the waters, you will no longer excel."*       GENESIS 49:4

Jacob summed up the life of Reuben best when he said that he was "turbulent as the waters." He meant that Reuben could be dependable one moment and treacherous the next. Consider the highlights (and lowlights) of his life:

Reuben displayed a lack of courage when his brothers concocted a plot to kill Joseph. Reuben gave tacit approval while scheming to save Joseph, a hope that was dashed when the brothers sold him to some Ishmaelites. Perhaps Reuben only went along with the plot in order to save Joseph. But Reuben also demonstrated a severe lack of self-control when he slept with his father's concubine Bilhah.

Later in life Reuben offered to take responsibility for the safety of young Benjamin on a proposed trip to Egypt. "You may put both of my sons to death if I do not bring him back to you," Reuben told Jacob (Genesis 42:37). Some see this offer as courageous. Others view it as still another example of Reuben's weakness, since he was willing to sacrifice his sons but not himself.

All in all, Reuben's life was ambiguous. He is not the most evil character we find in Scripture. Yet nothing about him is really worthy of emulation.

Spend some time today evaluating your character. Would those who know you well describe you as "turbulent as the waters"? Or are you reliable and committed to your beliefs? Do you stand out as someone who compromises or someone with deep-seated convictions?     ❖

**PRAYER**

*Lord, make my convictions yours ...*

**READ**

The story of Reuben is told in Genesis 29–50.

## RHODA
### *EXPECTING THE UNEXPECTED*

*When [Rhoda] recognized Peter's voice, she was so overjoyed she ran back without opening it and exclaimed, "Peter is at the door!"*                                    ACTS 12:14

We know nothing about Rhoda except for her delightful response to an unexpected event. She was among a group of Christians who gathered to pray for the release of Peter. Herod had already put to death the apostle James and promised to do the same to Peter. Christians felt helpless to do anything except pray, which they did persistently, even though hope of a miracle seemed slight.

Meanwhile, Peter slept soundly in his chains. An angel appeared in his cell, released the chains and led the sleepy apostle out of prison. Once outside, Peter finally came fully awake and hurried to the home where he knew the Christians were keeping a prayerful vigil.

When Peter rattled the outside gate, a servant girl named Rhoda came to answer. Hearing Peter's voice, she got so excited she forgot to open the door but instead ran inside to tell everyone.

Rhoda's oversight underscores how many times we only half expect God to answer our pleas. In fact, immediate answers usually astound us. But to those who persist in specific prayer, such answers are not surprising.

What discoveries have you made about prayer? Is there any situation in particular for which you are waiting for an answer to prayer?                                    ❖

**PRAYER**

*Surprise me, Lord ...*

**READ**

Rhoda appears in Acts 12:1–17.

## RUTH AND NAOMI
### INTRODUCING OTHERS TO GOD

*Ruth replied, "Don't urge me to leave you or to turn back from you. Where you go I will go, and where you stay I will stay. Your people will be my people and your God my God."*
RUTH 1:16

Logic tells us that Ruth and Naomi should not have been close. Ruth was young, Naomi was old. Ruth was from Moab, Naomi was from Israel. Most likely there were religious and language barriers. Throw in the customary potential for in-law friction, and it's truly a wonder that Ruth and Naomi were so close.

What enabled these women to forge such a close relationship? As Naomi prepared to leave Moab and return to her homeland, Ruth voiced her strong commitment to her mother-in-law. Her final statement is compelling, "Your God [will be] my God" (Ruth 1:16). Apparently Naomi was instrumental in introducing Ruth to the one true God! Naomi's testimony and walk with God had been so real and vibrant that Ruth was motivated to know him and follow him—even if that meant leaving Moab.

We can find similar success in relationships if we will let the love of Christ flow through us. When our lives are yielded to God, we exhibit the fruit of the Spirit: love, joy, peace, forbearance, kindness, goodness, faithfulness, gentleness and self-control. These are the qualities that make for incredible relationships— even between people who have little in common.                ❖

**PRAYER**

*Flow, River of Life, through me ...*

**READ**

The story of Ruth and Naomi is found in the book of Ruth. Matthew 1:5 also mentions Ruth.

## RUTH AND NAOMI
### *WORTHY OF TRUST*

*"I will do whatever you say," Ruth answered.*                    RUTH 3:5

Imagine being in a foreign culture; then imagine being there with the mother of your deceased spouse. Suddenly your mother-in-law is trying to play matchmaker. She is describing for you a plan to get you engaged to a distant relative of hers. And she is urging you to trust her. Would you?

That was the dilemma Ruth faced when Naomi was encouraging her to develop a relationship with Boaz. When we look beyond the ancient Jewish customs that come to play in this story, we discover a relationship marked by the highest levels of trust. Ruth followed her mother-in-law's instructions to the letter. Just as Naomi had said, Boaz ended up taking Ruth as his wife.

Trust like this only develops over time and only in relationships where both parties prove to be trustworthy, kind and unselfish. What about you? Do your friends and family members sense that you are looking out for their best interests? Do you keep your word? Have you proven to be consistently reliable, so that your spouse or children would willingly follow your advice (even when it seems a little scary or offbeat)?

Ask God to make you more and more trustworthy. Then make a concentrated effort today to demonstrate your unselfish concern for those you love.          ♣

**PRAYER**

*Lord, make me trustworthy ...*

**READ**

The story of Ruth and Naomi is found in the book of Ruth. Matthew 1:5 also mentions Ruth.

## SALOME
### *FOLLOWING WHOLEHEARTEDLY*

*In Galilee these women had followed [Jesus] and cared for his needs. Many other women who had come up with him to Jerusalem were also there.*      MARK 15:41

Salome's obscurity doesn't mean she was inactive or unimportant. She was part of an important group of women who supported Jesus and the disciples as they traveled around Galilee. She was the wife of Zebedee, and the mother of James and John. Women, including Salome, figure prominently in support of Jesus' ministry and are notably the first to receive the news of Jesus' resurrection (see Matthew 28:1–10).

Salome never wavered throughout Jesus' capture, trial, suffering and death. When those who seemed to be his strongest followers were afraid to appear in public, Salome and the other women boldly stood near the cross. Their faithfulness was rewarded when they made their way to Jesus' tomb on Easter morning, only to become the first to discover the glorious resurrection! Salome and the others literally kept their eyes on Jesus, even when they couldn't understand what was happening.

Salome reminds us we must, when all else fails, continue to trust! On a scale of one to ten, how quickly does your trust in God fade when trouble appears? What example from your own experience could you use to explain the principle that God does wonderful things for those who trust him? Resolve today to trust God wholeheartedly, even when the outlook is bleak.      ❖

**PRAYER**

*Lord, I trust you . . .*

**READ**

Salome's story is told in Matthew 20:20–28; 27:56; Mark 15:40–41; 16:1–8.

## SAMSON
### STAYING TOO CLOSE TO TEMPTATION

*Some time later, he fell in love with a woman in the Valley of Sorek whose name ˢ Delilah.*
JUDGES 16:4

Samson possessed unearthly strength. However, many people mistakenly identify Samson's famous long hair as the source of his great strength. Not so. The real reason for Samson's power was that God was with him and had chosen him to deliver the Israelite people from the Philistines.

So why the long hair? As an infant, Samson had been set apart as a servant of God known as a Nazirite. To symbolize their devotion to God, Nazirites vowed not to cut their hair. Cutting one's hair meant breaking the Nazirite vow and losing the sense of God's presence (a consequence that disobedience always brings).

Knowing this background information helps us better understand the episode involving Samson and Delilah. Delilah was a temptress hired by the Philistines to find out the reason for Samson's strength. She did her job well, whining and nagging until Samson caved in. The secrets Samson revealed ultimately cost him his life.

Even with all his mistakes, Samson is listed in Scripture as one of the heroes of the faith (see Hebrews 11:32). He believed in God and received strength from him, but ultimately he lacked self-control and lost his opportunity to deliver his people. We too often fight for self-control. When we stay in situations where our convictions are being challenged, we are more likely to compromise. We must not allow others, no matter how convincing or attractive, to entice us into doing something we know is wrong. The consequences of disobedience can be devastating!    ♣

### PRAYER

*Lord, grant me victory over this temptation . . .*

### READ

The story of Samson is found in Judges 13–16.

## SAMSON
### *ONE LAST CHANCE*

*Samson prayed to the LORD, "Sovereign LORD, remember me. Please, God, strengthen me just once more, and let me with one blow get revenge on the Philistines for my two eyes."* JUDGES 16:28

Samson had blown it. Chosen by God to deliver his people Israel from the Philistines, Samson had allowed lust to consume his life. Though married, he visited prostitutes and then met Delilah. Chasing after this infamous temptress, Samson was like an ox going to the slaughter. Delilah trapped him and turned him over to the Philistine leaders. They humiliated Samson, gouging out his eyes and putting him to work in a state of shameful bondage.

In spite of his disobedience, Samson at least had the sense to look to God one last time. He prayed for the strength to do what he had been chosen to do. And God heard his prayer. In pushing down the pillars of the temple of Dagon, the god of the Philistines, Samson killed thousands of prominent Philistines and their leaders.

What can we learn from this sad story? God never stops loving his children. When we cry out to him in humility, no matter what we have done, God hears us and can answer us.

Are you feeling guilty because of sinful choices? Are you reluctant to pray because of unwise decisions you have made? No matter how far you may feel you are from God, no matter how low you have sunk, God stands ready to hear from you and answer you. If God could still work in Samson's situation, he can still work in yours! ❖

### PRAYER

*Forgive me Lord, for ...*

### READ

The story of Samson is found in Judges 13–16.

## SAMUEL
### *RAISING GODLY CHILDREN*

*The boy Samuel continued to grow in stature and in favor with the LORD and with people.*      1 SAMUEL 2:26

Samuel, the last judge and first great prophet of Israel, had a rich spiritual heritage. His mother Hannah was a devout woman who dedicated him to God from birth. Consequently, Samuel grew up in and around the tabernacle, watching Eli the high priest offer sacrifices to God and helping him in his daily tasks.

Samuel became a godly leader. He anointed the first two kings of Israel. He stood up to King Saul when the monarch acted foolishly. He is also listed as a hero of the faith (see Hebrews 11).

What does the life of Samuel show us? Children (even at very young ages) are able to make significant spiritual commitments and substantial contributions to the work of God.

Are you making an effort to create a positive spiritual environment for your own children or the children within your extended family to grow up in? Do you give the kids in your life the opportunity to serve alongside you when you are doing the Lord's work? Teaching by doing is a great way to expose children to faith and faithful service. We can't afford to wait until they are teenagers to try to instill spiritual values in them. Begin today. Teach the children in your life about God's character and the importance of serving him. Perhaps one of them will become a modern-day Samuel!      ❖

### PRAYER

*Heavenly Father, may others see your character in me . . .*

### READ

The story of Samuel is found in 1 Samuel 1–28. He is also mentioned in Psalm 99:6; Jeremiah 15:1; Acts 3:24; 13:20 and Hebrews 11:32.

## SAMUEL
### POINTING OUR CHILDREN TO CHRIST

*When Samuel grew old, he appointed his sons as Israel's leaders.*     I SAMUEL 8:1

At least two facts are clear from the life of the prophet Samuel: (1) He was a faithful servant of God. (2) His sons were wicked men who used their power for selfish purposes. How can we reconcile these two facts? How is it possible for godly parents to have rebellious children?

Occasionally we hear stories about people with a public reputation for godliness but who are tyrants at home. Such hypocrisy was not present in Samuel's life—the Scriptures speak of him as a man of integrity. It's possible that Samuel was guilty of spiritual "workaholism," though again, the Scriptures never state that fact. Ultimately, whether a parent is good or bad, each and every child has a will and the freedom to make choices. Samuel's sons chose to reject the ways of their father.

Our children must grow up and decide for themselves whether they will believe and obey what we have taught them about God. We can pray diligently and model our faith. We can instruct and encourage. We can try to mold them and point them in the right way. But ultimately they will each decide to embrace or reject Christ. No one else can make that decision for them.

If your kids are walking with the Lord, thank God with a heart full of joy. If your children are not following God's ways, don't punish yourself. Take comfort in the fact that God can change even the most stubborn heart.     ♣

**PRAYER**

*You are all-powerful, O God . . .*

**READ**

The story of Samuel is found in 1 Samuel 1–28. He is also mentioned in Psalm 99:6; Jeremiah 15:1; Acts 3:24; 13:20 and Hebrews 11:32.

## SAMUEL
### *LIVING A LIFE OF INTEGRITY*

*"Here I stand. Testify against me in the presence of the LORD and his anointed."*

1 SAMUEL 12:3

As Samuel prepared to relinquish leadership to Saul, the new king of Israel, he gave a farewell speech. Samuel asked the assembled masses to judge his life. In so many words, he threw down a challenge: "Testify against me in the presence of the LORD and his anointed."

The crowd unanimously affirmed that Samuel lived his life with integrity. "'You have not cheated or oppressed us,' they replied. 'You have not taken anything from anyone's hand'" (1 Samuel 12:4). In other words, Samuel's reputation was spotless. God may have intended this testimony to challenge Saul, but it also honored Samuel's life of faithfulness.

Would you have the courage to stand up in front of your classmates, neighbors, family members, colleagues or church body and make a statement similar to the one Samuel made? Why or why not? Or imagine yourself nominated to a high government position. Suddenly the media is digging through your personal history looking for dirt. Would they find anything?

If you haven't lived a squeaky clean life, claim the forgiveness and cleansing offered by Christ. Then commit to one specific activity you need to stop doing and one you need to begin doing so that your behavior most accurately reflects what you say you believe. ♣

### PRAYER

*Purify my heart, Lord ...*

### READ

The story of Samuel is found in 1 Samuel 1–28. He is also mentioned in Psalm 99:6; Jeremiah 15:1; Acts 3:24; 13:20 and Hebrews 11:32.

# day315

## SANBALLAT
### *PROTECTING HIS TURF*

*When Sanballat the Horonite and Tobiah the Ammonite official heard about this, they were very much disturbed that someone had come to promote the welfare of the Israelites.*
NEHEMIAH 2:10

Sanballat opposed Nehemiah's efforts to rebuild the walls of Jerusalem. His opposition may have been provoked by ethnic hatred, greed or jealousy. Whatever his motives, he was intent on stopping Nehemiah.

Sanballat and his friends ridiculed Nehemiah and his plan. They questioned Nehemiah's authority and motives. As the restoration work continued, they threatened them and tried to lure Nehemiah into a situation where his character would be discredited.

Sanballat is definitely an all-time bad guy. But are we too often like Sanballat? How do you respond when a new worker is assigned to your "turf" in regard to your job or responsibilities? Do you welcome the new person and embrace their ideas and enthusiasm or do you resent their presence as a threat to you?

Welcoming and supporting a new leader assaults our pride. Even the strongest Christians can feel the temptation to talk negatively and wish for the new leader's failure. If pleasing God is our overriding desire, we don't have to worry about who gets the credit for a job well done. We can be pleased to be a small part of God's work being done. ❖

### PRAYER

*Lord, work through the leaders in my life...*

### READ

Sanballat's story is told in Nehemiah 2; 4 and 6.

## SAPPHIRA
### *TAKING SIN LIGHTLY*

*Peter said to her, "How could you conspire to test the Spirit of the Lord? Listen! The feet of the men who buried your husband are at the door, and they will carry you out also."*

ACTS 5:9

Surely the employees of the Internal Revenue Service would love to have the discernment Peter had the day he questioned Ananias and Sapphira about the amount of their gift to the church. How much would it be worth to know for certain if someone is telling the truth?

When Sapphira lied to Peter about the price of the land and the gift they were giving to the church, it wasn't a memory lapse or a slight exaggeration. She had full knowledge of what her husband was going to tell the leaders of the church. What she didn't know was that the consequences for lying were going to be severe and immediate.

When are you most tempted to lie? When you are trying to stay out of trouble or attempting to save money? If you knew lying would bring severe and immediate consequences, would you let even an exaggeration escape your lips?

Whatever lies you have told—big or small, recent or old—can be forgiven by confessing them to both God and the people involved. Why wait until you are in the presence of God to tell the truth? Sapphira was given the chance to tell the truth but wasted it. You also have the chance, so don't waste it.    ❖

### PRAYER

*Lord, I bow to your truth . . .*

### READ

Sapphira's story is told in Acts 5:1–11.

# day317

## SARAH
### *WAITING FOR THE PROMISE*

*Abraham fell facedown; he laughed and said to himself, "Will a son be born to a man a hundred years old? Will Sarah bear a child at the age of ninety?"*　　GENESIS 17:17

Think how hard it is to wait—for a vacation or in a long, slow line when you're running late or for the results of a medical test that could change your whole life.

Now imagine having to wait 90 years for something you want desperately. Would you have the patience to hang in there that long? That was the dilemma facing Sarah. She wanted children, but she was infertile. At age 65, she had long given up her dream of being a mom, when God suddenly announced that she would have a son. Then ten years dragged by and nothing happened.

Sarah eventually tired of waiting and tried to speed up the process. But God made it clear that Ishmael (the son of Sarah's servant Hagar) was not the child he had originally promised. Year after year continued to pass. Finally, after 15 more years (Sarah was then 90), God announced that the time was at last right. Abraham and Sarah got their bouncing baby, Isaac, and they learned—in the words of the old spiritual—that "God may make you wait, but he'll never be too late."

What are you waiting for today? Don't throw in the towel yet! It may be difficult, but resist the urge to rush things along. Too many times we get so caught up in our destination, we miss the wildness and wonder of the journey itself.　　❖

**PRAYER**

*I count on your promises, Lord . . .*

**READ**

The life of Sarah is depicted in Genesis 11–25.

## SARAH
### IS ANYTHING TOO HARD FOR HIM?

*"Is anything too hard for the LORD? I will return to you at the appointed time next year, and Sarah will have a son."* GENESIS 18:14

After waiting so long for a child, Sarah was skeptical, perhaps even cynical. Her 90-year-old skin was wrinkled. Her eyesight was failing. Her bones were creaking. No doubt her thoughts were focused on issues of geriatrics, not pediatrics! Yet here was God telling her and Abraham that they were about to become parents.

The thought was outrageous, ridiculous—laughable. And so that's what Sarah did—she laughed to herself. Was it a sneering laugh? Was it a laugh due to embarrassment or shock? The Bible doesn't say specifically, but God did confront her about it.

"You don't believe me," God seemed to be saying. "What's the big deal about me blessing you with a son late in life? I'm the God who created the universe out of nothing!"

Sarah tried to deny her disbelief, in much the same way we do. "I believe! I believe! Of course God is all-powerful! He can do anything!" we claim. But then we turn around in the next breath and focus on our problems. When we do we become disillusioned, depressed and despondent. "It's terrible!" we moan. "It's no use!" we yelp.

What hopeless situation are you facing today? Instead of looking at the size of your problem, why not meditate instead on the strength of your God? Nothing—nothing at all—is too hard for him. Will you trust him to work in your life today? ❧

**PRAYER**

*Lord, this situation is too hard for me ...*

**READ**

The life of Sarah is depicted in Genesis 11–25.

# day319

## SAUL
### *LOOKS CAN BE DECEIVING*

*Kish had a son named Saul, as handsome a young man as could be found anywhere in Israel, and he was a head taller than anyone else.* 1 SAMUEL 9:2

If you were looking for a king in 1050 BC (and the Israelites were), Saul definitely would have caught your eye. He was physically imposing and from a prominent, wealthy family. Some scholars even speculate that Saul was exceptionally handsome.

Saul's appearance, however, could not make up for some severe personal liabilities. As king, Saul repeatedly disobeyed God. He made unwise, impulsive decisions. Saul also lacked self-confidence, which led to extreme bouts of jealousy. He became a murderous, unstable, paranoid ruler. Who could have foreseen that such a promising guy would become such a terrible king?

If ever there was a culture that is hung up on appearance, it is today's culture. We spend billions of dollars every year on clothes, cosmetics and health equipment designed to make us look better on the outside. But how much time and money are we willing to invest to improve who we are on the inside?

Make the commitment today to spend some time strengthening your character and commitment to God's commands. Memorize the Beatitudes. Read a good book on some aspect of the Christian life in which you seek improvement. Spend half a day in prayer. Ask God for the strength to eliminate bad habits and begin good ones. ✤

### PRAYER

*Lord, grant me strength ...*

### READ

The story of Saul is found in 1 Samuel 9–31. He is also mentioned in Acts 13:21.

## SAUL
### SUBMITTING TO GOD

*Samuel replied: "Does the LORD delight in burnt offerings and sacrifices as much as in obeying the LORD? To obey is better than sacrifice, and to heed is better than the fat of rams."*                                                                    1 SAMUEL 15:22

It wasn't that King Saul couldn't get things right; it was that he wouldn't do the right things. His entire career was marked by rebellious attitudes and disobedient actions.

Early in his reign, Saul was faced with a crisis. The Philistines were gearing up for an attack on Israel. The Jewish troops were losing heart and beginning to go AWOL. The prophet Samuel had told Saul that he was coming to offer the necessary sacrifices so that Israel could enjoy the blessing and presence of God as they went into battle. Saul waited, and Samuel didn't come. Impatient and under increasing pressure, Saul brazenly assumed the role of the priest and offered the sacrifices himself. It was a serious offense that cost his descendants the throne.

Later, in another infamous act of disobedience, God gave Saul clear instructions to defeat the evil nation of Amalek and destroy it completely. Saul carried out only part of the Lord's command. He defeated the Amalekites but kept some of the plunder. Samuel rebuked Saul again. Saul's response was to offer rationalizations and excuses.

God doesn't want our justifications and explanations. God doesn't want us doing good and godly things in the wrong way, at the wrong time or for the wrong reasons. God wants our complete submission. Are you obeying God fully today?    ♣

### PRAYER

*Lord, make my half-hearted desires whole . . .*

### READ

The story of Saul is found in 1 Samuel 9–31. He is also mentioned in Acts 13:21.

## SAUL
### *AN UNREPENTANT HEART*

*Saul was afraid of David, because the LORD was with David but had departed from Saul.*      1 SAMUEL 18:12

The life of Saul is a sad illustration of the consequences of sin and being unwilling to turn to God for help. When we first meet Saul, he is a young, handsome man. He initially enjoys the filling of the Holy Spirit and seems to have a bright future as king.

Then he begins making selfish decisions. He inappropriately offers a sacrifice. He makes a rash vow that almost causes him to murder his son Jonathan. He keeps forbidden plunder from the defeat of Amalek. He is filled with jealousy and fear at the success and popularity of David. Paranoid, Saul orders the murder of 85 priests he suspects are loyal to David. His last spiritual consultation is with a witch. In the end, Saul commits suicide. Not a very impressive resume, is it?

Someone once said that every life is worth examining, even the bad ones, for they at least serve as examples of how *not* to live. Certainly that is the case with Saul. He expressed regret and sorrow for his deeds but never really repented of his sin. He allowed himself to become overcome by sinful attitudes that drove him away from God to the very brink of insanity and finally over the edge.

Don't let sin get a foothold in your life! If you are constantly angry, jealous or fearful, talk to a mature Christian leader. Get help before you drift into real danger.     ❖

### PRAYER

*Lord, I admit to being angry about . . .*

### READ

The story of Saul is found in 1 Samuel 9–31. He is also mentioned in Acts 13:21.

# day322

## SHADRACH, MESHACH AND ABEDNEGO
### *REFUSING TO BOW DOWN*

*"But even if he does not, we want you to know, Your Majesty, that we will not serve your gods or worship the image of gold you have set up."*  DANIEL 3:18

As young men, Hananiah, Mishael and Azariah were deported to Babylon. Given new names (Shadrach, Meshach and Abednego, respectively), they were encouraged to forsake their Hebrew heritage and faith in the God of Israel. They refused to compromise.

When Nebuchadnezzar erected a statue of himself for his subjects to worship, the Hebrew trio staunchly refused to bow to it. They trusted God to save them from a royal sentence of death by fire and assured the king that even if God did not spare their lives, they still would not cave in.

This was a bold stand. The men not only had faith in a big God but they also drew strength from each other. God spared them from death in the fiery furnace and went with them through the experience!

When you are faced with a situation in which holding to your convictions may result in unpleasant circumstances, how do you respond? Do you back down? Or do you stand up and stand firm? For extra strength to fight the temptation to compromise, find one or two committed Christian friends who can hold you accountable and encourage you to continue to do what is right. ❖

### PRAYER

*Lord, help me stand firm ...*

### READ

The story of Shadrach, Meshach and Abednego is found in Daniel 1–3.

## SHAPHAN
### *TAKING A RISK FOR THE TRUTH*

*Shaphan the secretary informed the king, "Hilkiah the priest has given me a book." And Shaphan read from it in the presence of the king.*      2 KINGS 22:10

It has always been a bit dangerous to serve kings and high officials. King Zedekiah had Jeremiah thrown into prison for predicting the fall of Jerusalem. King Nebuchadnezzar had all his advisors executed when they couldn't interpret his dream.

Shaphan, King Josiah's secretary, was given the Book of the Law, written by Moses that had been found in the temple while it was being repaired. For decades during the rule of evil kings, the books of the law had been destroyed or lost. How would King Josiah react to hearing the contents of this book? His reaction could either cost Shaphan his life or start a spiritual revival in the nation.

Delivering the truth is sometimes a risk. How will the hearers respond to what you tell them? We are commanded to "[speak] the truth in love" (Ephesians 4:15). The challenge is to tell the truth even when it may not please the hearers.

When Shaphan read the Book of the Law to King Josiah, the king repented and led the nation back to God. Delivering God's Word to your friends and family can change the direction of their lives for eternity.     ❖

**PRAYER**

*Lord, show me when to speak the truth in love . . .*

**READ**

Shaphan's story is told in 2 Kings 22:1–12 and 2 Chronicles 34:8–20.

## SHEBA
### *PRACTICING PREJUDICE*

*Now a troublemaker named Sheba son of Bikri, a Benjamite, happened to be there. He sounded the trumpet and shouted, "We have no share in David, no part in Jesse's son!"*

2 SAMUEL 20:1

Sheba led a rebellion against King David by inflaming tribal jealousy. He shouted that since David wasn't from the tribe of Benjamin, he wasn't one of them and would not give them fair treatment. The rebellion ended quickly when David's army besieged the city where Sheba was hiding and demanded his head be cut off and thrown over the city wall.

Sheba led his rebellion by appealing to prejudice. Racial and ethnic identity may make us proud, but they also can make us divisive. Sheba counted on that.

Some political leaders today still use the divide-and-conquer strategy. Like Sheba, they exalt themselves by emphasizing racial differences and charging that any leader from a different background cannot fairly represent or lead any people from another group. They talk unity and equality, but they practice division and prejudice.

What's more important to you: the differences or similarities between you and another person? Is your opinion of a leader influenced by their racial or ethnic background? An effective leader is much more than superficial qualities. A community and a nation can only be unified if we judge leaders (and all people) on the basis of their character and not the color of their skin.            ❖

### PRAYER

*Let unity start with me, Lord . . .*

### READ

Read Sheba's story in 2 Samuel 20:1–22.

## SHIPHRAH AND PUAH
### *FEARING GOD MORE THAN MEN*

*The midwives, however, feared God and did not do what the king of Egypt had told them to do; they let the boys live.* EXODUS 1:17

Shiphrah and Puah, two Hebrew midwives, were undoubtedly tense and a little confused when they were summoned to appear before the ruler of all Egypt. Yet that confusion must have given way to shock, fear and anger when they found out why they had been called. Pharaoh ordered them to kill all the boys born to Hebrew women from that moment forward. Even though they were placing their lives in jeopardy, the women refused to comply. They engineered a strategy of passive resistance that undermined Pharaoh's zero-population-growth plan. The births continued, and Israel grew to a mighty nation.

Shiphrah and Puah never hesitated when faced with the choice of serving God or obeying the sinful demands of a human ruler. They were confident that God would sustain them if they obeyed the Lord. Christians today may also be encouraged to join in causes or activities that clearly violate God's commands. Like the courageous midwives, we may face risks when obeying God—ridicule, isolation and even physical harm. But we can act knowing that God will honor our efforts as he did the efforts of Shiphrah and Puah. ❖

### PRAYER

*Heavenly Father, show me how to honor you ...*

### READ

The story of Shiphrah and Puah can be found in Exodus 1:15–21.

## SILAS
### *GIFTED ENCOURAGER*

*Judas and Silas, who themselves were prophets, said much to encourage and strengthen the believers.*                                                        ACTS 15:32

Silas was a Roman citizen and a leader in the Jerusalem church. He had a prophetic gift that enabled him to speak and teach with clarity and power. He became a traveling companion and colleague of the apostle Paul and a writing secretary for Paul and Peter.

We can't duplicate or emulate most of Silas's accomplishments (unless we want to travel thousands of miles and go back in time about 1900 years). However, we can, in the words of Acts 15:32, become people who encourage and strengthen others. Silas's life and words gave fellow believers in Antioch and elsewhere the courage to press on. Those who were slipping and struggling found the practical help they needed.

It is really a simple proposition. You can encourage and build others up, or you can discourage and tear others down. You have to choose which it will be. Why not make the choice to be an encourager? Without being preachy, you could remind a friend or family member of some Scriptural truth. Complimenting, affirming, cheerleading, supporting, caring, showing interest—these are ways we can encourage others in their faith.                                               ✤

**PRAYER**

*Encourage me, Lord, as I encourage others . . .*

**READ**

The story of Silas is told in Acts 15:22—19:10. He is also mentioned in 2 Corinthians 1:19; 1 Thessalonians 1:1; 2 Thessalonians 1:1 and 1 Peter 5:12.

# day**327**

## SILAS
### *AIM FOR FAITHFULNESS*

*With the help of Silas, whom I regard as a faithful brother, I have written to you briefly, encouraging you and testifying that this is the true grace of God.*　　1 PETER 5:12

Of all the words that could be used to describe a Christian, one of the best has to be the word "faithful." Faithfulness means you're dependable or reliable. It means you're trustworthy, steady and solid. It means others can count on you.

Peter wrote that Silas was a "faithful brother." Silas earned this description by becoming dedicated to the early church, by hanging in through all the ups and downs of missionary life with Paul. Nothing deterred Silas—not rough terrain, choppy seas, imprisonment, persecution, threats, hostile crowds or poor health. He plodded along, faithfully using his gifts and abilities, his time and energy in every situation. Perhaps he remembered (and longed to hear) the words uttered by Christ, "Well done, good and faithful servant!" (Matthew 25:23).

In our success-crazed culture, we think God is pleased with measurable results and large numbers and big programs. We like to use words like "victory" and "winning" and "excellence." To be sure, these concepts have a place in the Christian life. But the one ideal we ought to shoot for is faithfulness. If we plod along and carefully seek to do the will of God, we will bear fruit.　　✤

### PRAYER

*Increase my faith, Lord . . .*

### READ

The story of Silas is told in Acts 15:22—19:10. He is also mentioned in 2 Corinthians 1:19; 1 Thessalonians 1:1; 2 Thessalonians 1:1 and 1 Peter 5:12.

## SIMEON
### *REJOICING IN FULFILLED PROMISES*

*When the parents brought in the child Jesus to do for him what the custom of the Law required, Simeon took him in his arms and praised God.*                    LUKE 2:27–28

Many of us have hopes and dreams we want to see fulfilled. We dream of retirement and being able to travel; getting that job we've always wanted; or we dream of our children making good in the world.

Simeon also had a hope and a dream. God had promised Simeon he would live to see the long-awaited Messiah. Each year as Simeon grew older he must have wondered if this year would bring the fulfillment of the promise.

When he saw the baby Jesus in the temple with Mary and Joseph, God let him know the promise of the Messiah had been fulfilled. Simeon praised God from the depths of his heart.

Waiting for God to fulfill his promises or to answer our prayers can be a real test of our endurance and faith. We are often tempted to stop praying or to settle for something less than God's best plan for us.

Don't lose confidence in God's promises each passing day. Your wait may be as long as Simeon's, but when you see it fulfilled, you will have reason to rejoice as he did.                                                                        ✤

**PRAYER**

*Lord, I have been waiting for . . .*

**READ**

Simeon's story is told in Luke 2:21–35.

## SIMON THE PHARISEE
### *GRUDGING GENEROSITY*

*When the Pharisee who had invited [Jesus] saw this, he said to himself, "If this man were a prophet, he would know who is touching him and what kind of woman she is—that she is a sinner."*　　　　　　　　　　　　　　　　　　　　　　　　　Luke 7:39

Simon probably was quite proud of himself the day he asked Jesus to dine with him. After all, he was being a model of tolerance and goodwill, wasn't he? Not many Pharisees would have mingled with a controversial teacher who associated with sinners. Simon may have expected Jesus to be grateful for being admitted to the company of such a distinguished religious authority as himself.

The unexpected arrival of a prostitute exposed the hospitality of Simon for what it was: calculated and stingy. The lavish gift of perfume that the woman poured on Jesus' feet contrasted with the lack of courtesy Simon had shown to his guest. He had neglected the essential practices of wiping the dust off of Jesus' feet, giving the customary kiss and anointing his guest's head. Even after Jesus had called this to Simon's attention, we are left wondering whether or not the Pharisee felt any remorse for his behavior.

It is too easy to write Simon off because he belonged to a group known for its hypocrisy. We can—and do—behave much the way Simon did when we assume smugly that God is pleased with our token efforts of service to others. Take time today to reflect on what you are doing for others. Are you motivated by the desire to look good in the eyes of others, or are you looking for the good you can do without thought of reward?　　　　　　　　　　　　　　　　　　　　　　❖

**PRAYER**

*Lord, make me genuine ...*

**READ**

Simon's story is found in Luke 7:36–50.

## SIMON THE SORCERER
### *GIFTS FOR HIRE*

*When Simon saw that the Spirit was given at the laying on of the apostles' hands, he offered them money and said, "Give me also this ability so that everyone on whom I lay my hands may receive the Holy Spirit."*      ACTS 8:18–19

Simon the sorcerer thought he could buy God's power, as if it were some sort of potion that could be doled out to talented magicians. Peter and John rebuked Simon harshly and urged him to turn from his selfish and misguided plans. To his credit, Simon responded with a humble request for prayer.

We get the word "simony," which refers to the sin of buying or selling spiritual things, from this man's market-driven attitude toward God. It is a great perversion of Christianity to use God for our own purposes rather than letting God use us for accomplishing his purposes.

Serving God is not a franchise operation. We don't pay a fee and get a proven product to market to others for our personal gain. There are too many modern examples of people who use God's name for their own fame and financial benefit.

Listen to your own prayers. Are you asking God for help for your own gain? Do you go to church expecting to get something for yourself, or do you go to worship God and encourage and serve others? Depending on how you answer these questions, are there any changes to your attitude you need to make?     ❖

**PRAYER**

*Lord, I want to serve you out of love . . .*

**READ**

Simon's story is told in Acts 8:9–25.

# day331

## SOLOMON
### *A WISE AND DISCERNING HEART*

*"I will do what you have asked. I will give you a wise and discerning heart, so that there will never have been anyone like you, nor will there ever be."*          1 KINGS 3:12

With the death of King David, the mantle of leadership passed to his son Solomon. Early in his reign as Israel's third king, Solomon had a dream in which the Lord spoke to him. Essentially, he told the new monarch, "Ask for whatever you want, and I will give it to you." Imagine such an offer. The options are staggering!

Solomon didn't hesitate. He immediately requested wisdom. "Give your servant a discerning heart to govern your people and to distinguish between right and wrong" (1 Kings 3:9). This humble response thrilled the heart of God. He granted Solomon's request and added, "Moreover, I will give you what you have not asked for—both wealth and honor—so that in your lifetime you will have no equal among kings" (1 Kings 3:13).

Wisdom differs from knowledge in that wisdom is "skill in living." Wisdom is knowing not only facts but also what to do in life's various situations. According to the Bible, someone with an IQ of 180 can be a fool, while a high school dropout can be extremely wise (see Proverbs 17:24). The difference lies in the ability to understand and live out God's truth.

Ask God to make you a wise person. Then spend some time today reading the wise sayings of Solomon in the book of Proverbs.                                        ❖

### PRAYER

*Make me wise, Lord . . .*

### READ

The life of Solomon is told in 2 Samuel 12:24—1 Kings 11:43.

## SOLOMON
### *CLOSE ENCOUNTERS OF THE WRONG KIND*

*As Solomon grew old, his wives turned his heart after other gods, and his heart was not fully devoted to the LORD his God, as the heart of David his father had been.*

1 KINGS 11:4

Solomon was a mediocre king. He didn't mess up as badly as Saul, but he also never lived up to the promise of his father David. Solomon was a guy who began well but faded fast. He inherited a prosperous, thriving kingdom. He reigned during a time of great peace. He enjoyed wealth and wisdom. He had a chance to leave a mark. Instead, he left behind a kingdom that divided soon after his death, never to reunite. What happened?

Solomon's marriages to foreign wives were a big part of the problem. When Solomon brought these women into his palace, they invariably brought with them their unhealthy religious beliefs and practices. Before long, Solomon was making concessions and compromising his faith to please the numerous women in his life.

Solomon's sad end reminds us of the importance of not entering into intimate relationships with unbelievers. We can and should befriend them. After all, how else can we share the love of Christ with them? However, we must not risk an emotional bond that jeopardizes our devotion to God. Solomon became more concerned with pleasing his wives than with pleasing his God.

Are you too close to someone who doesn't share your belief in Christ? Ask God for the strength to make whatever change is needed in that relationship. ✤

**PRAYER**

*Guard me, O God, from unwise relationships . . .*

**READ**

The life of Solomon is found in 2 Samuel 12:24—1 Kings 11:43.

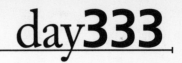

## SOLOMON
### *HAPPINESS IS KNOWING GOD*

*Fear God and keep his commandments, for this is the duty of all mankind.*
ECCLESIASTES 12:13

Everyone has ideas about where to find lasting happiness. Some people search for satisfaction in wealth. Some believe meaning and purpose are found in acquiring power or prestige. Some are convinced the way to find fulfillment is through pleasure. Some put their faith in the acquisition of knowledge. Others believe if they can accomplish certain goals or feats, they will achieve a sense of wholeness.

Solomon has a unique message for those who are traveling all these avenues in the quest for ultimate meaning. During his life, he searched exhaustively for something to give his life purpose. He tried it all (and had it all). After sampling in abundance everything this world has to offer, he concluded that the way to escape a dull, meaningless existence is to enter into a relationship with God.

Whatever we are looking to for happiness and purpose in life, we must realize this: We will never amass more money, more fame, more accomplishments or more wisdom than Solomon did. If he was unable to find fulfillment in those things, what makes us think we will be different?

If you have never opened yourself to Christ, do so today. Welcome him wholeheartedly into your life; invite him to infuse you with peace and purpose. ❧

**PRAYER**

*Jesus, I invite you . . .*

**READ**

The life of Solomon unfolds in 2 Samuel 12:24—1 Kings 11:43.

## SOSTHENES
### *SUFFERING IS NOT WASTED*

*The crowd there turned on Sosthenes the synagogue leader and beat him in front of the proconsul; and Gallio showed no concern whatever.*　　　　Acts 18:17

Sosthenes was the ruler of the Jewish synagogue in Corinth when the apostle Paul was there. On each Sabbath Paul would speak about Jesus, the Christ. Many Jews didn't like this. When they couldn't get the proconsul Gallio to punish Paul, they turned on Sosthenes and beat him in frustration. Eventually this man became a believer.

We don't know if Sosthenes became a believer in Christ before or after that beating, but he is mentioned as a brother in Christ in 1 Corinthians 1:1.

Jesus promised his disciples that suffering for him would not be wasted: "Blessed are you when people insult you, persecute you and falsely say all kinds of evil against you because of me. Rejoice and be glad, because great is your reward in heaven, for in the same way they persecuted the prophets who were before you" (Matthew 5:11–12).

What kind of persecution have you faced because of your commitment to Christ? While some Christians around the world often risk their lives living for Christ, most believers in North America often risk little, if anything, when they publicly identify with Christ.

How can God use you as a witness for Christ among your friends and family? What fears do you have about clearly identifying yourself as a follower of Jesus? ✤

### PRAYER

*Make me your witness, Lord . . .*

### READ

Sosthenes' story is told in Acts 18:17 and 1 Corinthians 1:1.

## STEPHANAS
### *REFRESHING BELIEVERS*

*Such men deserve recognition.*              1 CORINTHIANS 16:18

Stephanas and his family were the first to convert to Christianity when Paul came to Corinth. Paul baptized them himself. In the closing chapter of 1 Corinthians, Paul aimed the spotlight at this relatively unknown ordinary guy (and his likeminded cohorts): "I was glad when Stephanas, Fortunatus and Achaicus arrived, because they have supplied what was lacking from you. For they refreshed my spirit and yours also" (1 Corinthians 16:17–18). Stephanas was a hero of sorts.

Stephanas was also the kind of person who said what he said and did what he did to serve others. This is what it meant for him to serve his Lord. This is what it means for us too.

Consider those who have encouraged you throughout your life. Such people deserve recognition. Think of a way to shine the spotlight on them.

Consider someone whom you can encourage today. Perhaps by finding a tangible way to help them, your words and service will be much-needed refreshment for their soul.          ♣

**PRAYER**

*Lord, instill in me the desire to affirm others …*

**READ**

Stephanas's story is told in 1 Corinthians 1:16 and 16:15–18.

## STEPHEN
### *SHINING FOR CHRIST*

*Stephen, full of the Holy Spirit, looked up to heaven and saw the glory of God, and Jesus standing at the right hand of God.*      ACTS 7:55

Stephen, a man of achievement, was one of seven leaders chosen to supervise food distribution to the elderly in the early church. He was an outstanding administrator, teacher and debater. But he is chiefly remembered as the church's first martyr.

More significant than what Stephen did, however, was how he lived. Acts describes a man who was full of God's grace and power, and full of faith. Twice we find references to the fact that Stephen was a man who was filled with the Holy Spirit, bearing the fruits of love, joy, peace, forbearance, kindness, goodness, faithfulness, gentleness and self-control.

What we are is more important than what we do. Before we busy ourselves with serving God, we need to make sure we have fully yielded our will to God's will. When we give the Spirit of God the freedom to change us, we become walking billboards—testimonies to the life-changing power of God.

It's worth noting that as Stephen prepared to address the Jewish religious leaders, everyone in attendance noticed that "his face was like the face of an angel" (Acts 6:15). In other words, Stephen's countenance was radiant! Does your love for Christ show outwardly? If so, how?     ♣

**PRAYER**

*Shine, Jesus, shine...*

**READ**

The story of Stephen is found in Acts 6:3—8:2.

## STEPHEN
### *NO ACTION IS INSIGNIFICANT*

*Then he fell on his knees and cried out, "Lord, do not hold this sin against them." When he had said this, he fell asleep.*                    ACTS 7:60

Stephen's sermon to the Jewish ruling council started off like a pleasant review of Jewish history. But the more he preached, the more pointed his words became. By the end, Stephen was shouting, "You stiff-necked people! Your hearts and ears are still uncircumcised. You are just like your ancestors: You always resist the Holy Spirit!" (Acts 7:51).

Enraged, the Jews began to stone Stephen. As he lay dying, he scanned the crowd (which included Saul of Tarsus) and prayed, "Lord, do not hold this sin against them" (Acts 7:60). The whole episode seemed like such a waste ... Stephen, the gifted servant of God, dying before he could ever make an impact. But is that the whole story?

Stephen's last prayer was a plea that his murderers might find forgiveness. In other words, it was a prayer for their salvation! At least in the case of Saul, God heard and answered this request. Stephen's prayer contributed to Saul's conversion. Later Saul, who became known as Paul, went on to become God's leading spokesman for the good news of Christ!

You may think you are leading a quiet, ineffective life. You may not see any tangible fruit. But continue to be faithful and continue to pray. Some small, "insignificant" action on your part may one day be revealed as a crucial turning point in salvation history. Without knowing it, you might play a role in the conversion of the next Paul, Martin Luther or Billy Graham! We never know what great things God may do through us.                                                              ❖

**PRAYER**

*Lord, help me to see my part in your kingdom ...*

**READ**

The story of Stephen is found in Acts 6:3 — 8:2.

## SUFFERING WOMAN
### *THE GOD BEHIND THE HEALING*

*"Who touched me?" Jesus asked.*        LUKE 8:45

How long did she follow Jesus in the crowd, hesitating? Did she avoid asking Jesus for help because she feared he would regard her like other Jewish men who refused to touch an unclean woman? Fully believing in his power to heal, yet not wanting to attract his attention, she struggled her way through a crowd and lightly touched a fringe of his coat.

Two things happened instantly. Her bleeding stopped and so did Jesus. He wasn't angry, but he was firm: "Who touched me?" For a moment she thought she might slip away unnoticed, for Peter pointed out that many people were pressing in. But Jesus insisted that someone had tapped healing power from him.

The woman came forward trembling. She had taken without asking. Would the gift have to be returned? Unmasked, she fell at Jesus' feet and told him her story. How relieved she must have been after he addressed her lovingly as "daughter" (Luke 8:48) and assured her release from suffering.

No doubt the woman believed in the awesome power of Jesus and expected to be healed. What she didn't expect was the boundless love and assurance from the person behind the power. Behind every answered prayer and powerful miracle in our lives is a God who loves to surprise us with his love. Give thanks to God for the ways in which he has pleasantly surprised you recently.     ✤

**PRAYER**

*O God, I give you thanks for . . .*

**READ**

The story of the suffering woman is told in Matthew 9:20–22; Mark 5:25–34 and Luke 8:43–48.

## SUSANNA
### *GIVING THANKS*

*Susanna; and many others. These women were helping to support them out of their own means.*　　　　　　　　　　　　　　　　　　　　Luke 8:3

Several women accompanied Jesus and his twelve disciples as they traveled to the cities and villages of Galilee announcing the coming kingdom of God. Susanna was one of three women Luke mentions who had been healed by Jesus and were helping to support his ministry financially.

Jesus gave these women the recognition and responsibility often denied to them in their culture. Traveling and learning with the disciples served as an example to all women that Jesus valued them. He taught them. In gratitude, they gave generously from their own money to support Jesus and his disciples.

In what ways has God helped you? In what ways has he healed you? How are you showing your appreciation to Jesus for all he has done for you? Are you like Susanna, who gave financially to support the spreading of the message of Christ?

❖

**PRAYER**

*Lord, I will give . . .*

**READ**

Susanna's story is told in Luke 8:1–3.

## SYNTYCHE AND EUODIA
### RESTORING UNITY IN THE CHURCH

*I plead with Euodia and I plead with Syntyche to be of the same mind in the Lord.*

PHILIPPIANS 4:2

Who knows how it started … perhaps a disagreement, an unkind word or a simple misunderstanding. The rift between Euodia and Syntyche had grown to the point that Paul wrote about it from a prison cell in another city. Apparently these prominent women in the church were making no moves to resolve their conflict.

Conflict is a normal part of life even for the most committed Christian. Following the Lord doesn't remove conflict, but it does provide direction for handling and resolving it. We are told not to let the sun go down on our anger or to give the devil a foothold in our lives (see Ephesians 4:26–27) and to forgive each other just as God in Christ forgives us (see Ephesians 4:32).

Paul gave these women the key to finding resolution—they were to agree with each other in the Lord. This same advice may help you mend some of the rifts in your own relationships. You too can determine what would please the Lord and do it. When you sincerely seek to please the Lord, you are more willing to be honest, humble and ready to forgive.

What conflicts in your life are presently unresolved? What can you do to resolve them? How can this passage from Philippians help you find a resolution?   ❖

**PRAYER**

*Lord, I need your help to resolve …*

**READ**

Paul addresses these women in Philippians 4:2–3.

## THE SYROPHOENICIAN WOMAN
### *PUTTING PRIDE ASIDE*

*The woman was a Greek, born in Syrian Phoenicia. She begged Jesus to drive the demon out of her daughter.*                                                            MARK 7:26

Desperation had wiped clean any trace of sinful pride in this mother. She broke through the cultural barriers to seek help from Jesus. While Jesus' fellow Jews argued about his teaching and rejected him as the promised Messiah, this non-Jewish woman ran to him seeking help for her demon-possessed daughter. When Jesus explained that his primary mission was to his own people, she replied that she was ready to take whatever leftovers of time and attention he could give to her. Jesus recognized her humble faith and healed her daughter.

When you read the story of the Syrophoenician woman, can you sense the desperation she felt as she addressed Jesus? Can you relate to her situation? Her boldness and her willingness to risk rejection saved her daughter.

Often the first step to healing is realizing we don't have all the solutions to our problems and surrendering our stubborn pride to God. What has kept you from bringing your life with all its problems to Jesus? Today is the day to begin intently seeking God for his help.                                                            ✜

### PRAYER

*Lord, I need your help ...*

### READ

The story of the Syrophoenician woman is told in Matthew 15:21–28 and Mark 7:24–30.

## TAMAR
### *VICTIM OF LUST*

*"No, my brother!" she said to him. "Don't force me! Such a thing should not be done in Israel! Don't do this wicked thing."*                    2 SAMUEL 13:12

The life of Tamar, the daughter of King David by his third wife, Maacah, changed forever when her half brother, Amnon, devised a plan to seduce her. When Tamar refused Amnon's advances, he overpowered and raped her.

After he attacked her, Amnon's intense lust changed to hatred. Absalom, her brother, became angry when David did not punish Amnon. Absalom took matters into his own hands and killed Amnon, starting a feud with David that would eventually lead to Absalom's attempted rebellion and death.

Tamar's life was torn apart by sexual abuse at the hands of her own family member, and she spent the remainder of her life suffering the consequences of this violent act against her.

It's easy to look around and see how lust has polluted modern culture—pornography, human trafficking and other sexually-related businesses are prevalent across the globe. Media uses sex both to entertain and to sell everything from cars to shoes. Sex is everywhere we turn.

But misguided sexual desire can have far-reaching consequences. How does lust affect how you live? If you are ensnared in a sinful habit related to lust or have suffered sexual abuse, God can heal you and give you a new life. Seek the help of a close friend or family member. Or try to find a caring church or ministry that can help you in your situation. There is help and hope available.                    ❖

**PRAYER**

*Holy One, I can't do this alone . . .*

**READ**

Tamar's story is told in 2 Samuel 13:1–34.

## TAMAR
### *THE LONG SHADOWS OF THE PAST*

*"What about me? Where could I get rid of my disgrace?"*     2 SAMUEL 13:13

Tamar voices our heart's deep concern when we are overcome with guilt and shame. Whether it is a result of our own doing, or, like Tamar, through no fault of our own, we desperately seek to somehow get rid of our disgrace. Those closest to us may dismiss or downplay our situation. Phrases like, "Everything will be fine" or "Try to forget it" don't console us. We do not find the strength within ourselves. Only God knows the depth of human shame, and only he can heal life's pain.

Sometimes we do not have a choice about what happens to us. But the choices we make concerning the disgraceful incidents in our lives are crucial to our overall well-being. We can choose to depend on God's power for healing. We don't know if Tamar turned to God in answer to her question. Perhaps she did and was able to relieve some of her guilt or perhaps she lived the rest of her life feeling disgraced. What about you? How will you choose to let your past influence your future? ✤

**PRAYER**

*Lord, let my past be a roadmap to you . . .*

**READ**

Tamar's tragedy is described in 2 Samuel 13:1 – 34.

## THE TEN LEPERS
### *THE THANKS GOD DESERVES*

*"Has no one returned to give praise to God except this foreigner?"*  LUKE 17:18

Familiarity breeds contempt, the old saying goes. Perhaps that adage is applicable here in the story of ten men who were healed of leprosy. Luke tells us that this group begged Jesus to heal them, and he granted their request. Only one returned to thank him.

What about the other nine? One can speculate that they had heard it all before. They lived in a culture in which God was talked about openly. They knew it was just and right to give thanks to God for his blessings. They knew that God was the source of all healing. Yet somehow it didn't register when the reality of those words became apparent. Perhaps they were so caught up in their healing that they forgot to consider its source. By contrast, a Samaritan gave thanks to God. It is to him that Jesus says, "Your faith has made you well" (Luke 17:19), implying that he was healed spiritually as well as physically.

In Christian circles, it is easy to slip into a comfortable pattern of "God-talk." We can know all about evangelism, salvation and discipleship but ignore the God who stands behind everything. Does your spiritual life run on secondhand knowledge of God? Are you ignoring God's mighty works in your life? Today, pause to give him the thanks he deserves. ✤

**PRAYER**

*Lord, thank you . . .*

**READ**

The story of the ten lepers is found in Luke 17:11–19.

## THEOPHILUS
### *TALKING ABOUT GOD*

*That you may know the certainty of the things you have been taught.*     LUKE 1:4

What's in a name? Theophilus literally means "one who loves God." Luke wrote his Gospel to Theophilus, his friend and fellow believer of Greek descent, to describe the life of Jesus; he wrote the book of Acts to describe the life of the early church.

Apparently Theophilus's name also reflected his attitude and interests. He wanted to know about what God was doing in the world through the lives of other people.

What do you and your friends talk about when you are together? Discussing the weather, sports, our families and our work is more than enough to exhaust our time. But how often do you talk with your family and friends about God and his work in the world and in your life?

We need friends who love God and with whom we can talk about the Bible and our own spiritual interests. When we focus our conversation on God, we often find new insights and inspiration. What have you learned about God through intimate conversations with believers who are close to you?    ✤

**PRAYER**

*Heavenly Father, all of my relationships are before you . . .*

**READ**

Theophilus's story is told in Luke 1:1–4 and Acts 1:1.

## THOMAS
### *TIME TO STOP DOUBTING*

*Thomas said to him, "My Lord and my God!"*     JOHN 20:28

The disciples were chattering excitedly about their visit with the resurrected Christ. Thomas listened to their eager claims, but part of him was still unconvinced. He voiced his doubts. Because of that moment of honest questioning, he has been tagged with the unflattering nickname "Doubting Thomas." The label stuck. How unfortunate! Most of us probably would have responded in a similar way.

A week later, Thomas got his wish. As the men gathered in a locked room, Jesus suddenly materialized. The Savior looked at Thomas and said, "Stop doubting and believe." (John 20:27). Whatever uncertainty Thomas had gave way to immediate and total trust. "My Lord and my God!" (John 20:28) he exclaimed. By his response, it is apparent that Thomas wanted to believe. He was honestly searching for the truth. When Jesus revealed himself, Thomas's doubts dissolved.

It is normal for Christians to have temporary, occasional doubts. They can even be a good thing if they motivate us to seek a closer connection with God. It is only when we languish in unbelief that we displease the Lord.

If you are struggling with doubts today, ask God to give you a fresh glimpse of Jesus. When he does, stop doubting and believe!     ❖

**PRAYER**

*Lord, I confess that I doubt...*

**READ**

The story of Thomas is found in the Gospels. He is also mentioned in Acts 1:13.

## TIMOTHY
### *AN INHERITANCE OF FAITH*

*To Timothy my true son in the faith.*      1 TIMOTHY 1:2

Given the Scriptural evidence, it is not too difficult to trace Timothy's spiritual heritage (see 2 Timothy 1:5). His family lived in Lystra, a region of Galatia. The son of a devout Jewish mother, Timothy had been exposed to the Hebrew Scriptures since early childhood. His father was probably an unbelieving Greek, who doesn't seem to have been involved in his life.

When Paul visited Lystra on his first missionary journey and preached the good news that Jesus is the Messiah, Lois and Eunice — and possibly Timothy — put their faith in Christ. By the time Paul returned to Lystra on his second missionary journey, Timothy was mature enough to be invited to accompany Paul on his journey. Paul called Timothy his "true son in the faith" (1 Timothy 1:2). Even so, it is obvious that Lois and Eunice deserve at least some of the credit for Timothy's spiritual progress.

As parents we have great influence on the shaping of our children's spiritual destinies. Family prayer times, spontaneous conversations about God during life's everyday moments and reading our children Bible stories contribute to a spiritual foundation that can withstand the ups and downs of life.

What family habit or tradition can you begin this week that will help to root your child(ren) in the Christian faith?      ❖

**PRAYER**

*God, you have been our help …*

**READ**

Timothy appears in Acts 16, as Paul's frequent companion, and in several of Paul's letters, including two directly addressed to him.

## TIMOTHY
### *RISING ABOVE OUR WEAKNESSES*

*For the Spirit God gave us does not make us timid, but gives us power, love and self-discipline.*      2 TIMOTHY 1:7

The Scriptures make it seem that Timothy had a timid personality, or that he was sometimes plagued by self-doubt, though no one knows why. His ministry may have lacked assertiveness due to his mixed family background (his mother was Jewish, his father a Gentile). Perhaps Timothy suffered a lack of self-confidence because of his relatively young age. He may have been overawed by the confident, talented apostle Paul. Some have even speculated that Timothy's mission to the Corinthian church had not gone well, fueling his self-doubt.

Whatever the case, you'll notice that Paul never scolded Timothy for his timidity. He challenged him instead to concentrate on (1) using his gifts, (2) modeling his changed character and (3) fulfilling his God-given responsibilities.

Those who struggle with a sense of inadequacy would be wise to follow the same prescription: (1) Quit becoming despondent over your weaknesses. Instead, discover your spiritual gifts. Do you know what they are? Are you using your God-given abilities to serve Christ and others? (2) As a Christian, God is in the process of transforming you. Let others see the changes God is making in your life. (3) Remember that God has made you an ambassador of heaven. God wants to work in and through you.      ❖

**PRAYER**

*Lord, work through me ...*

**READ**

Timothy appears in Acts 16 and in several of Paul's letters.

## TITUS
### A DEDICATED WORKER

*The reason I left you in Crete was that you might put in order what was left unfinished and appoint elders in every town, as I directed you.*      TITUS 1:5

Some of the best and most capable people have a low profile. Not celebrities, not famous, not loud, they make their mark in quiet ways. Those people who know and rely on them could hardly live without them. Such was the case with Titus. For someone who received a major New Testament letter, we know remarkably little about Titus's background. All we know for sure is that he was Greek.

Titus made a profound impact on the early church. To this faithful and skilled man of God the apostle Paul entrusted great responsibilities, some that even Paul's favored Timothy could not handle. In fact, Titus was such a strong and dedicated Christian that Paul relied on him for many critical tasks.

Indeed, Paul took Titus as a prime example of a believing Gentile. When Timothy could not get the Corinthians to accept Paul, Paul sent Titus to "put in order what was left unfinished" on Crete (Titus 1:5). Titus's most challenging assignment was to oversee the immature Christians of Crete, an island where immorality ruled.

Titus, in other words, was a reliable servant of God. The early church took root and grew to a large extent because of Titus's influence.      ❖

**PRAYER**

*Lord, please show me those in need of my help ...*

**READ**

Titus's story is told in 2 Corinthians 2:13; 7:6–16; 8:6,16–24; 12:18; Galatians 2:1–5; 2 Timothy 4:10 and Titus 1–3.

## TROPHIMUS
### A CHEERFUL GIVER

*[Paul] was accompanied by ... Trophimus from the province of Asia.*     ACTS 20:4

Have you ever helped collect the offering in your church? Paul recruited Trophimus to help collect the church's offering. He didn't just have to carry a plate down the aisle, he was one of several men Paul designated to take it from their churches in Asia Minor (modern-day Turkey) across the Mediterranean Sea to Jerusalem.

Paul wanted the new churches he was starting in Asia to help the church in Jerusalem with its great financial needs. Trophimus was the representative from the church in Ephesus. Sending the men with the money gave the gift a personal touch and promoted unity among the believers from these diverse cultures. Trophimus was part of that human connection.

A plethora of natural disasters in recent years have left many churches in great need of financial assistance and physical repairs. You and your church could be a major encouragement to another church in need. It is more blessed to give than to receive. Find out what Trophimus learned when he presented the gift in Jerusalem. In addition to the blessing you will be to those in need, God may grant a blessing of joy and satisfaction to you.      ❖

**PRAYER**

*What can I offer, Lord, to bless your people ...*

**READ**

Trophimus's story is told in Acts 20:3−5; 21:29 and 2 Timothy 4:20.

## TYCHICUS
### *ALWAYS FINISHING THE JOB*

*Tychicus will tell you all the news about me. He is a dear brother, a faithful minister and fellow servant in the Lord.*        COLOSSIANS 4:7

Do you ever stay in the theater to read the credits that roll at the end of a movie or take time to read the acknowledgments of a book? The credits and acknowledgments point to a special person who tirelessly ran errands and provided service and support for the stars of the movie or the author of the book.

Tychicus provided that kind of help to Paul. He delivered at least two of the New Testament letters Paul wrote. He carried messages and represented Paul. While Paul had the gifts to preach and write, Tychicus exhibited the priceless quality of simply being a reliable helper. Paul could send him on any task, confident that he would complete the job.

A few people engage in public ministry, but everyone in such work depends on the dedication of reliable helpers. Success and recognition is the product of commitment, attention to detail, trustworthiness, honesty and perseverance.

Can people count on you? Are you a helper? When people think of you, does your reliability stand out?      ❖

**PRAYER**

*Lord, I want to honor you through ...*

**READ**

Tychicus's story is told in Colossians 4:7–9 and 2 Timothy 4:9–13. He is also mentioned in Acts 20:4; Ephesians 6:21–22 and Titus 3:12.

# day352

## URIAH
### *A PRINCIPLED MAN*

*Uriah said to David ... "As surely as you live, I will not do such a thing!"*

2 Samuel 11:11

On this night Uriah was a better man drunk than King David was sober. David had impregnated Uriah's wife, Bathsheba, while Uriah was away serving in the war. David brought him home to cover his adultery. If he could get him to sleep with his wife no one would suspect anything unusual.

But Uriah would not sleep with his wife even after David got him drunk. His thoughts were on the men he commanded on the battlefield. Uriah would not grant himself privileges his men could not also enjoy, even with the king's permission.

Uriah's strict adherence to his principles cost him his life. When King David purposely put him in harm's way, not even the mighty Uriah could single-handedly hold off the enemy forever. Rightly so, he is remembered as one of the great men of Israel (see 2 Samuel 23:24,39).

True leaders display great personal integrity and commitment to their cause. Leading others means leading by example. Leaders can't tell their followers what to do if they are not willing to operate by the same standards. They will not be respected. ❖

**PRAYER**

*Lord, make me consistent ...*

**READ**

Uriah's story is told in 2 Samuel 11:3–24.

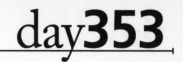
## UZZAH
### *STRUCK DOWN BY CARELESSNESS*

*The LORD's anger burned against Uzzah because of his irreverent act; therefore God struck him down, and he died there beside the ark of God.*        2 SAMUEL 6:7

Uzzah was struck dead by the Lord when he ignored God's longstanding command against touching the ark of the covenant. The ark had been housed in Uzzah's house for many years while David was seeking a permanent home for it. When the time came to move the ark, the Lord's commands for how to move it were ignored and it started to fall to the ground. Uzzah reached out to stop the fall of the ark and was immediately struck dead for touching the sacred box.

Perhaps housing the ark for so many years had reduced Uzzah's awe and respect for it. God's clear instructions were ignored; the people who were moving this sacred object treated it with little regard for its significance.

Likewise, becoming involved in the inner workings of a church or ministry can reduce our sense of awe and wonder about its services and events. Watching the human efforts required to operate a church can diminish our reliance on God's supernatural power.

We can keep a healthy view of the church by maintaining an active prayer life and studying God's Word. We can keep God's commands fresh in our minds, respect what is holy and focus not on human efforts but on God's supernatural powers within the church.                                                ✤

**PRAYER**

*Lord, keep my eyes on you ...*

**READ**

Uzzah's story is told in 2 Samuel 6:1–8 and 1 Chronicles 13:1–11.

# day354

## UZZIAH
### *A MOMENT OF FOOLISHNESS*

*After Uzziah became powerful, his pride led to his downfall. He was unfaithful to the LORD his God, and entered the temple of the LORD to burn incense on the altar of incense.*
2 CHRONICLES 26:16

It's interesting how a little bad can overshadow a lot of good. A bad score on just one hole can mar a great golf round. An otherwise fun vacation can be ruined by one bad experience. A great race can be lost by a slight misstep near the end. A life begun well can be tarnished by the failure to end well. Such was the case with King Uzziah (sometimes known as King Azariah).

Early in his reign, Uzziah sought the Lord. He enjoyed military success and gained fame for his innovative weaponry. He was an accomplished builder. The nation prospered for most of his 52-year reign.

But late in life, Uzziah became prideful. Forgetting that God was the source of all his success, Uzziah began to think he was above the law. One day he brashly entered the temple, brushed past the priests and attempted to burn incense before God. For this act of disobedience, God struck him with leprosy. For the rest of his life, Uzziah was disfigured and unclean, a visible testimony of his failure to remain faithful to God.

Uzziah reminds us of the sobering truth that a lifetime of good and wise living can be marred by a single moment of foolishness. Are you walking with God? Ask God for the grace to finish the race with humility and obedience. ❧

### PRAYER

*Giver of grace, I am grateful for your strength to ...*

### READ

The story of Uzziah is told in 2 Kings 15:1–7 and 2 Chronicles 26:1–23.

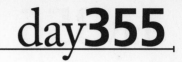

## VASHTI
### *A PART OF GOD'S PLAN*

*When the attendants delivered the king's command, Queen Vashti refused to come. Then the king became furious and burned with anger.* ESTHER 1:12

Vashti lost her position as queen of Persia when she refused King Xerxes' command to display her beauty at a party for the king's guests. Her clash with the king paved the way for Esther to become queen.

While Vashti's strength of character may earn our admiration, we also see God's sovereign hand at work in her situation, for Esther's resulting "promotion" enabled her to save her people, the Jews, from being massacred. God had prepared Esther "for such a time as this" (Esther 4:14).

Can you see God at work for good even when you suffer for doing what is right? Resist the temptation to feel sorry for yourself. God may be using your circumstances for his good purpose. Although you may not see the results immediately, you can be confident that God is at work for the best. ✤

**PRAYER**

*Work for good, Lord, in this situation . . .*

**READ**

Vashti's story is told in Esther 1:1 — 2:17.

## THE WISE MEN
### STAY AND FOLLOW

*On coming to the house, they saw the child with his mother Mary, and they bowed down and worshiped him ... And having been warned in a dream not to go back to Herod, they returned to their country by another route.*                              MATTHEW 2:11–12

We know little about the wise men who came to see the young Jesus. In fact, some of what we "know" comes from legend, not Scripture. Despite what some have said, we don't know their names. Though we assume there were three, the Bible never says how many came, only that they presented three gifts. And they came to see Jesus some time after he was born—probably when he was a toddler, rather than an infant.

Why did the magi—the wise men—come? We really don't know that either. They said they saw his star in the east and came to worship him (see Matthew 2:2). As soon as they found him and gave him their gifts, they went back home. What did they get out of this trip? Did they ever think about Jesus again?

Many people, like the magi, honor Jesus. A few also follow him. There is a difference between the magi and the disciples. The one pays his or her respects and returns home; the other stays, sits at Jesus' feet and learns. Ponder this question today: are you making occasional visits to fellowship with God, or do you take every opportunity available to be with him?                              ♣

**PRAYER**

*King of kings, I honor you ...*

**READ**

The story of the wise men can be found in Matthew 2:1–18.

## THE WITCH OF ENDOR
### *DABBLING WITH THE DEMONIC*

*Saul then said to his attendants, "Find me a woman who is a medium, so I may go and inquire of her." "There is one in Endor," they said.*      1 SAMUEL 28:7

King Saul, who had made a lifetime of foolish decisions, was about to make one of his worst. Afraid because a large Philistine army was poised to attack, he sought guidance from the Lord. He received no answer. When he ran out of patience, he consulted a medium for answers.

He found a woman in Endor willing to do the dirty work. This woman feared Saul but did not fear God. She knew that God had commanded the Jews to have nothing to do with mediums, divination, sorcery, spirits or witchcraft, but she practiced these evil arts anyway. After receiving assurances that she would not be harmed, she called up Samuel's spirit.

Samuel provided no consolation to the troubled king. He reminded Saul that God had turned away from him because of his sin. Worse still, Samuel revealed that Saul and his sons would die the next day. Indeed, Samuel's revelation came true (see 1 Samuel 31).

Most Christians know that dabbling in tarot cards, palmistry and other occult practices can seriously harm their spiritual lives. And, as Saul discovered, knowing the future is pointless if it is a future without God's guidance and blessing. What about you? Are you trifling with sin in a vain attempt to control your own destiny? Remember that dependence on God is the only hope we have for a secure future.      ♣

---

**PRAYER**

*Lord, root out any "harmless" activities in my life that are really harmful . . .*

---

**READ**

The witch of Endor's story is told in 1 Samuel 28:1–25.

## YOUNG JEWISH SLAVE GIRL
### *USING US AS WE ARE*

*Now bands of raiders from Aram had gone out and had taken captive a young girl from Israel, and she served Naaman's wife.*                    2 KINGS 5:2

Life can take unexpected and painful turns. One young woman in Israel found herself a prize of war. She became a slave, the property of Naaman's family. And yet the story that unfolds is contrary to what we might expect. Instead of indulging in self-pity, we find her pitying her master; instead of wishing evil upon those who had captured her, she hoped for their well-being. She wasn't crushed by her misfortune; she rose above it.

Naaman, this young slave's master, was a successful Syrian commander. He was also a leper. In Israel, a person with leprosy was shunned. Sufferers were forced to announce their uncleanness to anyone who came near.

In simple faith this young woman suggested to her mistress that Naaman ought to see Elisha, prophet of God in Samaria. She was sure Elisha would be able to bring about his healing. There must have been a note of conviction in her suggestion, because Naaman took her seriously. Eventually, he was healed by God.

Sometimes, all we can do is point people toward God. The faith of one young woman set in motion a chain of events through which God received glory. You can be alert this Christmas Eve to the same opportunities. God can accomplish miracles with our small actions.                                        ❖

**PRAYER**

*Do wonders through me, Lord . . .*

**READ**

The young Jewish slave girl is introduced in Naaman's story, found in 2 Kings 5:1–27.

# day359

## ZACCHAEUS
### GETTING GOD'S ATTENTION

*[Zacchaeus] wanted to see who Jesus was, but because he was short he could not see over the crowd.*                    Luke 19:3

Zacchaeus's approach to life involved compensating for his physical shortness by elevating himself in other ways. He was too short to be noticed, but as a rich tax collector he got plenty of attention. He came late to the parade and couldn't see over the crowd, so he climbed a tree. Zacchaeus wanted to see Jesus but suddenly found himself the object of observation.

As you pass through the world today, remember Zacchaeus in two ways. First, do you identify with his lack of being noticed? Do you sometimes wonder whether or not Jesus would have glanced your way if you had been in Zacchaeus's place? Remember that Jesus knew Zacchaeus's heart as well as he knew the man's name. Jesus knows you too and would never miss you in a crowd. Second, how many people will go unnoticed by you today? Make an extra effort to give special attention to as many people as you can—use people's names and look them in the eye; speak to people who don't expect it; show an interest in others' lives.

Since God showed his interest in us by sending his Son, why not celebrate Christmas by rereading Zacchaeus's story? You may experience some wonderful surprises when you make a specific effort to notice others.                    ✤

**PRAYER**

*Lord, I want to see you . . .*

**READ**

Zacchaeus's story is told in Luke 19:1–10.

## ZECHARIAH THE PRIEST
### *UNPREDICTABLE AND WONDERFUL*

*Zechariah ... belonged to the priestly division of Abijah; his wife Elizabeth was also a descendant of Aaron. Both of them were righteous in the sight of God, observing all the Lord's commands and decrees blamelessly.*                                   LUKE 1:5–6

Zechariah was an aged Jewish priest. He and his wife, Elizabeth, despite a lifetime of praying, were childless. One day Zechariah's priestly division was on duty at the temple, and he was selected to burn incense before God.

While praying at the altar, Zechariah was visited by the angel Gabriel, who announced a message of good news. The frightened priest learned that he and Elizabeth were going to become parents! Their child, who would be called John, would be a great man who would turn many in Israel back to God. Zechariah could not believe his ears—and because of this initial unbelief, he was struck dumb until John's birth.

The story of Zechariah reminds us of God's unpredictable and unusual ways. He often confounds conventional wisdom in accomplishing his plans. He chooses unlikely people. He disregards manmade customs and defies human reason. He overcomes staggering odds. His character is never inconsistent, but his boldness and knack for surprise often leave us marveling with delight.

Rejoice in the fact that your God is omnipotent. He can do anything! He is also good. Whatever dilemma we find ourselves in, we can be sure that God is in control and at work for his own glory and our own good.                    ❖

**PRAYER**

*Lord, you are worthy ...*

**READ**

The story of Zechariah is found in Luke 1.

## ZECHARIAH THE PROPHET
### *RELYING ON THE WORD OF GOD*

*Now Haggai the prophet and Zechariah the prophet, a descendant of Iddo, prophesied to the Jews in Judah and Jerusalem in the name of the God of Israel, who was over them.*

ᴇᴢʀᴀ 5:1

The best way to judge preaching is not by how eloquent or clever the words sound, but by whose words they are. Are they God's?

Zechariah (together with Haggai) prophesied during a time when the Jews of Jerusalem were trying to rebuild their city. Catcalls from the neighbors had slowed the people down, so Zechariah's message was clear and forceful: Keep building! It's what God wants! You can do it! Too determined to let a little opposition spoil the Jews' resolve to finish what God had called them to do, Zechariah encouraged and helped the people. It made a big difference. The people listened to the words and were stirred to take action.

Common sense and experience-based wisdom have their place, but there's no substitute for the Word of God. Put another way, sometimes we get discouraged unnecessarily. We hear bad news, or face a setback, or think that all is lost, and we want to give up. We want to quit. We feel hopeless.

With God, there is no such thing as hopelessness. God is still alive. His ways are going to prevail. Nothing is impossible with God. ❖

**PRAYER**

*Lord, I'm grateful that you are real . . .*

**READ**

Zechariah's story is told in Ezra 5–6 and in the Old Testament book bearing his name.

## ZEPHANIAH
### *GOD'S LOVING YOKE*

*Seek the LORD, all you humble of the land, you who do what he commands. Seek righteousness, seek humility; perhaps you will be sheltered on the day of the LORD's anger.*

ZEPHANIAH 2:3

Zephaniah prophesied in Judah during the reign of King Josiah, making him a contemporary of Jeremiah, Nahum and perhaps Habakkuk. He influenced King Josiah and his efforts to turn the nation back to God. Zephaniah's message was simple and clear: God will judge and punish the people for their disobedience, but he will also show mercy to all who are faithful to him.

That same prophetic message is still true today. We will be judged and punished for our disobedience to God. The punishment God brings isn't vengeful. It humbles us and purifies our desires. Through the disciplining process of judgment, we learn how much we were created to live in relationship with God and how foolish we are to ignore him.

Many Christians ride a spiritual roller coaster, drifting away from God and returning to worship and serve him when crises arise. But do you consider that the difficulties of our lives are often God's way of getting our attention and disciplining us? He still loves us and wants to purify us so that we can serve him. Decide today to submit to God's loving yoke of discipline.                    ❖

### PRAYER

*Lord, I submit to . . .*

### READ

Zephaniah's story is told in the Old Testament book bearing his name.

## ZERUBBABEL
### *HOW TO ACCOMPLISH GREAT THINGS*

*He said to me, "This is the word of the LORD to Zerubbabel: 'Not by might nor by power, but by my Spirit,' says the LORD Almighty."* ZECHARIAH 4:6

When the Persians conquered the Babylonians in 539 BC, the Persian king Cyrus gave the Jews exiled in Babylon permission to return to their homeland and rebuild their temple. Zerubbabel, a descendant of King David, was the man chosen to lead these exiles back to the promised land.

Under Zerubbabel's leadership, the people arrived in Judah and began the task. They built homes and laid a foundation for the temple. However, the rebuilding effort ground to a halt when Zerubbabel and his workers faced stern opposition from without, discouraging criticism from within, and distraction in constructing their own comforts. For 16 years, the Jews looked daily at that desolate foundation, a constant reminder of their failure to finish the task assigned by God. It took the prophets Haggai and Zechariah to come along and challenge the people to complete the task. In a mere four years, the project was complete.

Why did Zerubbabel fail? Perhaps because he was easily discouraged. Or maybe because he was relying on his own strength and ability to get the job done. Rather than trusting in our own power, we need to remember the word of the prophet Zechariah to Zerubbabel: It is by the Spirit of the Living God that we accomplish big and lasting things. Whatever you are doing today, draw on God's power. ❖

**PRAYER**

*Spirit of the Living God, fall afresh on me ...*

**READ**

The story of Zerubbabel is found in Ezra 2:2—5:2. See also Haggai 1–2 and Zechariah 4:6–10.

## ZIBA
### *SELFISH MOTIVES*

*"Ziba my servant betrayed me."*                    2 SAMUEL 19:26

Ziba's job was to take care of Saul's crippled grandson, Mephibosheth. But Ziba spent most of his time taking care of himself. He turned his responsibility to feed Mephibosheth into a meal ticket for himself.

When Absalom's rebellion against David was underway, Ziba put himself in the king's path and misrepresented the intentions of Mephibosheth in order to gain David's gratitude. He hoped that his revelations would lead to a privileged position once David was restored. He transformed from protector to predator.

Obviously Ziba failed to adhere to a respectable work ethic. But what about you? What are your motives in the professional and personal work you do? Are you dedicated to serving your own interests or the interests of others? Remember the story of Ziba. Time eventually exposed Ziba and his true motives. It will do the same to you, in this life or the next. Examine yourself to see whose best interest you have in mind.                    ✤

**PRAYER**

*Examine my heart, O God . . .*

**READ**

Ziba's story is told in 2 Samuel 9:1–13; 16:1–4; 19:17,24–30.

## ZIPPORAH
### *SEARCHING OUT UNCONFESSED SIN*

*"Surely you are a bridegroom of blood to me," [Zipporah] said.*      EXODUS 4:25

In the days after he had killed the Egyptian, Moses lived in the desert tending flocks. Here he married Zipporah and fathered two sons. Sometime later, God told Moses to return to Egypt to lead the Hebrews out of slavery.

On the journey there, Moses was reminded of some unfinished business. He had forgotten or ignored God's command to circumcise his second son. Now God was angry with him, and his life was in danger. Zipporah quickly performed the operation on her son. After she finished, the danger to Moses passed.

Zipporah's act was one of genuine repentance. Not only did she and Moses say they were sorry for disobeying the Lord, they corrected their mistake immediately. God's response was to restore Moses to safety.

When we suffer physically or emotionally we should examine our lives to see if we are harboring any deliberate sin. God could be using the ailment to focus our attention on our unconfessed thoughts and deeds. If our suffering results from disobeying God's commands, James 5:14–16 promises we can find the same quick relief by decisive confession and obedience in faith. If your well-being has been affected by sin, take to heart Zipporah's cure. Don't leave your sin unconfessed and unrepented.     ❖

**PRAYER**

*Lord, cure me of . . .*

**READ**

Zipporah's story is told in Exodus 2:21–22; 4:18–26; 18:1–6.

# SCRIPTURE INDEX

| SCRIPTURE | DATE | TITLE |
|---|---|---|
| Genesis 3:6 | April 20 | Eve: Following Dangerous Desires |
| Genesis 3:13 | April 21 | Eve: Passing the Buck |
| Genesis 3:10,15 | January 18 | Adam: Failure, Frustration and Hope |
| Genesis 4:1–14 | January 4 | Abel: Speaking Without Words |
| Genesis 4:4 | January 3 | Abel: Give Your Best |
| Genesis 4:9,13 | March 4 | Cain: Full Pardon Is Available |
| Genesis 4:24 | August 19 | Lamech: The Rapid Growth of Sin |
| Genesis 5:24 | April 10 | Enoch: Long-Term Faithfulness |
| Genesis 5:27 | September 10 | Methuselah: Living Life to the Fullest |
| Genesis 6:9 | October 1 | Noah: A Righteous Reputation |
| Genesis 6:22 | October 2 | Noah: Doing What God Commands |
| Genesis 13:12 | August 22 | Lot: High Plains Drifter |
| Genesis 14:18–19 | September 7 | Melchizedek: King of Righteousness |
| Genesis 16:9 | May 10 | Hagar: Running Away From Problems |
| Genesis 17:17 | November 13 | Sarah: Waiting for the Promise |
| Genesis 17:19 | June 2 | Isaac: The Importance of a Name |
| Genesis 18:14 | November 14 | Sarah: Is Anything Too Hard for Him? |
| Genesis 19:26 | August 23 | Lot's Wife: Don't Look Back |
| Genesis 21:9 | June 7 | Ishmael: Discovering God's Faithfulness |
| Genesis 22:5 | January 15 | Abraham: Taking God at His Word |
| Genesis 25:1 | August 15 | Keturah: Smoothing Over a Rough Situation |
| Genesis 25:28 | October 29 | Rebekah: Family Favorites |
| Genesis 26:22 | June 3 | Isaac: Keeping the Peace |
| Genesis 27:13 | October 30 | Rebekah: Deception's Price Tag |
| Genesis 27:41 | April 14 | Esau: Redirecting Anger |
| Genesis 28:15 | June 9 | Jacob: Uniquely Blessed |
| Genesis 29:17 | October 26 | Rachel: Beauty Secret |
| Genesis 30:1 | October 27 | Rachel: The Trap of Envy |
| Genesis 30:20 | August 21 | Leah: Prisoner of Insecurity |
| Genesis 30:21 | March 23 | Dinah: Shamed and Forgotten |
| Genesis 30:27 | August 18 | Laban: Riding a Coattail of Blessings |
| Genesis 32:28 | June 10 | Jacob: Clinging to God |
| Genesis 35:18 | February 25 | Benjamin: A Family Man |
| Genesis 37:8 | July 28 | Joseph: Holding Your Tongue |
| Genesis 39:5 | October 23 | Potiphar: Recognizing the True Source of Our Blessing |
| Genesis 39:9 | July 29 | Joseph: No Excuses for Sin |
| Genesis 39:10 | October 24 | Potiphar's Wife: Satisfying Selfish Desires |
| Genesis 42:37; 49:4 | November 1 | Reuben: Turbulent Character |
| Genesis 44:34 | August 9 | Judah: The Difference God Has Made |
| Genesis 50:20 | July 30 | Joseph: The Sovereign Hand of God |
| Exodus 1:17 | November 21 | Shiphrah and Puah: Fearing God More Than Men |
| Exodus 2:2 | July 14 | Jochebed: Entrusting Children to God's Care |
| Exodus 4:25 | December 31 | Zipporah: Searching Out Unconfessed Sin |

| SCRIPTURE | DATE | TITLE |
|---|---|---|
| Exodus 4:10 | September 18 | Moses: No Excuse Will Suffice |
| Exodus 7:2 | January 2 | Aaron: A Team Player |
| Exodus 18:12 | July 4 | Jethro: Watching the Evidence |
| Exodus 18:24 | July 5 | Jethro: Prescription for Spiritual Health |
| Exodus 20:3 | August 8 | Jotham: Leaving the Job Unfinished |
| Exodus 31:2–5 | February 27 | Bezalel: God's Craftsman |
| Exodus 32:24 | January 1 | Aaron: A Crowd Pleaser |
| Exodus 35:34 | February 27 | Bezalel: God's Craftsman |
| Exodus 38:21 | June 8 | Ithamar: Attention to Small Details |
| Leviticus 10:1 | September 23 | Nadab and Abihu: Doing What We Know |
| Numbers 10:31 | May 28 | Hobab: A Trustworthy Guide |
| Numbers 12:1–2 | September 14 | Miriam: Wanting Back in the Spotlight |
| Numbers 13:30; 14:24 | March 5 | Caleb: Boundless Faith |
| Numbers 16:1–2 | August 17 | Korah: Cultivating Bitterness |
| Numbers 20:12 | September 19 | Moses: A Moment to Regret |
| Numbers 20:23–26 | March 28 | Eleazar: The Value of Godly Role Models |
| Numbers 23:18–24 | February 12 | Balaam: Prophet for Hire |
| Numbers 25:13 | October 19 | Phinehas: A Necessary Zeal |
| Numbers 27:22–23 | August 3 | Joshua: Training a Leader |
| Joshua 1:3,5,8–9 | August 4 | Joshua: Being Strong and Courageous |
| Joshua 6:18; 7:25 | January 17 | Achan: The Cost of Selfishness |
| Joshua 9:14 | August 5 | Joshua: Forgetting to Ask God |
| Joshua 14:11 | March 6 | Caleb: Ready and Hopeful |
| Judges 3:15 | March 27 | Ehud: Faith and Preparation |
| Judges 4:8 | February 14 | Barak: Reluctant Warrior |
| Judges 4:9,17 | June 11 | Jael: Ready to Obey |
| Judges 5:31 | March 19 | Deborah: A Song for God's People |
| Judges 6:12 | May 4 | Gideon: Preparing for God's Work |
| Judges 6:14 | May 5 | Gideon: God's Strength, Not Our Weakness |
| Judges 6:36–37 | May 6 | Gideon: Waiting for Another Sign |
| Judges 9:5 | January 9 | Abimelek: Pray for the Day |
| Judges 11:12 | June 27 | Jephthah: The Way of Reconciliation |
| Judges 11:30 | June 28 | Jephthah: Promises That Shouldn't Be Made |
| Judges 13:20 | August 29 | Manoah: Awestruck by God's Goodness |
| Judges 16:4 | November 6 | Samson: Staying Too Close to Temptation |
| Judges 16:28 | November 7 | Samson: One Last Chance |
| Judges 16:16–17,20 | March 20 | Delilah: How to Lose Friends the Fast Way |
| Ruth 1:16 | November 3 | Ruth and Naomi: Introducing Others to God |
| Ruth 2:12 | February 28 | Boaz: Giver of Refuge |
| Ruth 3:5 | November 4 | Ruth and Naomi: Worthy of Trust |
| Ruth 3:18 | March 1 | Boaz: A Holy Reason for Hard Work |
| 1 Samuel 1:6 | October 12 | Peninnah: Protecting Ourselves from the Hurt |
| 1 Samuel 1:8 | April 8 | Elkanah: Reason to Obey |
| 1 Samuel 1:27–28 | May 14 | Hannah: On Loan From God |
| 1 Samuel 2:12 | July 15 | Joel, Son of Samuel: Shaping Our Children's Character |

| SCRIPTURE | DATE | TITLE |
|---|---|---|
| 1 Samuel 2:26 | November 8 | Samuel: Raising Godly Children |
| 1 Samuel 3:14 | March 29 | Eli: Backing Down From Confrontation |
| 1 Samuel 4:18 | March 30 | Eli: The Source of Our Power |
| 1 Samuel 8:1 | November 9 | Samuel: Pointing Our Children to Christ |
| 1 Samuel 8:3 | July 15 | Joel, Son of Samuel: Shaping Our Children's Character |
| 1 Samuel 9:1 | August 16 | Kish: Passing on Family Values |
| 1 Samuel 9:2 | November 15 | Saul: Looks Can Be Deceiving |
| 1 Samuel 12:3–4 | November 10 | Samuel: Living a Life of Integrity |
| 1 Samuel 14:6 | July 25 | Jonathan: Defying the Odds |
| 1 Samuel 15:22 | November 16 | Saul: Submitting to God |
| 1 Samuel 16:1,7,11 | July 3 | Jesse: Challenging Our Expectations |
| 1 Samuel 17:26 | May 7 | Goliath: Fighting Against God |
| 1 Samuel 17:45 | March 15 | David: Training for Our Mission |
| 1 Samuel 18:3 | July 26 | Jonathan: The Covenant of Friendship |
| 1 Samuel 18:12 | November 17 | Saul: An Unrepentant Heart |
| 1 Samuel 20:42 | March 16 | David: A Cherished Friendship |
| 1 Samuel 21:1–3 | March 25 | Doeg: The (Temporary) Triumph of Evil |
| 1 Samuel 22:2 | March 18 | David's Mighty Warriors: All for One and One for All |
| 1 Samuel 25:10–11 | September 21 | Nabal: Single-Minded Selfishness |
| 1 Samuel 25:24 | January 6 | Abigail: Stepping Into the Line of Fire |
| 1 Samuel 26 | January 12 | Abner: Learning From Past Mistakes |
| 1 Samuel 28:7 | December 23 | The Witch of Endor: Dabbling With the Demonic |
| 1 Samuel 30:4 | January 7 | Abigail: Expecting a Rescue |
| 1 Samuel 30:6 | March 18 | David's Mighty Warriors: All for One and One for All |
| 2 Samuel 3:16 | January 13 | Abner: The Need for Decisiveness |
| 2 Samuel 4:1 | June 6 | Ish-Bosheth: An Unlikely King |
| 2 Samuel 6:7 | December 19 | Uzzah: Struck Down by Carelessness |
| 2 Samuel 6:16 | September 13 | Michal: Consumed by Jealousy |
| 2 Samuel 9:8 | September 8 | Mephibosheth: Marveling at Grace |
| 2 Samuel 11:4 | February 21 | Bathsheba: God Sees It All |
| 2 Samuel 11:11 | December 18 | Uriah: A Principled Man |
| 2 Samuel 11:13 | March 17 | David: One Sin Leads to Another |
| 2 Samuel 12:1,5,7 | September 25 | Nathan: Confronting Sin |
| 2 Samuel 13:3 | July 22 | Jonadab: Deadly Advice |
| 2 Samuel 13:12 | December 8 | Tamar: Victim of Lust |
| 2 Samuel 13:13 | January 31 | Amnon: A Chain Reaction of Sin |
| 2 Samuel 13:13 | December 9 | Tamar: The Long Shadows of the Past |
| 2 Samuel 15:4 | January 16 | Absalom: Fallen Youth |
| 2 Samuel 15:31 | January 28 | Ahithophel: Good Advice and Godly Advice |
| 2 Samuel 19:13 | January 29 | Amasa: A Rebel Is Restored |
| 2 Samuel 19:26 | December 30 | Ziba: Selfish Motives |
| 2 Samuel 19:30 | September 9 | Mephibosheth: A Reliable Master |
| 2 Samuel 20:1 | November 20 | Sheba: Practicing Prejudice |
| 2 Samuel 21:17 | January 11 | Abishai: Loyal to a Fault |
| 2 Samuel 22:2; 23:20 | February 24 | Benaiah: A Trustworthy Follower |
| 2 Samuel 23 | March 18 | David's Mighty Warriors: All for One and One for All |

| SCRIPTURE | DATE | TITLE |
|---|---|---|
| 2 Samuel 23:39 | December 18 | Uriah: A Principled Man |
| 1 Kings 1:4 | January 10 | Abishag: We Matter to God |
| 1 Kings 1:5 | January 19 | Adonijah: Ambition Without Wisdom |
| 1 Kings 1:15 | February 22 | Bathsheba: A Promise Remembered |
| 1 Kings 2:5 | July 7 | Joab: Failing to Meet His Potential |
| 1 Kings 2:7 | February 20 | Barzillai: A Friend Indeed |
| 1 Kings 2:26 | January 5 | Abiathar: The Gift of Mercy |
| 1 Kings 3:9,12–13 | November 27 | Solomon: A Wise and Discerning Heart |
| 1 Kings 5:1 | May 26 | Hiram, King of Tyre: Making Friendships That Count |
| 1 Kings 11:4 | November 28 | Solomon: Close Encounters of the Wrong Kind |
| 1 Kings 12:8,10–11 | October 31 | Rehoboam: Not-So-Wonderful Counselors |
| 1 Kings 14:2 | January 27 | Ahijah: Small Acts of Faithfulness |
| 1 Kings 14:7 | July 1 | Jeroboam: Sin's Consequences Guaranteed |
| 1 Kings 15:3 | January 8 | Abijah: Half-Hearted Devotion |
| 1 Kings 18:17 | January 21 | Ahab: The Blame Game |
| 1 Kings 18:36 | April 1 | Elijah: Knowing God Above All |
| 1 Kings 19:3 | April 2 | Elijah: The Anxious Prophet |
| 1 Kings 21:3 | September 22 | Naboth: Bringing Injustice to Light |
| 1 Kings 21:4 | January 22 | Ahab: The Pouting King |
| 1 Kings 21:25 | July 6 | Jezebel: A Life of Treachery |
| 1 Kings 22:8,14 | September 12 | Micaiah: Facing Unpleasant Facts |
| 1 Kings 22:53 | January 25 | Ahaziah, King of Israel: A Legacy of Sin |
| 2 Kings 2:9 | April 4 | Elisha: A Double Portion of Service |
| 2 Kings 3:2,11 | July 27 | Joram, King of Israel: Presuming on God's Patience |
| 2 Kings 5:2 | December 24 | Young Jewish Slave Girl: Using Us as We Are |
| 2 Kings 5:10 | September 20 | Naaman: The Barrier of Pride |
| 2 Kings 5:20 | May 2 | Gehazi: Deception's Reward |
| 2 Kings 7:2 | April 5 | Elisha: Faith in a Tight Spot |
| 2 Kings 8:13 | May 16 | Hazael: Deceiving Ourselves |
| 2 Kings 10:16 | June 25 | Jehu: Settling for Mediocrity |
| 2 Kings 10:31 | June 26 | Jehu: A Lack of Heartfelt Obedience |
| 2 Kings 11:1 | February 11 | Athaliah: Killer Queen |
| 2 Kings 14:24–25 | July 2 | Jeroboam II: Sharing the Wealth |
| 2 Kings 15:35 | August 8 | Jotham: Leaving the Job Unfinished |
| 2 Kings 20:3 | May 23 | Hezekiah: The Courage to Resist Sin |
| 2 Kings 20:19 | May 24 | Hezekiah: No Regard for the Future |
| 2 Kings 22:8 | May 25 | Hilkiah: Experiencing Revival |
| 2 Kings 22:10 | November 19 | Shaphan: Taking a Risk for the Truth |
| 1 Chronicles 16:37 | February 10 | Asaph: A Man of Worship |
| 1 Chronicles 16:41 | June 17 | Jeduthun: Minister of Thanksgiving |
| 1 Chronicles 19:2 | May 15 | Hanun: Defending a Mistake |
| 1 Chronicles 21:9–10 | April 26 | Gad: Telling the Truth When It Hurts |
| 1 Chronicles 27:33 | May 31 | Hushai: Loyal in All Circumstances |
| 2 Chronicles 2:13 | May 27 | Hiram: Pursuing Excellence |
| 2 Chronicles 14:11; 15:16 | February 8 | Asa: Taking a Tough Stand |
| 2 Chronicles 16:10 | February 9 | Asa: Love Grown Cold |
| 2 Chronicles 18:31 | June 22 | Jehoshaphat: Turning Back to God |

| SCRIPTURE | DATE | TITLE |
|---|---|---|
| 2 Chronicles 20:35 | June 23 | Jehoshaphat: Faithfulness in the Little Things |
| 2 Chronicles 21:13,18–19 | June 21 | Jehoram of Judah: Miserable Monarch |
| 2 Chronicles 22:3 | June 21 | Jehoram of Judah: Miserable Monarch |
| 2 Chronicles 22:3 | January 26 | Ahaziah, King of Judah: Mother Didn't Know Best |
| 2 Chronicles 22:11 | June 24 | Jehosheba: Resisting Evil in Small Ways |
| 2 Chronicles 24:2 | July 9 | Joash: The Tragedy of Borrowed Faith |
| 2 Chronicles 24:16 | June 19 | Jehoiada: A Wise Mentor |
| 2 Chronicles 25:2 | January 30 | Amaziah: Halfhearted Obedience |
| 2 Chronicles 26:16 | December 20 | Uzziah: A Moment of Foolishness |
| 2 Chronicles 28:22 | January 24 | Ahaz: The Root of Spiritual Illness |
| 2 Chronicles 33:13 | August 28 | Manasseh: Changing the Hardest Heart |
| 2 Chronicles 34:3 | August 6 | Josiah: Tearing Down the Idols |
| 2 Chronicles 34:19 | August 7 | Josiah: A Blueprint for Action |
| 2 Chronicles 34:22 | May 30 | Huldah: Preparing for the Right Moment |
| 2 Chronicles 36:5 | June 20 | Jehoiakim: Royal Rebel Against God |
| Ezra 5:1 | December 27 | Zechariah the Prophet: Relying on the Word of God |
| Ezra 7:10 | April 23 | Ezra: Growing in God's Word |
| Nehemiah 1:4–11; 2:4; 4:4–5,9; 6:9; 12 | September 28 | Nehemiah: A Life of Prayer |
| Nehemiah 2:10 | November 11 | Sanballat: Protecting His Turf |
| Nehemiah 4:9 | September 29 | Nehemiah: Taking the Wisest Course of Action |
| Nehemiah 6:3 | May 3 | Geshem: An Unholy Alliance |
| Esther 1:12 | December 21 | Vashti: A Part of God's Plan |
| Esther 4:11 | January 23 | Ahasuerus: The Center of His Universe |
| Esther 4:14 | April 15 | Esther: Not Just a Coincidence |
| Esther 4:14 | December 21 | Vashti: A Part of God's Plan |
| Esther 4:16 | April 16 | Esther: Faith and True Security |
| Esther 3:5 | May 12 | Haman: Pride and Destruction |
| Esther 10:3 | September 15 | Mordecai: Working for the Good of His People |
| Job 2:6 | July 10 | Job: God Is in Control |
| Job 2:9 | July 13 | Job's Wife: Missing the Point |
| Job 2:10 | July 11 | Job: What Hard Times Can Teach Us |
| Job 2:11 | April 3 | Eliphaz, Bildad and Zophar: Friendly Advice Worth Forgetting |
| Job 16:2 | July 12 | Job: Being There |
| Psalm 46:10 | September 2 | Mary, Mother of Jesus: Reflecting on God's Kindness |
| Psalm 52:1 | March 25 | Doeg: The (Temporary) Triumph of Evil |
| Psalm 73:25 | October 27 | Rachel: The Trap of Envy |
| Proverbs 26:6,17 | January 6 | Abigail: Stepping Into the Line of Fire |
| Proverbs 27:2 | July 28 | Joseph: Holding Your Tongue |
| Ecclesiastes 12:13 | November 29 | Solomon: Happiness Is Knowing God |
| Isaiah 6:1 | June 4 | Isaiah: A Life-Changing Event |
| Isaiah 6:8 | June 5 | Isaiah: Planting the Seeds |
| Isaiah 53 | April 17 | The Ethiopian Eunuch: A Responsive Heart |
| Jeremiah 1:8 | June 29 | Jeremiah: The Prophet Who Endured |

| SCRIPTURE | DATE | TITLE |
|---|---|---|
| Jeremiah 8:21 | June 30 | Jeremiah: Sharing in the Suffering |
| Jeremiah 22:13–19 | June 20 | Jehoiakim: Royal Rebel Against God |
| Jeremiah 22:24,30 | June 18 | Jehoiachin: Going With the Flow |
| Jeremiah 26:20–23 | June 20 | Jehoiakim: Royal Rebel Against God |
| Jeremiah 28:15 | May 13 | Hananiah: Sweet-Sounding Lies |
| Jeremiah 36:4; 45:5 | February 19 | Baruch: Faithful Scribe |
| Jeremiah 40:6 | May 1 | Gedaliah: Resting in a False Security |
| Ezekiel 3:11 | April 22 | Ezekiel: Our Responsibility to Others |
| Daniel 1:8–15 | March 13 | Daniel: Fit for God's Service |
| Daniel 3:18 | November 18 | Shadrach, Meshach and Abednego: Refusing to Bow Down |
| Daniel 4:37 | September 27 | Nebuchadnezzar: Humbled by God |
| Daniel 5:22 | February 23 | Belshazzar: Weighed and Found Wanting |
| Daniel 6:23 | March 14 | Daniel: Trusting in God's Goodness |
| Hosea 1:3 | May 8 | Gomer: Love Without Conditions |
| Hosea 2:20 | May 29 | Hosea: Extraordinary Obedience |
| Obadiah 4 | October 4 | Obadiah: The Proud Brought Low |
| Jonah 1:3 | July 23 | Jonah: God's Patience With His Children |
| Jonah 4:1–2 | July 24 | Jonah: Desiring Mercy |
| Micah 3:8; 6:8; 7:7,18–20 | September 11 | Micah: Strong Faith for Tough Times |
| Nahum 1:7 | September 24 | Nahum: Messenger of Doom |
| Habakkuk 2:4 | May 9 | Habakkuk: The Timetable of Heaven |
| Zephaniah 2:3 | December 28 | Zephaniah: God's Loving Yoke |
| Haggai 1:4 | May 11 | The One-Year Prophet |
| Zechariah 4:6 | December 29 | Zerubbabel: How to Accomplish Great Things |
| Matthew 1:19 | July 31 | Joseph, Mary's Husband: |
| Matthew 1:24 | August 1 | Joseph, Mary's Husband: |
| Matthew 2:2,11–12 | December 22 | The Wise Men: Stay and Follow |
| Matthew 2:3 | May 21 | Herod the Great: The Disease of Self-Centeredness |
| Matthew 5:11–12 | November 30 | Sosthenes: Suffering Is Not Wasted |
| Matthew 9:10 | September 4 | Matthew: Seeing Jesus as He Really Is |
| Matthew 10:2–3 | September 5 | Matthew: Attention to Detail |
| Matthew 11:2–3 | July 19 | John the Baptist: Honest Doubter |
| Matthew 11:11 | July 18 | John the Baptist: Pointing Others to Jesus |
| Matthew 17 | April 1 | Elijah: Knowing God Above All |
| Matthew 25:23 | November 23 | Silas: Aim for Faithfulness |
| Matthew 26:49 | August 11 | Judas: Phony Commitment |
| Matthew 27:17 | February 13 | Barabbas: The Unexpected Reprieve |
| Matthew 27:24 | October 21 | Pilate: The Price of Indecision |
| Mark 3:17 | July 17 | John the Apostle: Transformed by God |
| Mark 4:1–20 | March 21 | Demas: Loving the World |
| Mark 5:7 | April 27 | The Gadarene Demoniac: Released From Bondage |
| Mark 5:36 | June 12 | Jairus: Time to Trust |
| Mark 6:19 | May 22 | Herodias: Turning Toward the Darkness |
| Mark 6:20 | May 20 | Herod Antipas: Hearing Without Listening |

| SCRIPTURE | DATE | TITLE |
|---|---|---|
| Mark 7:26 | December 7 | Syrophoenician Woman: Putting Pride Aside |
| Mark 10:37 | June 14 | James, Brother of John: A Heavenly Perspective |
| Mark 10:43 | March 31 | Eliezer: The Honor of Service |
| Mark 10:47,51 | February 18 | Bartimaeus: A Demonstration of Gratitude |
| Mark 14:38 | April 19 | Eutychus: A Sound Sleeper |
| Mark 14:51–52 | July 21 | John Mark: Coming to Maturity |
| Mark 15:41 | November 5 | Salome: Following Wholeheartedly |
| Mark 15:43 | August 2 | Joseph of Arimathea: Acting in Spite of Fear |
| Luke 1:3 | August 25 | Luke: The Doctor Has Good News |
| Luke 1:4 | December 11 | Theophilus: Talking About God |
| Luke 1:5–6 | December 26 | Zechariah the Priest: Unpredictable and Wonderful |
| Luke 1:7 | April 6 | Elizabeth: God's Perfect Timing |
| Luke 1:38 | September 1 | Mary, Mother of Jesus: A Faithful Response |
| Luke 1:41 | April 7 | Elizabeth: Rejoicing With God's People |
| Luke 2:19 | September 2 | Mary, Mother of Jesus: Reflecting on God's Kindness |
| Luke 2:27–28 | November 24 | Simeon: Rejoicing in Fulfilled Promises |
| Luke 2:37 | February 4 | Anna: The Rewards of Waiting |
| Luke 4:27 | September 20 | Naaman: The Barrier of Pride |
| Luke 5:5 | October 13 | Peter: Obeying When It Doesn't Make Sense |
| Luke 7:37 | November 25 | Simon the Pharisee: Grudging Generosity |
| Luke 8:2 | August 31 | Mary Magdalene: Overflowing Gratitude |
| Luke 8:3 | December 5 | Susanna: Giving Thanks |
| Luke 8:45,48 | December 4 | Suffering Woman: The God Behind the Healing |
| Luke 10:1,17 | October 25 | Quartus: The Value of Encouragement |
| Luke 10:40 | August 30 | Martha: Caught Up in the Urgent |
| Luke 17:18–19 | December 10 | The Ten Lepers: The Thanks God Deserves |
| Luke 17:32 | August 23 | Lot's Wife: Don't Look Back |
| Luke 19:3 | December 25 | Zacchaeus: Getting God's Attention |
| Luke 22:32–34 | October 14 | Peter: Standing Against the Evil One |
| Luke 24:10 | July 8 | Joanna: Celebrity Servant |
| Luke 24:32 | March 8 | Cleopas: Keeping Your Eyes Open |
| John 1:36 | July 18 | John the Baptist: Pointing Others to Jesus |
| John 1:41; 6:9 | February 3 | Andrew: A Hopeful Disciple |
| John 1:47 | September 26 | Nathanael: Working in Unexpected Ways |
| John 3; 7:51; 19:39 | September 30 | Nicodemus: Growing in Boldness |
| John 3:30 | July 18 | John the Baptist: Pointing Others to Jesus |
| John 6:70 | August 11 | Judas: Phony Commitment |
| John 9:2,7,25 | August 27 | The Man Born Blind: A Reason for Rejoicing |

| SCRIPTURE | DATE | TITLE |
| --- | --- | --- |
| John 11:43 | August 20 | Lazarus: Obeying the Call |
| John 11:49–50 | March 2 | Caiaphas: Recipes for Success |
| John 12:3 | September 3 | Mary, Sister of Lazarus: Lavish Gifts |
| John 13:2 | August 10 | Judas: The Wrong Agenda |
| John 13:23 | July 16 | John the Apostle: Love With No S Attached |
| John 14:6 | January 4 | Abel: Speaking Without Words |
| John 14:6 | October 22 | Pilate: Searching for the Truth |
| John 17:12 | August 11 | Judas: Phony Commitment |
| John 18:38 | October 22 | Pilate: Searching for the Truth |
| John 19:26 | July 16 | John the Apostle: Love With No Strings Attached |
| John 20:27–28 | December 12 | Thomas: Time to Stop Doubting |
| John 21:7,20 | July 16 | John the Apostle: Love With No Strings Attached |
| John 21:17 | October 15 | Peter: Feeding His Sheep |
| Acts 1:23 | February 17 | Barsabbas: Disappointment Is Not Doubt |
| Acts 1:26 | September 6 | Matthias: Laboring Out of the Public Eye |
| Acts 3; 4:13 | March 3 | Caiaphas: Confounding the Wise |
| Acts 5:3 | February 2 | Ananias of Jerusalem: God Is Not Divided |
| Acts 5:9 | November 12 | Sapphira: Taking Sin Lightly |
| Acts 5:39 | April 30 | Gamaliel: An Unlikely Advocate |
| Acts 6:3 | October 8 | Parmenas: A Matter of Serving |
| Acts 6:15; 7:55 | December 2 | Stephen: Shining for Christ |
| Acts 7:25 | September 16 | Moses: Running Ahead of God |
| Acts 7:51,60 | December 3 | Stephen: No Action Is Insignificant |
| Acts 8:18–19 | November 26 | Simon the Sorcerer: Gifts for Hire |
| Acts 8:27–28 | April 17 | The Ethiopian Eunuch: A Responsive Heart |
| Acts 8:29–30,39 | October 17 | Philip: Chance Encounter? |
| Acts 9:10 | February 1 | Ananias of Damascus: Obedience Overcomes Fear |
| Acts 9:27 | February 15 | Barnabas: The Encourager |
| Acts 9:36 | March 26 | Dorcas: Devoted to Good Works |
| Acts 10:2 | March 9 | Cornelius: The Quiet Revolution |
| Acts 10:45 | March 10 | Cornelius: God's New Community |
| Acts 11:19–21 | August 24 | Lucius: Obscure Obedience |
| Acts 12:2 | June 15 | James, Brother of John: Suffering and Endurance |
| Acts 12:14 | November 2 | Rhoda: Expecting the Unexpected |
| Acts 12:23 | May 17 | Herod Agrippa I: Giving Credit Where It Is Due |
| Acts 13:1 | August 24 | Lucius: Obscure Obedience |
| Acts 13:10 | April 9 | Elymas: Blinded by Sin |
| Acts 15 | June 13 | James, Brother of Jesus: Faith Leads to Action |
| Acts 15:32 | November 22 | Silas: Gifted Encourager |
| Acts 15:37 | July 20 | John Mark: Overlooking Our Past |
| Acts 16:1 | April 18 | Eunice: Passing on Our Faith |
| Acts 16:15 | August 26 | Lydia: Household of Hospitality |
| Acts 17:6–7 | June 16 | Jason: A Costly Investment |

| SCRIPTURE | DATE | TITLE |
|---|---|---|
| Acts 17:34 | March 12 | Damaris: Responding to the Truth |
| Acts 18:7 | August 14 | Justus: An Open Heart, an Open Home |
| Acts 18:8 | March 11 | Crispus: Leading by Example |
| Acts 18:17 | November 30 | Sosthenes: Suffering Is Not Wasted |
| Acts 18:24 | February 5 | Apollos: Serving With Heart and Mind |
| Acts 18:26 | February 6 | Aquila and Priscilla: A Faithful Team |
| Acts 19:25–26 | March 22 | Demetrius: The Gods of Our Making |
| Acts 20:4 | April 29 | Gaius, Friend of Paul: Friendships Rooted in Faith |
| Acts 20:4 | December 16 | Trophimus: A Cheerful Giver |
| Acts 20:10 | April 19 | Eutychus: A Sound Sleeper |
| Acts 21:10 | January 20 | Agabus: Bad News and More Bad News |
| Acts 22:3 | February 2 | Ananias of Jerusalem: God Is Not Divided |
| Acts 22:28 | March 7 | Claudius Lysias: Every Deed an Act of Service |
| Acts 24:25 | April 24 | Felix: Avoiding the Good News |
| Acts 25:13 | May 18 | Herod Agrippa II: Bad Blood |
| Acts 25:20 | April 25 | Festus: The Hope Within Us |
| Acts 26:28 | May 19 | Herod Agrippa II: Missed Opportunity |
| Acts 26:31 | February 26 | Bernice: Hearing Problem |
| Acts 27:1 | August 13 | Julius: Influencing the Authorities |
| Romans 12:11 | October 9 | Paul: The Source of Spiritual Fervor |
| Romans 12:13 | April 28 | Gaius, Friend of John: The Ministry of Hospitality |
| Romans 16:2 | October 20 | Phoebe: A Proven Disciple |
| Romans 16:10,12 | October 10 | Paul: The Difference Praise Makes |
| Romans 16:13 | April 29 | Gaius, Friend of Paul: Friendships Rooted in Faith |
| Romans 16:20 | July 10 | Job: God Is in Control |
| Romans 16:23 | October 25 | Quartus: The Value of Encouragement |
| 1 Corinthians 1:1 | November 30 | Sosthenes: Suffering Is Not Wasted |
| 1 Corinthians 16:17–18 | December 1 | Stephanas: Refreshing Believers |
| 1 Corinthians 16:17–18 | October 10 | Paul: The Difference Praise Makes |
| 2 Corinthians 12:7 | October 11 | Paul: The Thorn in the Flesh |
| Galatians 1:19 | June 13 | James, Brother of Jesus: Faith Leads to Action |
| Galatians 2:13 | February 16 | Barnabas: Taking Criticism the Right Way |
| Ephesians 3:19 | October 9 | Paul: The Source of Spiritual Fervor |
| Ephesians 4:15 | November 19 | Shaphan: Taking a Risk for the Truth |
| Ephesians 4:26,32 | December 6 | Syntyche and Euodia: Restoring Unity in the Church |
| Ephesians 6 | July 10 | Job: God Is in Control |
| Ephesians 6:10–18 | May 7 | Goliath: Putting on God's Armor |
| Ephesians 6:21 | October 10 | Paul: The Difference Praise Makes |
| Philippians 2:12–13 | September 29 | Nehemiah: Taking the Wisest Course of Action |
| Philippians 2:29–30 | October 10 | Paul: The Difference Praise Makes |
| Philippians 2:30 | April 12 | Epaphroditus: Our Expectations and God's Plans |
| Philippians 4:2 | December 6 | Syntyche and Euodia: Restoring Unity in the Church |

| SCRIPTURE | DATE | TITLE |
|---|---|---|
| Philippians 4:18 | April 12 | Epaphroditus: Our Expectations and God's Plans |
| Colossians 1:7 | April 11 | Epaphras: Hometown Hero |
| Colossians 4:7 | December 17 | Tychicus: Always Finishing the Job |
| Colossians 4:9 | October 5 | Onesimus: Running Back to the Problem |
| Colossians 4:10 | February 7 | Aristarchus: Exceptional Commitment |
| Colossians 4:12 | April 11 | Epaphras: Hometown Hero |
| Colossians 4:12 | October 10 | Paul: The Difference Praise Makes |
| Colossians 4:15 | October 3 | Nympha: An Oasis of Ministry |
| 1 Timothy 1:2 | December 13 | Timothy: An Inheritance of Faith |
| 1 Timothy 1:18–20 | June 1 | Hymenaeus: Shipwrecked Faith |
| 1 Timothy 5:5 | February 4 | Anna: The Rewards of Waiting |
| 2 Timothy 1:5 | April 18 | Eunice: Passing on Our Faith |
| 2 Timothy 1:5 | December 13 | Timothy: An Inheritance of Faith |
| 2 Timothy 1:7 | December 14 | Timothy: Rising Above Our Weaknesses |
| 2 Timothy 1:16 | October 6 | Onesiphorus: A Source of Refreshment |
| 2 Timothy 2:17 | October 17 | Philetus: Sincerely Wrong |
| 2 Timothy 4:10 | March 21 | Demas: Loving the World |
| 2 Timothy 4:11 | July 21 | John Mark: Coming to Maturity |
| 2 Timothy 4:19 | October 7 | Onesiphorus: Going Out of the Way to Help |
| Titus 1:5 | December 15 | Titus: A Dedicated Worker |
| Philemon 21 | October 16 | Philemon: Growing in Christ |
| Hebrews 11 | November 8 | Samuel: Raising Godly Children |
| Hebrews 11:4 | January 4 | Abel: Speaking Without Words |
| Hebrews 11:5–6 | April 10 | Enoch: Long-Term Faithfulness |
| Hebrews 11:8 | January 14 | Abraham: The Risk of Faith |
| Hebrews 11:19 | January 15 | Abraham: Taking God at His Word |
| Hebrews 11:25 | September 17 | Moses: Living With an Eternal Perspective |
| Hebrews 11:31 | October 27 | Rahab: God Can Change Anyone |
| Hebrews 11:32 | February 14 | Barak: Reluctant Warrior |
| Hebrews 12:16 | April 13 | Esau: Ruined by an Impulse |
| Exodus 4:26 | December 31 | Zipporah: Searching Out Unconfessed Sin |
| James 5:14–16 | November 23 | Silas: Aim for Faithfulness |
| 1 Peter 5:13 | July 21 | John Mark: Coming to Maturity |
| 2 Peter 2:5 | October 1 | Noah: A Righteous Reputation |
| 2 Peter 2:15 | February 12 | Balaam: Prophet for Hire |
| 1 John 4:10 | July 16 | John the Apostle: Love With No Strings Attached |
| 3 John 5 | April 28 | Gaius, Friend of John: The Ministry of Hospitality |
| 3 John 9 | March 24 | Diotrephes: Authority Problems |
| Jude 1,3 | August 12 | Jude: Contender for the Faith |
| Revelation 2:4 | October 9 | Paul: The Source of Spiritual Fervor |
| Revelation 2:20–21 | July 6 | Jezebel: A Life of Treachery |

# TOPICAL INDEX

| SCRIPTURE | DATE |
| --- | --- |

Character . . . . . . . . . . . . . . . . . .Jan. 16; Feb. 12; Mar. 21; Apr. 9; May 5, 16, 26; June 17; July 11, 15; July 29; Sept. 2, 11; Oct. 11, 16, 23, 26; Nov. 1, 8–10, 15; Dec. 2, 14, 18

Choices (*see* Decisions)

Commitment . . . . . . . . . . . . . .Jan. 8; Feb. 2, 7; Mar. 12, 21; Apr. 23; May 21; June 26, 28; July 4, 9, 17, 26; Aug. 2, 8, 11, 18; Sept. 7; Oct. 9, 24; Nov. 1, 3, 5, 8, 30; Dec. 17–18

Community . . . . . . . . . . . . . . .Feb. 16; Mar. 9–10; July 4; Sept. 1; Nov. 20

Compassion . . . . . . . . . . . . . . .Mar. 9; Apr. 3–4; June 30; July 12; Aug. 15; Oct. 7, 12

Confession . . . . . . . . . . . . . . . .Jan. 12; Mar. 17; Apr. 21; June 4, 21; July 24; Sept. 20; Nov. 12; Dec. 31

Confrontation . . . . . . . . . . . . .Jan. 1–2, 6, 18, 21; Feb. 2, 23; Mar. 11, 24, 29; Apr. 9, 26; May 22; June 27; Sept. 22, 25; Oct. 5

Consequences. . . . . . . . . . . . . .Jan. 17, 22, 26; Feb. 2, 21; Mar. 29; Apr. 13, 21–22, 26, 30; May 19, 24, 30; June 1, 19, 21–22; July 1, 6–7, 22; Aug. 8, 17; Sept. 19, 21–25; Oct. 4, 30; Nov. 6, 12, 16–17, 28; Dec. 8

Counsel . . . . . . . . . . . . . . . . . .Jan. 6–7, 21, 26, 28; Feb. 16, 26; Mar. 28; Apr. 26; May 4, 30–31; June 19, 23; July 3, 5, 22; Aug. 5, 29; Sept. 25; Oct. 31; Dec. 23

Courage . . . . . . . . . . . . . . . . . .Feb. 8; Mar. 15; June 16; Sept. 30; Oct. 21; Dec. 14

Deception. . . . . . . . . . . . . . . . .Feb. 2; Mar. 20, 25; May 2, 13, 16; Sept. 12; Oct. 30; Nov. 12

Decisions . . . . . . . . . . . . . . . . .Jan. 13; Mar. 29; Apr. 13–14, 20; May 24; June 11, 14, 23–24; July 9; Aug. 4–5, 10; Oct. 21, 30; Nov. 22; Dec. 9, 23

Desires . . . . . . . . . . . . . . . . . . .Jan. 17, 23, 31; Mar. 21; Apr. 13, 20; May 21; July 7; Aug. 26; Sept. 16–17; Oct. 24; Dec. 8, 28, 30

Difficult circumstances (*See* Trials)

Discouragement. . . . . . . . . . . . .Jan. 18; Mar. 5–6; Apr. 2; Sept. 28; Dec. 14, 27, 29

Doubts . . . . . . . . . . . . . . . . . . .May 9; July 19; Sept. 18; Dec. 12, 26

Encouragement . . . . . . . . . . . . .Feb. 3, 9, 15; Mar. 5; July 20; Sept. 15; Oct. 7, 10, 25; Nov. 22; Dec. 1, 11, 25

Eternal life . . . . . . . . . . . . . . . .Jan. 4; May 19; Sept. 17, 30; Oct. 18

Evangelism. . . . . . . . . . . . . . . .Apr. 17, 24–25, 27; July 4, 18; Aug. 14; Sept. 4; Oct. 13, 18; Nov. 3, 28, 30; Dec. 24

Evil. . . . . . . . . . . . . . . . . . . . . .Jan. 4, 9, 25; Feb. 11; Mar. 15, 25; May 16, 22; June 24; July 6, 10; Sept. 24

Faith. . . . . . . . . . . . . . . . . . . . .Jan. 14–15, 22; Feb. 9, 23; Mar. 5, 11, 13–15, 22, 27; Apr. 2, 5–6, 10, 16, 18, 22; May 4, 7, 11, 19; June 1, 12–13; July 9, 13, 17, 19, 25, 30; Aug. 4, 12–13; Sept. 5, 30; Oct. 11, 16–17, 29; Nov. 5, 14, 18, 21, 30; Dec. 2, 23

Faithfulness . . . . . . . . . . . . . . .Jan. 27; Feb. 6; Mar. 13, 26, 31; Apr. 5–6, 10, 18; June 7, 16; July 11; July 21; Aug. 13, 24; Sept. 1, 6, 9, 14; Oct. 20, 23; Nov. 5, 10, 23; Dec. 3, 15, 17

Family, dysfunctional. . . . . . . .Jan. 4, 25, 31; Feb. 11; Mar. 23, 29; Apr. 14; May 18; June 18; Aug. 15, 21; Sept. 13; Oct. 12, 27, 29–30

Family, godly . . . . . . . . . . . . . . Feb. 25; Apr. 18; May 14, 28; Aug. 16; Nov. 3–4; Dec. 13

Fear . . . . . . . . . . . . . . . . . . . . . .Feb. 1; June 12; July 23; Aug. 2, 4; Dec. 14

Forgiveness. . . . . . . . . . . . . . . . .Feb. 13, 21; Mar. 4; May 15; June 4; July 1; Aug. 28; Sept. 19; Oct. 5, 14; Dec. 6

Friendship . . . . . . . . . . . . . . . .Feb. 20; Mar. 16, 20; Apr. 3; May 27; July 26; Sept. 4; Oct. 6; Nov. 18, 28; Dec. 11

Generosity . . . . . . . . . . . . . . . .Feb. 28; Apr. 12; July 2; Sept. 3, 8; Oct. 3; Nov. 25; Dec. 5, 16

God's gifts . . . . . . . . . . . . . . .Jan. 20; Feb. 27; Apr. 4; June 6, 25; Sept. 5, 8, 10; Nov. 22–23; Dec. 14

God's judgment . . . . . . . . . . . .Jan. 9; Feb. 23; June 18; July 24; Sept. 19, 22–25; Oct. 1–2, 4, 19; Dec. 28

God's love. . . . . . . . . . . . . . . .Jan. 10; Mar. 16; May 8, 29; June 29; July 16, 24; Aug. 21; Nov. 7; Dec. 4, 25

God's mercy. . . . . . . . . . . . . . .Jan. 5, 29; Feb. 18, 28; Mar. 14; Apr. 26; May 8; June 18; July 23–24; Oct. 16

God's power. . . . . . . . . . . . . . .Mar. 3, 19; Apr. 5, 9; May 5; June 2, 26; July 10; Sept. 18; Oct. 11, 29; Nov. 26; Dec. 4, 9, 19, 29

God's presence . . . . . . . . . . . .Mar. 8; June 25; July 27; Aug. 30

God's promises. . . . . . . . . . . . .Jan. 15, 18; Apr. 5; May 13; June 2, 5, 7; July 10; Aug. 4; Nov. 24

God's protection . . . . . . . . . . .Feb. 19, 28; May 1

God's provision . . . . . . . . . . . .Feb. 28; Apr. 5; May 4–5, 7; June 29; Aug. 29

God's will. . . . . . . . . . . . . . . .Jan. 3, 19; Feb. 17, 23; Apr. 6, 12, 15; May 1, 4–5, 13; June 14; July 3, 7, 23, 30; Aug. 5, 10, 22; Sept. 1, 5, 16, 18, 26; Dec. 21, 26

God's Word . . . . . . . . . . . . . . .Feb. 5; Mar. 30; Apr. 17, 23; May 6, 25; July 1, 3; Aug. 7; Oct. 18; Nov. 19; Dec. 7, 19, 27

Greed . . . . . . . . . . . . . . . . . . .Jan. 3; Feb. 12; Apr. 20; June 10, 20; Sept. 22

Guilt. . . . . . . . . . . . . . . . . . . .Jan. 18; Feb. 13, 21–23; Mar. 29; May 20; June 22, 28,; Oct. 21, 23, 29; Nov. 7; Dec. 9

Hope/hopefulness . . . . . . . . . . .Feb. 3, 21; Mar. 6, 8; Apr. 25; June 12; Nov. 14

Hospitality. . . . . . . . . . . . . . . .Jan. 20; Feb. 6, 15; Mar. 24; Apr. 28–29; Aug. 14, 26; Oct. 3

Idolatry. . . . . . . . . . . . . . . . . .Jan. 1, 25, 30; Mar. 22; May 23; Aug. 6, 28; Oct. 19

Injustice . . . . . . . . . . . . . . . . .Jan. 9; Aug. 27; Sept. 11, 16, 22, 24

Integrity (see Character)

Jealousy . . . . . . . . . . . . . . . . .Jan. 3; Apr. 7, 14; May 21; Aug. 17; Sept. 13; Oct. 12, 26–27; Nov. 15, 17, 20

Leadership . . . . . . . . . . . . . . . .Jan. 2, 11, 13, 16, 26; Feb. 8, 14, 24; Mar. 18–19, 23–24, 27–28; May 28; June 19; July 3, 7; Aug. 3; Sept. 15, 28; Oct. 8; Nov. 11, 20; Dec. 18

Listening to God . . . . . . . . . . .Jan. 21; Feb. 26; Mar. 27; Apr. 1, 22; May 20; June 5; Aug. 1, 20, 30; Sept. 2; Oct. 18, 22

Love . . . . . . . . . . . . . . . . . . . .Mar. 1, 16; May 8, 29; July 28; Aug. 21; Oct. 9, 15, 29; Nov. 3–4

Loyalty. . . . . . . . . . . . . . . . . .Jan. 11; Feb. 24; Mar. 16, 18, 20; May 31; July 26; Oct. 12; Nov. 3

Lust . . . . . . . . . . . . . . . . . . . .Feb. 21; July 29; Oct. 24; Nov. 7; Dec. 8

Obedience . . . . . . . . . . . . . . . .Jan. 30; Feb. 1, 14; Mar. 13, 25; Apr. 8; May 3–4, 29–30; June 8–9, 11, 13, 19, 24, 26, 28; July 27; Aug. 1, 7–8, 23–24, 28; Sept. 10, 19, 23; Oct. 2, 13, 16, 19; Nov. 16, 21; Dec. 20, 28, 31

Opposition. . . . . . . . . . . . . . . .Feb. 8; Mar. 11, 25; Apr. 9; May 3, 12; Sept. 28–29; Nov. 11; Dec. 27, 29

Parenting . . . . . . . . . . . . . . . . . .Jan. 31; Mar. 23, 29; Apr. 18; May 14, 18, 27; June 2,
18, 19–20; July 14–15; Aug. 16, 29; Sept. 15; Nov. 8–9;
Dec. 13

Patience (*see* Perseverance)

Peacemaking . . . . . . . . . . . . . . .Jan. 31; May 15; June 3, 27; Aug. 15

Peer Pressure . . . . . . . . . . . . . . .Jan. 1; Apr. 13; May 22; July 5; Aug. 2; Oct. 21

Perseverance. . . . . . . . . . . . . . . .Mar. 4, Mar. 21; June 29; July 4; Sept. 28–29; Nov. 13;
Dec. 17, 20

Plans. . . . . . . . . . . . . . . . . . . . .Jan. 17, 19, 22, 28; Apr. 6, 12; May 1, 13, 24; June 22;
July 7; Aug. 5; Sept. 18; Nov. 26, 29

Prayer. . . . . . . . . . . . . . . . . . . .Jan. 7; Mar. 14–15; Apr. 11; May 9; June 5–6, 9; Sept.
28–29; Nov. 2, 7; Dec. 3

Prejudice. . . . . . . . . . . . . . . . . .Mar. 10, 12; May 15, 23; Sept. 26; Nov. 11, 20

Pride (*see* Self-centeredness)

Problem solving . . . . . . . . . . . . .Jan. 22; Apr. 14; May 10, 23; July 31; Aug. 15; Sept. 29;
Oct. 26, 30; Dec. 6

Quitting (*see* Perseverance)

Relationship with God . . . . . . .Mar. 7, 30; Apr. 1, 22–23; May 8, 11, 25–26; June 10,
17; Aug. 14, 18, 23, 30; Sept. 2, 10, 20; Oct. 5, 9, 13, 16,
19; Nov. 29; Dec. 22, 28

Repentance. . . . . . . . . . . . . . . . .Mar. 17; Apr. 22; May 23; June 21–22; Aug. 7, 28; Sept.
20; Oct. 14; Nov. 7, 17; Dec. 31

Revenge . . . . . . . . . . . . . . . . . . .Jan. 6; July 7, 30

Security . . . . . . . . . . . . . . . . . . .Jan. 14; Feb. 23; Apr. 16; May 1; July 2, 6

Self-centeredness . . . . . . . . . . . .Jan. 3, 17, 19, 23, 31; Feb. 11, 23; Mar. 24; May 12, 15,
17, 21; June 30; July 28; Aug. 19; Sept. 13, 20–21, 27;
Oct. 4, 24; Nov. 17; Dec. 7, 20, 30

Service . . . . . . . . . . . . . . . . . . . .Feb. 1, 4–7, 17; Mar. 1, 7, 9, 31; Apr. 4, 12, 15, 28–29;
May 23, 31; June 16, 26; July 8, 12, 14; Aug. 25; Sept. 3,
5–6, 10, 14–16; Oct. 7–9, 13, 15; Nov. 8, 25–26; Dec.
1–2, 15, 30

Sorcery . . . . . . . . . . . . . . . . . . . .Nov. 26

Success, worldly . . . . . . . . . . . . .Mar. 2; May 17; July 2; Sept. 17, 21, 27

Suffering (*see* Trials)

Temptation. . . . . . . . . . . . . . . . .Apr. 19; May 12–13, 16; June 1; July 29; Aug. 23;
Nov. 6, 18

Thankfulness. . . . . . . . . . . . . . .Jan. 5; Feb. 18, 25; Mar. 26; Apr. 7, 29; May 2, 14, 28;
June 17; Aug. 9, 17, 27, 31; Sept. 8, 14; Dec. 5, 10

Transformation . . . . . . . . . . . . .Apr. 27; July 17; Aug. 9, 28; Oct. 28; Dec. 2

Trials . . . . . . . . . . . . . . . . . . . . .Jan. 4, 24 Feb. 19; Mar. 21; Apr. 3; May 1, 9–10; June
15, 29–30; July 11–13, 29, 31; Sept. 9, 11, 24, 28–29;
Oct. 11–12, 27; Nov. 14, 30; Dec. 21, 24, 28, 31

Trust (*see* Faith)

Truth . . . . . . . . . . . . . . . . . . . . .Jan. 1; Feb. 2, 5; Mar. 2, 12; Apr. 17, 26, 30; May 2, 22;
July 19; Aug. 7, 22; Sept. 11–12; Sept. 26; Oct. 17, 22,
31; Nov. 12, 19

Unity . . . . . . . . . . . . . . . . . . . . .Mar. 10; Dec. 6, 16

Vocation . . . . . . . . . . . . . . . . . . .Jan. 28; Feb. 27; Mar. 1

Waiting . . . . . . . . . . . . . . . . . . .Feb. 4; May 6; June 5; Nov. 13, 24

Watchfulness . . . . . . . . . . . . . . .Mar. 8; Apr. 19, 22; Aug. 23

Wisdom . . . . . . . . . . . . . . . . . . .Jan. 11; Mar. 3; Apr. 30; May 30; July 21, 28; Aug. 5, 16;
Oct. 8 ; Nov. 27–28

Work (*see* Vocation)

Worship . . . . . . . . . . . . . . . . . . .Feb. 10, 27; Mar. 15, 19, 30; Apr. 1; May 25; Aug. 14;
Sept. 7

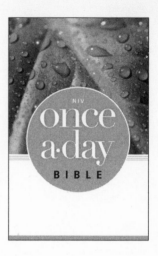
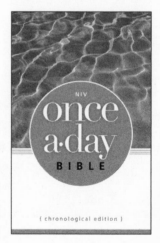